Frommer's®

P

Las V

Non-Gamblers

4th Edition

by Mary Herczog

Here's what critics say about Frommer's:

"Amazingly easy to use. Very portable, very complete."

—*Booklist*

"Detailed, accurate, and easy-to-read information for all price ranges."

—*Glamour Magazine*

WILEY

Wiley Publishing, Inc.

Published by:

WILEY PUBLISHING, INC.

111 River St.
Hoboken, NJ 07030-5774

ISBN 978-0-470-40293-1

Editor: Ian Skinnari
Production Editor: Lindsay Conner
Cartographer: Guy Ruggiero
Photo Editor: Richard Fox
Production by Wiley Indianapolis Composition Services

For information on our other products and services or to obtain technical support, please contact our Customer Care Department within the U.S. at 877/762-2974, outside the U.S. at 317/572-3993 or fax 317/572-4002.

Wiley also publishes its books in a variety of electronic formats. Some content that appears in print may not be available in electronic formats.

Manufactured in the United States of America

5   4   3   2   1

Contents

List of Maps   vi

1 Introducing Las Vegas   1

   1 Favorite Vegas Experiences 2
   2 Best Hotel Bets 4
   3 Best Dining Bets 6

2 Planning Your Trip to Las Vegas   8

   1 Visitor Information 8
       Winning Websites 9
   2 Entry Requirements & Customs 9
   3 When to Go 11
       Las Vegas Calendar of Events 12
       New Year's Eve in Las Vegas 14
   4 Getting There & Getting Around 15
   5 City Layout 21
   6 Money & Costs 24
   7 Specialized Travel Resources 27

3 Where to Stay   29

   1 The Top Hotels 31
       So Your Trip Goes Swimmingly 37
   2 Best Casino Hotels 38
   3 Best Casino-Free Hotels 52
   4 When the Others Are Booked 55
       Spa Life 56

4 Where to Dine   62

   1 South Strip 62
       You Gotta Have a Theme 70
   2 Mid-Strip 73
   3 North Strip 85

4 East of the Strip 88
   Las Vegas Is for (Wine) Lovers 90

5 West Las Vegas 96

6 Downtown 100

7 Buffets & Sunday Brunches 102

5   What to See & Do in Las Vegas   108

   Suggested Itineraries 109

1 The Top Attractions 110
   Free Vegas 114
   When Temptation Strikes 118

2 Getting Married 123
   Photo Ops 126

3 Especially for Kids 128
   Hotel Arcades 131

4 Organized Tours 131
   Going Vegas 132

5 Fore! Great Desert Golf 133

6 Staying Active 135
   Desert Hiking Advice 137

6   Shopping   139

1 The Malls 139

2 Outlet Centers 141

3 Hotel Shopping Arcades 142

4 Vintage Clothing 146

5 Souvenirs 146

6 Candy 147

7 Antiques 147

8 Wigs 148

7   Las Vegas After Dark   149

1 The Major Production Shows 151
   Family-Friendly Shows 153

2 Headliner Showrooms 161

3 Comedy Clubs 163

4 Gay Bars 163

Lounge Lizard Supreme 165

5 Other Bars 166

6 Dance Clubs 171

7 Strip Clubs 176

8 Side Trips from Las Vegas   **181**

1 Hoover Dam & Lake Mead 181

2 Valley of Fire State Park 189

3 Red Rock Canyon 192

Appendix: Fast Facts   **194**

Index   **198**

General Index 198

Accommodations Index 203

Restaurants Index 204

List of Maps

Las Vegas at a Glance   23

Accommodations on the Strip   33

Dining on the Strip   63

Accommodations, Dining & Nightlife East of the Strip   89

Dining & Nightlife West of the Strip   97

Las Vegas Attractions   111

Excursions from Las Vegas   183

ABOUT THE AUTHOR

Mary Herczog writes a great many books for Frommer's (*Frommer's Las Vegas, Frommer's New Orleans, California For Dummies,* and *Las Vegas For Dummies,* among others) and lives in the hopes of writing a great many more. When she is not traveling or writing, she lives in Los Angeles and works for Hollywood. She has spent upwards of a week in Vegas and not so much as touched a slot machine.

AN INVITATION TO THE READER

In researching this book, we discovered many wonderful places—hotels, restaurants, shops, and more. We're sure you'll find others. Please tell us about them, so we can share the information with your fellow travelers in upcoming editions. If you were disappointed with a recommendation, we'd love to know that, too. Please write to:

Frommer's Portable Las Vegas for Non-Gamblers, 4th Edition
Wiley Publishing, Inc. • 111 River St. • Hoboken, NJ 07030-5774

AN ADDITIONAL NOTE

Please be advised that travel information is subject to change at any time—and this is especially true of prices. We therefore suggest that you write or call ahead for confirmation when making your travel plans. The authors, editors, and publisher cannot be held responsible for the experiences of readers while traveling. Your safety is important to us, however, so we encourage you to stay alert and be aware of your surroundings. Keep a close eye on cameras, purses, and wallets, all favorite targets of thieves and pickpockets.

Frommer's Star Ratings, Icons & Abbreviations

Every hotel, restaurant, and attraction listing in this guide has been ranked for quality, value, service, amenities, and special features using a **star-rating system.** In country, state, and regional guides, we also rate towns and regions to help you narrow down your choices and budget your time accordingly. Hotels and restaurants are rated on a scale of zero (recommended) to three stars (exceptional). Attractions, shopping, nightlife, towns, and regions are rated according to the following scale: zero stars (recommended), one star (highly recommended), two stars (very highly recommended), and three stars (must-see).

In addition to the star-rating system, we also use **seven feature icons** that point you to the great deals, in-the-know advice, and unique experiences that separate travelers from tourists. Throughout the book, look for:

Finds	Special finds—those places only insiders know about
Fun Fact	Fun facts—details that make travelers more informed and their trips more fun
Kids	Best bets for kids and advice for the whole family
Moments	Special moments—those experiences that memories are made of
Overrated	Places or experiences not worth your time or money
Tips	Insider tips—great ways to save time and money
Value	Great values—where to get the best deals

The following **abbreviations** are used for credit cards:

AE	American Express	DISC	Discover	V	Visa
DC	Diners Club	MC	MasterCard		

Frommers.com

Now that you have this guidebook to help you plan a great trip, visit our website at **www.frommers.com** for additional travel information on more than 4,000 destinations. We update features regularly to give you instant access to the most current trip-planning information available. At Frommers.com, you'll find scoops on the best airfares, lodging rates, and car rental bargains. You can even book your travel online through our reliable travel booking partners. Other popular features include:

- Online updates of our most popular guidebooks
- Vacation sweepstakes and contest giveaways
- Newsletters highlighting the hottest travel trends
- Podcasts, interactive maps, and up-to-the-minute events listings
- Opinionated blog entries by Arthur Frommer himself
- Online travel message boards with featured travel discussions

Introducing Las Vegas

Las Vegas is the city of sin and illusion, the town that Bugsy built, and it's like nothing you've seen before—a facade of a facade with some neon on it. And you're here! And you—don't gamble! Egads!

But don't despair. Las Vegas is many, many things—Sin City, Disneyland for Adults, A Stopover on a Drive Through the West, Convention Central—and just because you aren't all that interested in the main attraction doesn't mean you can't have a whale of a good time. Sure, Vegas would still prefer that you lighten your pockets the traditional way, and so you will still find casinos and slot machines nearly everywhere you go. But with our guidance, not only will you be able to avoid a great deal of exposure to the one-armed bandit, you will also find plenty to otherwise fill your time.

As a non-gambler, your biggest problem will be finding a hotel where the emphasis isn't on gambling. There are a few of these, most of them chain hotels without casinos, although the posh Four Seasons also remains unsullied by craps. But even the official casino hotels have come around to the idea that gambling may not be everyone's first reason for coming to Vegas, with two of them (Mandalay Bay's THEhotel and the Venetian's Venezia tower) built specifically as alternatives to casino hotels, though still attached to casino hotels. And so visitors now have swell pools, lush spas, and some of the best restaurants in the country—and if all that doesn't spell vacation, well, then you've also got access to some marvelous hiking in Red Rock Canyon, water fun on Lake Mead, stunning desert visits in Valley of the Fire State Park, and the engineering and architectural marvels at Hoover Dam. And back in town, there are shows—some hokey, and some on the level of the best in the world. There are even a couple real museums, with actual masterpieces.

But there are some things to bear in mind while navigating Vegas and avoiding the temptation of the dice or the cards or the slot machines. First of all, the casinos aren't easy to avoid. They generally stand between you and, well, anything you want. When staying inside a hotel, a casino can sometimes be between you and the entire outside world. In chapter 3, we will let you know how obtrusive the casino in question (if there is one) is and how much of a hindrance it can be. Anyone traveling with children should take special note of those descriptions; kids aren't allowed in casinos, though if the only way through the facility is through the gambling area, obviously that rule is relaxed. But kids are expected to stick to walkways between machines, and many a child who has stopped (and who can blame them?) because their attention was caught by noise or flashing lights have found themselves descended upon by security, who hustle them right along. If this sounds like the opposite of fun, you might want to avoid a casino hotel.

Second, the days of Vegas bargains are, for the most part, gone. Sure, hotel prices can dip quite low (provided that you travel during the off season or want a room Sun–Thurs nights), but the cost of everything else is high. The best restaurants are the expensive ones, with prices hitting nearly New York City levels. The better museums charge a bundle. Spa treatments? Ouch. And the best shows charge outrageous ticket prices.

But then again, you are on vacation. Or maybe you are in town for a convention. Either way, you deserve some foie gras. Or a little massage. See Cirque du Soleil and marvel. Then go outside and look at the lights of Las Vegas. Ever seen anything like it? Of course not. Remember, that's really why you are here.

1 Favorite Vegas Experiences

- **Taking a Stroll on the Strip:** Sure, it's a skyline made up entirely of the skylines of other cities, but where else can you see a glowing pyramid, a gleaming giant brass lion, a mini version of New York City, a volcano, the sights of Paris and Venice, and more, all in one day? The Strip, known officially as Las Vegas Boulevard South, is where it's at—and by "it" we mean "huge enormous hotels, most with a theme," and by "theme" we mean "copies, sometimes faithful, of some of the great sights of the world, plus some other stuff just for Vegas."

  So walk down the Strip during the day and giggle. And then do it again at night, when the lights turn it all into something magical. Get in your car and cruise, for maximum effect.

- **Checking Out the Inside of the Hotels:** Remember the part about the theme? Well, in some cases, it's continued inside— and how! Rome, Venice, Paris, just to name a few—all lovingly and cartoonishly evoked within. And even though the trend has been less about theme and more about grand elegance, said grandness is on such a scale of ridiculousness that the gawking opportunities are still plentiful.

- **Free Shows and Attractions:** To further lure you, many of the hotels provide free entertainment, of varying degrees of worth. The best, and not to be missed, are the fountains of Bellagio, which rise and fall in choreographed rhythms to tunes from Sinatra to opera during the day and part of the night. The Mirage's volcano "explodes" (spews light and fire). Treasure Island's pirates battle scantily clad "sirens" in a really stupid show. And the MGM Grand lets you get up close to a lion or two. Plus there are lounges with free music, live or otherwise, at just about every hotel.

- **The Dolphin Habitat at The Mirage:** Dolphins in the desert? Don't worry, these Atlantic bottlenose dolphins have one of the finest (admittedly manufactured) habitats in the world, and they get cosseted and coddled and stimulated by some marvelous handlers. Watching them frolic—leap, flop, and even toss balls around—is an utter delight. It's the best attraction in Vegas.

- **Eating Out:** No longer the joke of the foodie scene, Vegas has attracted many of the most prominent chefs in the country, from Food Network favorites such as Puck and Emeril, to Jean-Georges, Julian Serrano, and more, including Joël Robuchon, considered one of the finest chefs alive. You may well have one of the meals of your life here.

- **Binging at Buffets:** Of course, buffets are often quantity over quality, but nothing says "vacation" to us like unlimited mounds of shrimp and an endless flow of prime rib.

- **Cirque du Soleil:** It's a costly ticket, but it's also world-class entertainment. Cirque has six shows as we write this, with more on the way. The magical *Mystère* (at Treasure Island), the almost-cinematic *KÀ* (at the MGM Grand), and the other-worldly *O* (at Bellagio)—where the troupe's trademark acrobatics and surreal theatrics take place on, above, around, and in water—are the best, while you can skip *Zumanity* and Criss Angel. Then there is the new Beatles-themed *LOVE,* which is either a must-see or a bit overpriced and redundant or even a travesty, depending on how sacred you hold the Beatles.

- **Red Rock Canyon and Valley of the Fire State Park:** When visiting this Wonder of the Artificial World, it's important to remind yourself of the Natural World, and what better way to do it than with awe-inspiring desert rock formations? No money-grubbing businessperson caused these to be built, and they will be standing long after Vegas.

- **Shopping:** The above doesn't mean we don't have our materialistic side, and while Vegas has little in terms of unique shops, it does have pretty much every store you could want. Thoughs shopping at a Gap is nothing special, shopping at a Gap set in a Roman coliseum or a mock Venice is.

- **Liberace Museum:** While much fuss—some of it even justified—has been made about Vegas's additions to the cultural scene, you probably should not miss the most Vegas of Vegas attractions, the Liberace Museum. Who needs masterworks when you've got rhinestones?

2 Best Hotel Bets

- **Best for Business Travelers:** If you have a good expense account, head over to the **Four Seasons,** 3960 Las Vegas Blvd. S. (© **877/632-5000;** www.fourseasons.com), and let them soothe and pamper you. Otherwise, you can join the other business travelers who have made the **Las Vegas Hilton,** 3000 Paradise Rd. (© **888/732-7117;** www.lvhilton.com), their stop for many years, or you can stretch out in the comfort of the mini-apartments found at the **Residence Inn,** 3225 Paradise Rd. (© **800/331-3131;** www.marriott.com).

- **Best for Families:** The **Four Seasons** (see above for contact info) is the only hotel in town that truly rolls out the red carpet for Junior (they will provide cribs, toys, and treats, and even baby-proof a room), plus guests have access to Mandalay Bay's ultra-kid-friendly pool area. If you want lower prices and little or no exposure to the Strip, try the **Desert Rose Resort,** 5051 Duke Ellington Way (© **888/732-8099;** www.shell hospitality.com), just a couple blocks away, with a free breakfast buffet, a good pool, and basketball and volleyball courts; and they allow pets.

- **Best Luxury Resorts:** It's a toss-up between the **Four Seasons** (see above for contact info) and **Ritz-Carlton, Lake Las Vegas** (1610 Lake Las Vegas Pkwy., Henderson, NV; © **800/ 241-3333;** www.ritzcarlton.com), with the more moderately priced **Green Valley Ranch Resort** also getting a nod (2300 Paseo Verde Dr., Henderson, NV; © **866/782-9487;** www. greenvalleyranchresort.com) and the most costly **Red Rock Resort** (10973 W. Charleston Rd.; © **866/767-7773;**

www.redrockstation.com) taking a well-deserved spot on the list. The Four Seasons sits atop Mandalay Bay but seems like a world away, whereas the Ritz-Carlton really is (it's about 30 min. away, in Henderson)—so much so (and now we are referring to gestalt, not geography) that once you arrive, it's very hard to leave. Green Valley Ranch is a winning combo of Ritz-Carlton posh and W Hotel hip. Red Rock sits next to the otherworldly scenery of the eponymous canyon, so you do get away from it all, without sacrificing a lick of luxury. If you want Strip proximity and brand-name comfort, the Four Seasons is for you. If you want a genuine luxury resort experience, then it's the Ritz. If you want a bargain as well, try Green Valley Ranch. If you want to see what Britney's up to, try Red Rock.

- **Best Swimming Pool:** The winner is the 11 acres of water fun (including a beach pool with regular waves, plus a long lazy river) at **Mandalay Bay,** 3950 Las Vegas Blvd. S. (© 877/632-7800; www.mandalaybay.com). But second is a tossup between the jungle fantasy at **The Mirage,** 3400 Las Vegas Blvd. S. (© 800/374-9000; www.mirage.com), and the one at **The Flamingo Las Vegas,** 3555 Las Vegas Blvd. S. (© 800/732-2111; www.flamingolv.com). Both are full of slides and waterfalls, plus lots of lush foliage.

- **Best Spa:** The designers of **Mandara Spa** at **Planet Hollywood** (formerly the Aladdin), 3667 Las Vegas Blvd. S. (© 866/935-3647 www.aladdincasino.com), were sent to Morocco for inspiration, and the result is the most beautiful spa in Vegas. We hope the new Planet Hollywood owners keep their mitts off it, as they swear they will. The greatest number of services can be found at the highly regarded (and highly expensive) **Canyon Ranch Spa** at **The Venetian,** 3355 Las Vegas Blvd. S. (© 877/220-2688; www.venetian.com), which also has the best health club.

- **Best Rooms:** THEhotel at Mandalay Bay, 3950 Las Vegas Blvd. S. (© 877/632-7800; www.thehotelatmandalaybay.com), with full one-bedroom suites with impressive bathrooms, beats out **The Venetian** (see above for address; © 877/883-6423), whose rooms include sunken living rooms. **Wynn Las Vegas** has the best non-suite rooms, all spacious clean-lined comfort (3131 Las Vegas Blvd. S.; © 888/320-9966; www.wynnlasvegas.com).

- **Best Beds: Ritz-Carlton, Lake Las Vegas,** and **Green Valley Ranch Resort** (see contact info above) both have plush beds, high-thread-count sheets, and down comforters; and it all comes together in a cocoon you will be hard-pressed to leave.

Palms Casino Resort, 4321 W. Flamingo Rd. (© 866/ 942-7777; www.palms.com), has a similar philosophy toward nighttime comfort.

- **Best Bathrooms: THEhotel at Mandalay Bay** (see contact info above) heads a pack of hotels (which includes Mandalay Bay, the Ritz, the Four Seasons, Green Valley Ranch, Bellagio, Wynn Las Vegas, and The Venetian) with marble tubs and large glass-and-marble showers, but THEhotel adds a flat-screen plasma TV and a chin-deep soaking tub.

- **Best Hotel Dining:** On one hand, it's hard to beat the lineup at **Bellagio; Picasso, Le Cirque, Circo, Prime Steakhouse**— these represent some important names in the restaurant world. But **Mandalay Bay's** wattage—**Fleur de Lys, Aureole, Border Grill,** even the amusing **Red Square**—may thrill us even more. And we do appreciate **Wynn Las Vegas'** hard line when it comes to those fancy-name chefs; they are required to actually work on the premises. The results—Bartolotta and Alex chief among them—demonstrate why this matters.

3 Best Dining Bets

- **Best Buffet:** You get what you pay for, so in the expensive category, try the incredible assortment offered at **Wynn Las Vegas** (see above for contact info) or Bellagio's **Buffet** (© 888/ 987-6667), or the buffet at the French-regional-themed **Le Village Buffet** (© 702/946-7000) at **Paris.** In the moderate category, try local favorite **Rio's Carnival World Buffet** (© 702/252-7777). And at the low end, head Downtown, where **Main Street Station's Garden Court** (© 702/ 387-1896) offers a well-priced and quite good buffet.

- **Best for Families:** Buffets work well for feeding bottomless-pit teenagers, but **Monte Carlo Pub & Brewery** (© 702/ 730-7777) has mounds of family-friendly food (Buffalo wings, pizza, ribs, large salads) for even better prices. **Cypress Street Marketplace** in Caesars Palace (© 702/731-7110) has such a wide variety of food booths (salads to fat Chicago hot dogs, to wraps, to Vietnamese noodle bowls) that there should be something there for even the most varied family tastes.

- **Best for a Romantic Dinner:** It's hard to beat the view found at **Alizé** (© 702/951-7000)—at the top of the Palms, with no other tall buildings around to obscure the twinkling city lights from three walls of windows. It's a wow.

- **Best Place to Impress a Date:** Take 'em to **Joël Robuchon at the Mansion** (© 702/891-7925). If the works of culinary art—prepared by a master chef and considered some of the best French food in the world—don't do the trick, the bill (a small fortune, but worth it) surely will.
- **Best Authentic Italian:** So simple, so sublime. Take fish flown straight from the Mediterranean, and then grill it. A little olive oil, a little fresh sautéed tomato. Say "grazie" to **Bartolotta** (© 888/352-3463).
- **Best for Sexy Food and Dining:** We mean this in a grown-up way, not in a tummy-bearing, sin-is-in way. The playful, teasing concoctions at the luscious **Fleur de Lys** (© 877/632-7800) make other attempts at fine dining in town look feeble. Food here is sensual in all ways.
- **Best Wine List:** Mandalay Bay's **Aureole** (© 877/632-7800) is renowned for its "wine angels," the catsuit-clad gals who rise to the top of a four-story tower of wine bottles to retrieve a patron's selection. It's a gimmick that may be misleading; they have a wonderful selection, as well as handheld computers that guide you through the selections.
- **Best Steak:** Fighting words for many. Not for us, though. We think it's at **Charlie Palmer Steak,** in the Four Seasons (© 702/632-5120). But others think it can be found in **Austins Steakhouse** (© 702/631-1033).
- **Best Bistro:** Thomas "Best Chef in America" Keller has a Vegas outlet; **Bouchon** in The Venetian (© 702/414-6200) surpasses the original in Napa. Not a misstep on the menu.
- **Best Decor:** Genuine works from the master on the wall (and the most lovely casual floral arrangements possible) at **Picasso** (© 877/234-6358) or the over-the-top-of-the-Iron-Curtain satirical fun of Mandalay Bay's **Red Square** (© 702/632-7407).

2

Planning Your Trip to Las Vegas

Before any trip, you need to do a bit of advance planning. You'll need to decide whether a package tour makes sense for you, when to go, and more. In the pages that follow, you'll find everything you need to know to handle the practical details of planning your trip to Las Vegas in advance: airlines and area airports, a calendar of events, a list of major conventions you may want to avoid, resources for those with special needs, and much more.

We also suggest that you check out chapter 7, "Las Vegas After Dark," before you leave home; if you want to see the most popular shows, it's a good idea to call ahead and order tickets well in advance to avoid disappointment. (Ditto if you want to dine in one of the city's top restaurants; head to chapter 4, "Where to Dine," for full reviews and contact information.)

1 Visitor Information

For information, contact the **Las Vegas Convention and Visitors Authority,** 3150 Paradise Rd., Las Vegas, NV 89109 (© **877/ VISIT-LV [847-4858]** or 702/892-0711; www.visitlasvegas.com). They can send you a comprehensive packet of brochures, a map, a show guide, an events calendar, and an attractions list; help you find a hotel that meets your specifications (and make reservations); and tell you if a major convention is scheduled during the time you would like to visit Las Vegas. They're open daily from 6am to 9pm.

Another excellent information source is the **Las Vegas Chamber of Commerce,** 3720 Howard Hughes Pkwy., #100, Las Vegas, NV 89109 (© **702/735-1616;** www.lvchamber.com). Their *Visitor's Guide* contains extensive information about accommodations, attractions, excursions, children's activities, and more. They can answer all your Las Vegas questions, including those about weddings and divorces. They're open Monday to Friday 8am to 5pm.

Tips **Winning Websites**

When you consider the enormous popularity of Las Vegas, it should come as no surprise that there are hundreds of websites devoted to the destination. There is a lot of good—and bad—information about everything from the casino hotels to dining suggestions.

Start your online journey to Sin City at **www.vegas4 visitors.com**. This small, family-run endeavor is packed full with information; unbiased reviews; contact info; maps; photos; and links to hotels, restaurants, and more. There's also a weekly news and events column.

If you want to pick the brains of the local populace—and whom better to ask about life in Las Vegas?—head over to **www.lasvegasweekly.com**. You'll find out where locals go for fun, and you can browse through reviews of bars, cafes, nightclubs, restaurants, and amusement parks.

For the most comprehensive Vegas dining resource on the Web, go to **www.nightonthetown.com**. The site arranges its plethora of restaurants by cuisine and location so you can find what you want, where you want it.

If you like your information with a side order of humor, then head to **www.cheapovegas.com**. This fun site offers lots of sassy reviews and unbiased opinions, especially on the Las Vegas casino hotels. There's also a small section on getting freebies while you're in town.

For information on all of Nevada, including Las Vegas, contact the **Nevada Commission on Tourism** (© **800/638-2328;** www.travelnevada.com). If you call or visit their website, they'll send you a comprehensive information packet on Nevada.

Additionally, all major Las Vegas hotels provide comprehensive tourist information at their reception and/or sightseeing and show desks.

2 Entry Requirements & Customs

ENTRY REQUIREMENTS

The U.S. State Department has a **Visa Waiver Program** allowing citizens of the following countries (at press time) to enter the United

States without a visa for stays of up to 90 days: Andorra, Australia, Austria, Belgium, Brunei, Denmark, Finland, France, Germany, Iceland, Ireland, Italy, Japan, Liechtenstein, Luxembourg, Monaco, the Netherlands, New Zealand, Norway, Portugal, San Marino, Singapore, Slovenia, Spain, Sweden, Switzerland, and the United Kingdom. Citizens of these nations need only a valid passport and a round-trip air or cruise ticket upon arrival. If they first enter the United States, they may also visit Mexico, Canada, Bermuda, and/or the Caribbean islands and return to the United States without a visa. Further information is available from any U.S. embassy or consulate. Canadian citizens may also enter the United States without visas; they need only a passport (if arriving by land or sea, some other forms of ID may be acceptable, but with entry requirements in flux, a passport is still strongly recommended).

Citizens of all other countries must have (1) a valid passport that expires at least 6 months later than the scheduled end of their visit to the United States, and (2) a tourist visa, which may be obtained without charge from any U.S. consulate.

CUSTOMS
WHAT YOU CAN BRING INTO LAS VEGAS
Every visitor more than 21 years of age may bring in, free of duty, the following: (1) 1 liter of wine or hard liquor; (2) 200 cigarettes, 100 cigars (but not from Cuba), or 3 pounds of smoking tobacco; and (3) $100 worth of gifts. These exemptions are offered to travelers who spend at least 72 hours in the United States and who have not claimed them within the preceding 6 months. It is altogether forbidden to bring into the country foodstuffs (particularly fruit, cooked meats, and canned goods) and plants (vegetables, seeds, tropical plants, and the like). Foreign tourists may carry in or out up to $10,000 in U.S. or foreign currency with no formalities; larger sums must be declared to U.S. Customs on entering or leaving, which includes filing form CM 4790. For details regarding U.S. Customs and Border Protection, consult your nearest U.S. embassy or consulate, or **U.S. Customs and Border Protection (© 202/927-1770;** www.customs.ustreas.gov).

WHAT YOU CAN TAKE HOME FROM LAS VEGAS
CANADIAN CITIZENS   For a clear summary of Canadian rules, write for the booklet *I Declare,* issued by the **Canada Border Services Agency (© 800/461-9999** in Canada, or 204/983-3500; **www.cbsa-asfc.gc.ca**).

U.K. CITIZENS   For information, contact **HM Revenue & Customs** at © **0845/010-9000** (from outside the U.K., 020/8929-0152), or consult their website at **www.hmrc.gov.uk**.

AUSTRALIAN CITIZENS   A helpful brochure available from Australian consulates or Customs offices is *Know Before You Go*. For more information, call the **Australian Customs Service** at © **1300/363-263,** or log on to **www.customs.gov.au**.

IRISH CITIZENS   **Irish** citizens can obtain up-to-date information through the **Embassy of the USA Dublin,** 42 Elgin Rd., Dublin 4, Ireland (© **353/1-668-8777**), or by checking the "Consular Services" section of the website at **http://dublin.uscmbassy.gov**.

NEW ZEALAND CITIZENS   Most questions are answered in a free pamphlet available at New Zealand consulates and Customs offices: *New Zealand Customs Guide for Travellers, Notice no. 4*. For more information, contact **New Zealand Customs Service,** the Customhouse, 17–21 Whitmore St., Box 2218, Wellington (© **04/473-6099** or 0800/428-786; **www.customs.govt.nz**).

3 When to Go

Since most of a Las Vegas vacation is usually spent indoors, you can have a good time here year-round. The most pleasant seasons are spring and fall, especially if you do want to experience the great outdoors.

Weekdays are slightly less crowded than weekends. Holidays are almost always a mob scene and are accompanied by high hotel prices. Room rates also skyrocket when big conventions and special events are taking place. The slowest times of year are June and July, the week before Christmas, and the week after New Year's.

If a major convention is to be held during your trip, you might want to change your date. Contact the **Las Vegas Convention and Visitors Authority** (p. 8), since convention schedules often change.

THE WEATHER

First of all, Vegas isn't always hot, but when it is, it's *really* hot. One thing you'll hear again and again is that even though Las Vegas gets very hot, the dry desert heat is not unbearable. This is true (we know this because we spent a couple days there in 104°F/40°C weather and lived to say, "It wasn't all that bad, not really"), except in most of the hotel pool areas; they are surrounded by massive buildings covered in mirrored glass, which act like a giant magnifying glass on the antlike people below. Still, generally the humidity averages a low 22%, and even on very hot days, there's apt to be a breeze. Also, except on the hottest summer days, there's relief at night, when temperatures often drop by as much as 20°F.

Las Vegas's Average Temperatures (°F/°C) & Precipitation

	Jan	Feb	Mar	Apr	May	June	July	Aug	Sept	Oct	Nov	Dec
Average Temp. (°F)	47	52	58	66	75	86	91	89	81	69	55	47
(°C)	8	11	14	19	24	30	33	32	27	21	13	8
Avg. High Temp. (°F)	57	63	69	78	88	99	104	102	94	81	66	57
(°C)	14	17	21	26	31	37	40	39	34	27	19	14
Avg. Low Temp. (°F)	37	41	47	54	63	72	78	77	69	57	44	37
(°C)	3	5	8	12	17	22	26	25	21	14	7	3
Average Precip. (in.)	.59	.69	.59	.15	.24	.08	.44	.45	.31	.24	.31	.40
(cm)	1.5	1.8	1.5	.4	.6	.2	1.1	1.1	.8	.6	.8	1.0

But this is the desert, and it's not hot all year round. It can get quite cold, especially in the winter, when at night it can drop to 30°F (–1°C) and lower. (In the winter of 2008–09, it actually snowed in Vegas, dropping nearly 2 in. on the Strip. There's nothing quite like the sight of Luxor's Sphinx covered in snow.) The breeze can also become a cold, biting, strong wind of up to 40 mph or more. And so there are entire portions of the year when you won't be using that hotel swimming pool at all (and even if you want to, be advised that most of the hotels close huge chunks of those fabulous swimming pool areas for "the season," which can be as long as from Labor Day to Memorial Day). If you aren't traveling in the height of summer, bring a wrap. Also, remember your sunscreen and hat—even if it's not all that hot, you can burn very easily and very fast. (You should see all the lobster-red people glowing in the casinos at night.)

LAS VEGAS CALENDAR OF EVENTS

You may be surprised that Las Vegas does not offer as many annual events as most tourist cities. The reason is Las Vegas's very raison d'être: the gaming industry. This town wants its visitors spending their money in the casinos, not at Renaissance fairs and parades.

When in town, check the local paper and call the **Las Vegas Convention and Visitors Authority** (© **877/VISIT-LV [847-4858]** or 702/892-7575; www.lvcva.com) or the **Chamber of Commerce** (© **702/735-1616**; www.lvchamber.com) to find out about events scheduled during your visit.

March

NASCAR/Winston Cup. The **Las Vegas Motor Speedway,** 7000 N. Las Vegas Blvd. (© **800/644-4444;** www.lvms.com), has become one of the premier facilities in the country, attracting races and racers of all stripes and colors. The biggest races of the year are the Sam's Town 300 and the UAW–DaimlerChrysler 400, held in early March, often drawing over 150,000 race fans to town.

June

CineVegas Film Festival. This annual event, usually held in early June, is growing in popularity and prestige, with film debuts from both independent and major studios, plus lots of celebrities hanging around for the big parties. Call ℂ **702/992-7979** or visit their website at **www.cinevegas.com**.

World Series of Poker. When Harrah's Entertainment bought the legendary Binion's Horseshoe in Downtown Vegas out of bankruptcy, they quickly turned around and sold the hotel, but kept the hosting rights to this famed event and moved its location and place on the calendar. Now held at the **Rio All-Suite Hotel and Casino** (3700 W. Flamingo Rd.; ℂ **800/PLAY-RIO [752-9746]**) in June, July, and August instead of April and May, the event features high-stakes gamblers and showbiz personalities competing for six-figure purses. There are daily events with entry stakes ranging from $125 to $5,000. To enter the World Championship Event (purse: $1 million), players must pony up $10,000. It costs nothing to go crowd around the tables and watch the action (which, in 2003, was televised for the first time on the Travel Channel). In 2005 they even added the world's first poker convention and trade show to capitalize on the growing popularity of the game. For more information, visit the official website at **www.worldseriesofpoker.com**.

September

Oktoberfest. This boisterous autumn holiday is celebrated from mid-September through the end of October at the **Mount Charleston Resort** (ℂ **800/955-1314** or 702/872-5408; www.mtcharlestonlodge.com) with music, folk dancers, sing-alongs around a roaring fire, special decorations, and Bavarian cookouts.

October

Frys.com Open. This 4-day championship golf event, played on three local courses (the main course is TPC Summerlin), is televised by ESPN. For details, call ℂ **702/242-3000.**

November

The Comedy Festival. Launched in 2005, this festival was such a hit that it has since been turned it into an annual event. Some of the world's top comics and comedy troupes perform and also

> ## ⟨Moments⟩   New Year's Eve in Las Vegas
>
> More and more people have been choosing Las Vegas as their party destination for New Year's Eve. In fact, some estimates indicate that there are more people ringing in the New Year in Nevada than in New York City's Times Square.
>
> From experience, we can tell you that there are a lot of people who come here on December 31. We mean a *lot* of people. Figure on just about every room being sold out. Traffic is a nightmare, parking is next to impossible, and there is not a square inch of the place that isn't occupied by a human being.
>
> A major portion of the Strip is closed down, sending the masses and their mass quantities of alcohol into the street. Each year's celebration is a little different but usually includes a streetside performance by a major celebrity, confetti, the obligatory countdown, fireworks, and, if you're lucky, maybe even a building implosion. This has become one of the city's biggest annual events.

includes workshops, film festivals, and more. It's held in mid-November and although events take place in several locations, the primary host hotel is Caesars Palace. For details, call the hotel at ⓒ **800/634-6661** or check out the festival's website at **www.the comedyfestival.com**.

December

Western Athletic Conference (WAC) Football Championship. This collegiate championship event takes place the first week in December in Sam Boyd Stadium. Call ⓒ **702/731-5595** for ticket information. Ticket prices start around $20 and go up over $100 for the best seats.

National Finals Rodeo. This is the Super Bowl of rodeos, attended by close to 170,000 people each year and offering nearly $5 million in prize money. The top 15 male rodeo stars compete in six different events: calf roping, steer wrestling, bull riding, team roping, saddle bronco riding, and bareback riding. The top 15 women compete in barrel racing. An all-around "Cowboy of the Year" is chosen. In connection with this event, hotels book country stars in their showrooms, and there's even a cowboy shopping opportunity—the **NFR Cowboy Christmas Gift Show,** a trade show for Western gear—at Cashman Field. The NFR runs for 10 days during the first 2 weeks of December at the 17,000-seat Thomas and Mack Center of the University of Nevada, Las Vegas (UNLV). It usually begins on the first Friday in December and lasts through the following Sunday. Order tickets as far in advance as possible (② 702/895-3900). For more information, see **www.nfrexperience.com**.

Las Vegas Bowl Week. A championship football event in mid-December pits the winners of the Mid-American Conference against the winners of the Big West Conference. The action takes place at the 32,000-seat Sam Boyd Stadium. Call ② **702/895-3900** or visit **www.lvbowl.com** for ticket information.

New Year's Eve. This is a biggie (reserve your hotel room early). Downtown, on the Fremont Street Experience, there's a big block party with two dramatic countdowns to midnight (the first is at 9pm, midnight on the East Coast). The Strip is usually closed to street traffic, and hundreds of thousands of people pack the area for the festivities. There are, of course, fireworks.

4 Getting There & Getting Around

GETTING THERE
BY PLANE
Most major North American airlines, and a number of regional airlines, offer regularly scheduled flights into Las Vegas's **McCarran International Airport,** 5757 Wayne Newton Blvd. (② **702/261-5211;** www.mccarran.com).

BY CAR
The main highway connecting Las Vegas with the rest of the country is I-15; it links Montana, Idaho, and Utah with Southern California. The drive from Los Angeles is quite popular and, thanks to the narrow two-lane highway, can get very crowded on Friday and Sunday afternoons with hopeful weekend gamblers making their way to and from Vegas.

From the east, take I-70 or I-80 west to Kingman, Arizona, and then U.S. 93 north to Downtown Las Vegas (Fremont St.). From the south, take I-10 west to Phoenix and then U.S. 93 north to Las Vegas. From San Francisco, take I-80 east to Reno and then U.S. 95 south to Las Vegas. *Note:* If you're driving to Las Vegas, be sure to read the driving precautions below.

BY TRAIN

Amtrak (© 800/872-7245; www.amtrak.com) does not currently offer direct rail service to Las Vegas. However, you can take the train to Los Angeles or Barstow, California, and Amtrak will get you to Vegas by bus.

GETTING AROUND

Located in the southernmost precincts of a wide, pancake-flat valley, Las Vegas is the biggest city in the state of Nevada. Although it is one of the fastest-growing cities in America, for tourism purposes, the city is quite compact.

ARRIVING AT THE LAS VEGAS AIRPORT

Las Vegas is served by **McCarran International Airport,** 5757 Wayne Newton Blvd. (© 702/261-5211; www.mccarran.com). It's just a few minutes' drive from the southern end of the Strip. This big, modern airport is perhaps unique in that it includes several casino areas with more than 1,000 slot machines. You non-gamblers will save lots of money bypassing the machines (they are avoidable).

Getting to your hotel from the airport is a cinch. **Bell Trans** (© 800/274-7433 or 702/739-7990; www.bell-trans.com) runs 20-passenger minibuses between the airport and all major Las Vegas hotels and motels daily from 7:45am to midnight. Several other companies run similar ventures—just stand outside on the curb, and one will be flagged down for you. Buses from the airport leave about every 10 minutes. When you want to check out of your hotel and head back to the airport, call at least 2 hours in advance to be safe (though often you can just flag down a shuttle outside any major hotel). The cost is $5.50 per person each way to the Strip and Convention Center area hotels, $7 to Downtown or other off-Strip properties (any place north of the Sahara Hotel and west of I-15). Other

---

Tips   Help for Troubled Travelers

The **Traveler's Aid Society** is a social-service organization geared to helping travelers in difficult straits. If you're in trouble, seek them out. In Las Vegas, there is a Traveler's Aid office at McCarran International Airport (© 702/798-1742; daily 8am–5pm). Similar services are provided by **Help of Southern Nevada** (© 702/369-4357; www.helpsonv.org; Mon–Fri 8am–4pm).

similarly priced shuttles run 24 hours daily and can be found in the same place.

Less expensive than shuttles are **Citizens Area Transit (CAT)** buses (© 702/CAT-RIDE [228-7433]; www.catride.com). The no. 108 bus departs from the airport and will take you to the Stratosphere, where you can transfer to the Deuce (p. 20). The no. 109 bus goes from the airport to the Downtown Transportation Center at Casino Center Boulevard and Stewart Avenue. The fare is $1.25 for adults, 60¢ for ages 62 and older and children 5 to 17, and free for those 4 and under. (The Deuce, p. 20, costs $2, $1 for seniors and children 5–17 for a one-way ticket, or $5 for an all-day pass.) ***Note:*** You might have a long walk from the bus stop to your door (even if it's right in front of your hotel); keep this in mind if you have heavy luggage.

All the major car-rental companies are represented in Las Vegas. See "Renting a Car," below.

BY CAR

If you plan to confine yourself to one part of the Strip (or one cruise down it) or to Downtown, your feet will suffice. Otherwise, we highly recommend that visitors rent a car. The Strip is too spread out for walking (and is often too hot or too cold to make strolls pleasant), Downtown is too far away for a cheap cab ride, and public transportation is ineffective, at best. Plus, further visits call for exploration of still more parts of the city, and a car brings freedom (especially if you want to take any side trips—bus tours are available, but a car lets you explore at your own pace).

You should note that places with addresses some 60 blocks east or west from the Strip are actually less than a 10-minute drive—provided there is no traffic.

Having advocated renting a car, we should warn you that the growing population of Vegas means a proportionate increase in the number of cars. Traffic is getting worse, and it's harder and harder to get around town with any certain swiftness. A general rule of thumb is to avoid driving on the Strip whenever you can, and avoid driving at all during peak rush hours, especially if you have to make a show curtain.

Parking is usually a pleasure because all casino hotels offer valet service. That means that for a mere $1 to $2 tip, you can park right at the door (though the valet usually fills up on busy nights).

Renting a Car

National car-rental companies with outlets in Las Vegas include **Alamo** (© 877/227-8367; www.alamo.com), **Avis** (© 800/230-4898; www.avis.com), **Budget** (© 800/527-0700; www.budget.com), **Dollar** (© 800/800-3665; www.dollar.com), **Enterprise** (© 800/736-8227; www.enterprise.com), **Hertz** (© 800/654-3131; www.hertz.com), **National** (© 800/227-7368; www.nationalcar.com), **Payless** (© 800/729-5377; www.paylesscarrental.com), and **Thrifty** (© 800/847-4389; www.thrifty.com).

Car-rental rates vary even more than airline fares. The price you pay will depend on the size of the car, where and when you pick it up and drop it off, the length of the rental period, where and how far you drive it, whether you purchase insurance, and a host of other factors. A few key questions could save you hundreds of dollars.

- Are weekend rates lower than weekday rates? Ask if the rate is the same for pickup Friday morning, for instance, as it is for pickup Thursday night.
- Is a weekly rate cheaper than the daily? Even if you need the car for only 4 days, it may be cheaper to keep it for 5.
- Does the agency assess a drop-off charge if you don't return the car to the same location where you picked it up? Is it cheaper to pick up the car at the airport than at a Downtown location?
- Are special promotional rates available? If you see an advertised price in your local newspaper, be sure to ask for that specific rate; otherwise, you may be charged the standard cost. Terms change constantly, and reservations agents are notorious for not mentioning available discounts unless you ask.
- Are discounts available for members of AARP, AAA, frequent-flier programs, or trade unions?
- How much tax will be added to the rental bill?
- What is the cost of adding an additional driver's name to the contract?
- How many free miles are included in the price? Free mileage is often negotiable.
- How much does the rental company charge to refill your gas tank if you return with the tank less than full? Though most rental companies claim these prices are "competitive," fuel you purchase yourself is almost always cheaper.

Some companies offer "refueling packages," in which you pay for an entire tank of gas upfront. The price is usually fairly competitive with local gas prices, but you don't get credit for any gas remaining in the tank. If a stop at a gas station on the way to the airport will make you miss your plane, then by all means take advantage of the fuel purchase option. Otherwise, skip it.

Many packages are available that include airfare, accommodations, and a rental car with unlimited mileage. Compare these prices with the cost of booking airfare and renting a car separately to see if these offers are good deals.

Internet resources can make comparison shopping easier. An excellent car-rental website is **BreezeNet,** at **www.bnm.com**.

DEMYSTIFYING RENTER'S INSURANCE   Before you drive off in a rental car, be sure you're insured. Hasty assumptions about your personal auto insurance or a rental agency's additional coverage could end up costing you tens of thousands of dollars—even if you are involved in an accident that was clearly the fault of another driver.

If you already hold a **private auto insurance** policy, you are most likely covered in the United States for loss of or damage to a rental car and liability in case of injury to any other party involved in an accident. Be sure to find out whether you are covered in the area you are visiting, whether your policy extends to all persons who will be driving the rental car, how much liability is covered in case an outside party is injured in an accident, and whether the type of vehicle you are renting is included under your contract. (Rental trucks, sports utility vehicles, and luxury vehicles such as a Jaguar may not be covered.)

Most **major credit cards** provide some degree of coverage as well—provided that they were used to pay for the rental. Terms vary widely, however, so be sure to call your credit card company directly before you rent.

If you are **uninsured,** the credit card you use to rent a car may provide primary coverage as long as you decline the rental agency's insurance. This means that the credit card company will cover damage or theft of a rental car for the full cost of the vehicle. If you already have insurance, your credit card may provide secondary coverage—which basically covers your deductible. *Credit cards will not cover liability* or the cost of injury to an outside party and/or damage to an outside party's vehicle. Bear in mind that each credit card company has its own peculiarities; call your own credit card company for details before relying on a card for coverage. If you do not hold an insurance policy, you may want to seriously consider purchasing additional liability insurance from your rental company. Be sure to check the terms, however: Some rental agencies cover liability only if the renter is not at fault; even then, the rental company's obligation varies from state to state.

The basic insurance coverage offered by most car-rental companies, known as the **loss/damage waiver (LDW)** or **collision damage waiver (CDW),** can cost as much as $20 per day. It usually covers the full value of the vehicle with no deductible if an outside party causes an accident or other damage to the rental car. In all states except California, you will probably be covered in case of theft as well. Liability coverage varies according to the company policy and state law, but the minimum is usually at least $15,000. If you are at fault in an accident, however, you will be covered for the full replacement value of the car—but not for liability. Some states allow you to buy additional liability coverage for such cases. Most rental companies require a police report in order to process any claims you file, but your private insurer will not be notified of the accident. Check your own policies and credit cards before you shell out money for this extra insurance because you may already be covered.

BY TAXI

Since cabs line up in front of all major hotels, an easy way to get around town is by taxi. Cabs charge $3.20 at the meter drop and 25¢ for each additional ⅛ mile, with an additional $1.20 fee for all fares originating from the airport and time-based penalties if you get stuck in a traffic jam. A taxi from the airport to the Strip will run you $12 to $20, from the airport to Downtown $15 to $20, and between the Strip and Downtown about $10 to $15. You can often save money by sharing a cab with someone going to the same destination (up to five people can ride for the same fare).

If you want to call a taxi, any of the following companies can provide one: **Desert Cab Company** (© 702/386-9102), **Whittlesea Blue Cab** (© 702/384-6111), and **Yellow/Checker Cab** (© 702/873-2000).

BY PUBLIC TRANSPORTATION

The Deuce (© **702/CAT-RIDE [228-7433];** www.thedeucelas vegas.com) is a fleet of modern double-decker buses that run the length of the Strip and should be operating expanded routes to Downtown, McCarran Airport, and the Paradise Road/Convention Center area by the time you read this. For a remarkably low $5 you get an all-day pass and can get on and off as many times as you like.

The **Las Vegas Monorail** (www.lvmonorail.com) runs from the Sahara Hotel, zigzagging out to the Hilton and the Convention Center, and then back down the east side of the Strip, making several stops along its 4-mile journey before ending at the MGM Grand and turning around. Prices are $5 one-way, $9 round-trip.

Or you can hop aboard a classic streetcar replica run by **Las Vegas Strip Trolley** (© 702/382-1404; www.striptrolley.com). These old-fashioned dark-green vehicles have interior oak paneling and are comfortably air-conditioned. Like the buses, they run northward from Hacienda Avenue, stopping at all major hotels en route to the Sahara, and then looping back via the Las Vegas Hilton. They do not, however, go to the Stratosphere or Downtown. Trolleys run about every 15 minutes daily between 9:30am and 2am. The fare is $4.25 (free for children 4 and under) for an all-day pass, and exact change is required.

There are also a few free transportation services, courtesy of the casinos. For example, a free tram shuttles between The Mirage and Treasure Island.

5 City Layout

There are two main areas of Las Vegas: the **Strip** and **Downtown.** For many people, that's all there is to Las Vegas. But there is actually more to the town than that, maybe not as glitzy and glamorous—okay, definitely not—but you will find still more casino action on Paradise Road and in east Las Vegas, mainstream and alternative culture shopping on Maryland Parkway, and different restaurant choices all over the city. Confining yourself to the Strip and Downtown is fine for a first-time visitor, but repeat customers should get out and explore. Las Vegas Boulevard South (the Strip) is the originating point for addresses; any street crossing it starts with 1 East and 1 West at its intersection with the Strip.

THE STRIP

The Strip is probably the most famous 4-mile stretch of highway in the nation. Officially called Las Vegas Boulevard South, it contains most of the top hotels in town and offers almost all of the major showroom entertainment. First-time visitors will, and probably should, spend the bulk of their time on the Strip. If mobility is a problem for you, then we suggest basing yourself in a South or Mid-Strip location.

For the purposes of organizing this book, we've divided the Strip into three sections. The **South Strip** is roughly defined as the portion of the Strip south of Harmon Avenue and north of Russell

Road. It's home to the MGM Grand, Mandalay Bay, the Monte Carlo, New York–New York, Luxor, the new CityCenter and many more hotels.

Mid-Strip is a long stretch of the street between Harmon Avenue and Spring Mountain Road. Hotels you'll find here include Bellagio, Caesars, The Mirage and Treasure Island, Bally's, Paris Las Vegas, the Flamingo Las Vegas, and Harrah's, among others.

North Strip stretches north from Spring Mountain Road all the way to the Stratosphere Tower and features the Wynn Las Vegas, Stardust, Sahara, Riviera, and Circus Circus, to name a few.

EAST OF THE STRIP/CONVENTION CENTER

This area has grown up around the Las Vegas Convention Center. Las Vegas is one of the nation's top convention cities, attracting more than 3 million conventioneers each year. The major hotel in this section of town is the Las Vegas Hilton, but in recent years, Marriott has built Residence Inn and Courtyard properties here, and a Hard Rock Hotel has opened. You'll find many excellent smaller hotels and motels southward along Paradise Road. All of these offer proximity to the Strip.

BETWEEN THE STRIP & DOWNTOWN

The area between the Strip and Downtown is a seedy stretch dotted with tacky wedding chapels, bail-bond operations, pawnshops, and cheap motels.

However, the area known as the **Gateway District** (roughly north and south of Charleston Blvd. to the west of Las Vegas Blvd. South) is slowly but surely gaining a name for itself as an actual artists' colony. Studios, small cafes, and other signs of life are springing up, and we hope this movement will last.

DOWNTOWN

Also known as **"Glitter Gulch"** (narrower streets make the neon seem brighter), Downtown Las Vegas, which is centered on Fremont Street between Main and 9th streets, was the first section of the city to develop hotels and casinos. With the exception of the Golden Nugget, which looks like it belongs in Monte Carlo, this area has traditionally been more casual than the Strip. But with the advent of the **Fremont Street Experience** (p. 113), Downtown has experienced a revitalization. The area is clean, the crowds are low-key and friendly, and the light show overhead is as silly as anything on the Strip. Don't overlook it. Las Vegas Boulevard South runs all the way into Fremont Street Downtown.

Las Vegas at a Glance

It shouldn't be too hard to navigate your way around Las Vegas. But keep in mind that, given the huge hotel acreage, increased and very slow traffic, and lots and lots of people like you, getting around takes a lot longer than you might think. Heck, it can take 15 to 20 minutes to get from your room to another part of your hotel! Always allow for plenty of time to get from point A to point B.

6 Money & Costs

MONEY

ATMs linked to both the **Cirrus** (© **800/424-7787;** www.master card.com) and **PLUS** (© **800/843-7587;** www.visa.com) networks can be found everywhere in Las Vegas; no one wants you to find yourself without cash you could lose in a slot! Beware of withdrawal charges, though, which can often run as high as $2 or $3 (the highest charges are usually for commercial machines in convenience stores and hotel lobbies). Also be aware that your own bank may impose a fee every time you use your card at an ATM in a different city or bank. To compare banks' ATM fees within the U.S., use **www.bankrate.com**.

Almost every credit card company has an emergency toll-free number that you can call if your wallet or purse is stolen. **Visa**'s U.S. emergency number is © **800/847-2911.** American Express cardholders and traveler's check holders should call © **800/221-7282.** **MasterCard** holders should call © **800/307-7309.**

MONEY-SAVING DEALS

Before you start your search for the lowest airfare, you may want to consider booking your flight as part of a travel package.

Package tours are not the same as escorted tours. They are simply a way to buy airfare and accommodations (and sometimes extras like sightseeing tours and hard-to-get show tickets) at the same time. When you're visiting Las Vegas, a package can be a smart way to go. In many cases, a package that includes airfare, hotel, and a rental car will cost you less than your hotel bill alone would have, had you booked it yourself. That's because packages are sold in bulk to tour operators, who then resell them to the public at a cost that drastically undercuts standard rates.

Packages, however, vary widely. Some offer a better class of hotels than others. Some offer the same hotels for lower prices. With some packagers, your choice of accommodations and travel days may be limited. Which package is right for you depends entirely on what you want. Prices vary according to the season, seat availability, hotel choice, whether you travel midweek or on the weekend, and other factors. But since even an advance-purchase round-trip fare between New York and Las Vegas can easily be $100 or $200 more than the figures quoted below, it seems almost insane *not* to book a less expensive package that includes so many extras.

Just to give you a couple of examples, at press time, a **Delta Vacations** package leaving from New York cost as little as $478 per person, based on double occupancy, including round-trip coach air transportation, 2 nights at your choice of several major casino hotels, a rental car, airport transfers, and bonus discounts and admissions. At press time, **Southwest Airlines Vacations** was offering round-trip airfare from Los Angeles with 2 nights at several different hotels; cost per person, based on double occupancy, was $269 for the Bellagio (before applicable taxes and fees).

Here are a few tips to help you tell one package from another and figure out which one is right for you:

- **Read this guide.** Do a little homework. Compare the rates that we've published to the discounted rates being offered by the packagers to see what kinds of deals they're offering—if you're actually being offered a substantial savings, or if they've just gussied up the rack rates to make their offer *sound* like a deal. If you're being offered a stay in a hotel we haven't recommended, do more research to learn about it, especially if it isn't a reliable franchise. It's not a deal if you end up at a dump.

- **Read the fine print.** Make sure you know *exactly* what's included in the price you're being quoted and what's not. Are hotel taxes included, or will you have to pay extra? Before you commit to a package, make sure you know how much flexibility you have if, say, your kid gets sick or your boss suddenly asks you to adjust your vacation schedule. Some packagers require ironclad commitments, while others will go with the flow, charging only minimal fees for changes or cancellations.

- **Use your best judgment.** Stay away from fly-by-nights and shady packagers. If a deal appears to be too good to be true, it probably is. Go with a reputable firm with a proven track record. This is where your travel agent can come in handy; he or she should be knowledgeable about different packagers, the deals they offer, and the general rate of satisfaction among their customers.

So how do you find a package deal? Perhaps the best place to start is with the airlines themselves, which often package their flights together with accommodations. **Southwest Airlines Vacations** (© 800/475-9792; www.swavacations.com) has dozens of flights in and out of Las Vegas every day, so the sheer volume allows them to offer some relatively inexpensive vacation deals with lots of options in terms of travel time and hotels.

Other airlines that offer air/land packages include **American Airlines Vacations** (© 800/321-2121; www.aavacations.com), **Continental Airlines Vacations** (© 800/301-3800; www.covacations.com), **Delta Vacations** (© 800/654-6559; www.deltavacations.com), **United Vacations** (© 888/854-3899; www.unitedvacations.com), and **US Airways Vacations** (© 800/455-0123; www.usairways vacations.com).

The biggest hotel chains, casinos, and resorts also offer package deals. If you already know where you want to stay, call the resort itself and ask if they can offer land/air packages.

Another place to start your search is the travel section of your local Sunday newspaper. Also check the ads in the back of national travel magazines like *Travel Holiday, National Geographic Traveler,* and *Arthur Frommer's Budget Travel.*

One of the biggest packagers in the Northeast, **Liberty Travel** (© 888/271-1584; www.libertytravel.com), boasts a full-page ad in many Sunday papers. You won't get much in the way of service from them, but you can get a good deal. **American Express Vacations** (© 800/297-2977; http://travel.americanexpress.com) is another option.

For one-stop shopping, **Vacation Together** (© 877/444-4547; www.vacationtogether.com) allows you to search for and book Las Vegas packages offered by a number of tour operators and airlines.

Finally, another good source for money-saving deals is online travel-planning sites, which frequently offer discounted packages to Las Vegas. The most long-standing and reputable sites, **Travelocity** (www.travelocity.com or http://frommers.travelocity.com) and **Expedia** (www.expedia.com), offer excellent selections and searches for complete vacation packages. Travelers search by destination and dates coupled with how much they are willing to spend.

Orbitz (www.orbitz.com), a site launched by United, Delta, Northwest, American, and Continental airlines, offers a huge range of airfares and hotel rooms, as well as complete vacation packages.

7 Specialized Travel Resources

TRAVELERS WITH DISABILITIES

On the one hand, Las Vegas is fairly well-equipped for those with disabilities, with virtually every hotel having accessible rooms, ramps, and other requirements. On the other hand, the distance between hotels (particularly on the Strip) makes a vehicle of some sort virtually mandatory for most travelers with disabilities, and it may be extremely strenuous and time-consuming to get from place to place (even within a single hotel because of the crowds). Even if you don't intend to gamble, you still may have to go through the casino, and casinos can be quite difficult to maneuver in, particularly for a guest in a wheelchair. Casinos are usually crowded, and the machines and tables are often laid out close together, with chairs, people, and such blocking easy access. You should also consider that it is often a long trek through larger hotels between the entrance and the room elevators (or, for that matter, anywhere in the hotel), and then add a crowded casino to the equation.

Southern Nevada Center for Independent Living, 6039 Eldora St., Suite H-8, Las Vegas, NV 89146 (© **800/870-7003** or 702/889-4216; www.sncil.org) can recommend hotels and restaurants that meet your needs, help you find a personal attendant, advise about transportation, and answer all sorts of other questions. The **Nevada Commission on Tourism** (© **800/638-2328;** www.travelnevada.com) offers a free accommodations guide to Las Vegas hotels that includes access information.

GAY & LESBIAN TRAVELERS

For such a licentious, permissive town, Las Vegas has its conservative side, and it is not the most gay-friendly city. This will not manifest itself in any signs of outrage toward open displays of gay affection, but it does mean that the local gay community is largely confined to the bar scene. This may be changing, with local gay pride parades and other activities gathering steam each year, including the first-ever nighttime parade through Downtown with the mayor in attendance in 2001. See listings for gay bars in chapter 7, "Las Vegas After Dark." Also, if you're on the Web, check out **www.gaylasvegas.com** or **Gayvegas.com,** both of which have helpful advice on lodging, restaurants, and nightlife.

QVegas, a monthly magazine serving the gay community, provides information about bars, workshops, local politics, support groups, shops, events, and more. You can find the magazine in bars,

music stores, and most libraries and bookstores. For details, call
© 702/650-0636 or check their online edition at **www.qvegas.com**.

SENIORS

Seniors, don't be shy about asking for discounts, but always bring an
ID card, especially if you've kept your youthful glow. Mention the
fact that you're a senior when you first make your travel reservations.
Most of the major domestic airlines offer discount programs for senior travelers, as does **Greyhound** (© 800/231-2222; www.grey
hound.com).

Members of **AARP** (formerly known as the American Association
of Retired Persons), 601 E St. NW, Washington, DC 20049
(© 888/687-2277; www.aarp.org), get discounts on hotels, airfares,
and car rentals. AARP offers members a wide range of benefits,
including *AARP The Magazine* and a monthly newsletter. Anyone 50
or over can join.

FAMILY TRAVEL

Vegas is a city that caters to the over-21 set and isn't the best destination to bring the kids to. For one thing, kids are not allowed in
casinos at all. Since most hotels are laid out so that you have to frequently walk through their casinos, you can see how this becomes a
headache. Some casino hotels will not allow the children of non-
guests on the premises after 6pm—and this policy is seriously
enforced. If you choose to travel here with the children, look for the
hotels, restaurants, and shows bearing the Kids icon in chapters 3, 4,
and 7.

If you do bring your children to Las Vegas during the summer,
you'll definitely want to book a place with a pool. Many hotels also
have enormous video arcades and other diversions.

WOMEN TRAVELERS

Thanks to the crowds, Las Vegas is as safe as any other big city for a
woman traveling alone. Take the usual precautions and be wary of
hustlers or drunken businessmen who may mistake a woman on her
own for a "working girl." (Alas, million-dollar proposals, a la Robert
Redford, are a rarity.) Many of the big hotels (most MGM-Mirage
hotels, for example) have security guards stationed at the elevators at
night to prevent anyone other than guests from going up to the
room floors. Ask when you make your reservation. If you're anxious,
ask a security guard to escort you to your room. *Always* lock your
door *and* deadbolt it to prevent intruders from entering.

3

Where to Stay

Accommodations in Vegas, if gambling is not your priority, are perhaps the trickiest part of a visit. Not because Vegas lacks for space. Goodness no; at last count, the city had nearly 140,000 hotel rooms and rising. It's because you aren't there specifically to indulge in the usual pastime of gaming, and the hotel owners, by and large, are going to do their darnedest to make you change your mind.

Everywhere else in the world, hotels are built near the top attractions. Here, they *are* the top attractions. A hotel's designers are considered failures if they have not made leaving the premises unnecessary, if not outright impossible, so you can see that your choice of lodging is going to be a challenge. Because as fantastical as these behemoths are, they exist for one reason: to trap their customers into using slot machines. Or blackjack tables. Whatever.

Consequently, the most common design of a casino hotel makes sure that all guests have to skirt, if not cross, the casino floor on their way from their room to anywhere else. Many make the layout as confusing as possible, in the hopes that you will grow so exhausted trying to find the exit, you will just give up and eat/play/gamble there. Why go find a curious little ethnic place when there is Chinese food right there? Why go see a show at some other hotel when they've got a circus act right there? And hey, I've got these quarters in my hand, I might as well play them instead of carting them around . . . There are alternatives: Can you say *chain hotel*? Name one, any one, and Vegas has it. They're designed for the comfort and anonymity of the business traveler. They're fine, for sure, but nothing special, and certainly offer no dazzle. On the other hand, they are without casinos, which brings their noise and chaos quotients way down. We list the best.

There are a number of things to keep in mind when booking accommodations in Vegas. The first and most significant is that rack rates have little to do with real rates. No one ever pays rack rates in Vegas. Ever. Vegas hotels change their prices at the drop of a hat. The same room can cost $39 one night and a couple nights later cost $239 if there is a convention, the Super Bowl, or a holiday going on.

This is why the rates listed in this chapter in some cases fluctuate wildly. What to do? Keep your eyes open for deals; the Internet will be your friend, with websites such as **www.hotels.com** offering a roundup of low prices on rooms. Newspapers often have ads offering terrific room rates. And you can also just call up a hotel and beg the person who answers to help you out. Note that for some reason, casino hotels are often considerably more affordable than the chains; though the days of rock-bottom room prices, figuring guests will then feel comfortable dropping more at the tables, are gone, that basic incentive is still at the back of the casino hotel's minds. Chain hotels, *sans* casino, don't have that kind of motivation. Web clearance sites, however, can often let you know if Marriott or whoever is offering a special.

If you have the chance, when booking your room, request a corner unit, for they tend to be larger and have more windows. Also, the higher up the room, the better the view; nearly every Strip hotel in Vegas has some special view to offer (The Mirage of the exploding volcano, Treasure Island of its siren-and-pirate battle, The Venetian of gondolas, and for every one, the bright lights that are the Strip in all its nightly glory). A room on a low floor will often get you only a view of other buildings.

Note also that while we will tell you if there are any differences in Vegas rooms, it can sometimes be hard to spot any such differences. There seem to be a few basic categories—okay, somewhat better than okay, somewhat nicer than that—but within those categories, with a few exceptions, there isn't that much to distinguish one room from another. After all, again we are talking cookie-cutter chain hotels or big giant enormous hotels—individuality is just difficult to produce when you are talking upward of 3,000 rooms. Speaking of which, if you are coming to Vegas because you've heard it's now focusing on

---

Tips **A Web Wonder**

A little-known gem, **Travelaxe (www.travelaxe.com)** offers a free, downloadable price-comparison program that will make your Las Vegas hotel search infinitely easier. The program searches the hotels and a host of discount travel websites for the best prices for your travel dates. Click on the price you like, and the program will send you straight to the website offering it. And, unlike most websites, Travelaxe prices include hotel tax, so you actually see the total price of the room.

being a luxury resort town, remind yourself that full service and Egyptian cotton sheets are not found in bulk. If you agree with us that those are not insignificant components in the concept of "luxury," head toward the smaller complexes.

The resorts are pretty smashing, in terms of all they offer, but there are hidden potholes. Like how those glorious spas cost dearly (p. 56). How the pools are shallow and the newer ones generally don't have much tree cover or other shade. There are usually cabanas, but there's a charge for using them. Actually, there's a charge for everything after the basic cost of your room, and it adds up.

The location of your hotel is also worth taking into consideration. All the Downtown hotels are totally skewed toward gamblers and would not be good choices for non-gamblers, so we have not reviewed any of them here. If you aren't going to gamble, but you do want to engage in the second-most-popular Vegas pastime, cruising the Strip uttering variations of "Wow!," you need to either rent a car (cabs add up, and while many off-Strip hotels have shuttle service, it may not be often enough for comfort and flexibility) or stay at a centrally located hotel, either at the corner of Tropicana Avenue and the Strip or no farther north than The Venetian. The Strip is long, the properties are bigger than they seem, and it gets really hot in the summer and cool and windy in the winter. On the other hand, if you want peace, stay away from the Strip, and in a non-casino hotel; the hustle-bustle factor goes way, way down.

Note: The star ratings we assign in this chapter reflect *the hotel's suitability for non-gamblers.* Thus, a hotel that might rate three stars for gamblers may rate only two stars for you.

1 The Top Hotels

The following are our absolute favorites for non-gambler accommodations, thanks to either layout or services.

SOUTH STRIP

Four Seasons Las Vegas ★★★ *Kids* We love the four three-star hotels in this section just about equally; each has something to recommend it over the others. But we give a slight edge to the Four Seasons because of the combination of location and service; it is right on the Strip (as opposed to the Ritz and Green Valley Ranch, both of which are in nearby Henderson), and the Four Seasons is one of the world's premier hotel conglomerates, so these people know all about pampering—from the moment you hit the portico, everyone is looking out for you.

Located on the top floors of Mandalay Bay, the entrance is located on the other side of that hotel, so you need never hear the clang of a slot if you so choose. The rooms, recently redone, are heavy on neutral tones and quiet good taste. The bathrooms are lush, stocked with pricey L'Occitane amenities. The hotel has all its own facilities, including a medium-size pool and a fully equipped health club with no fee (unique in Vegas). Despite the grown-up atmosphere, children are welcome; rooms can be baby-proofed, kids get a welcome gift of toys and goodies, and on it goes. Of the hotels in this category, it's the best place for children (provided that their parents have deep pockets).

Service is impeccable; one guest recalls asking for a Christmas tree during a holiday stay and finding said tree, fully decorated, waiting for her. The restaurants, Charlie Palmer Steak and Veranda Café, are good to even superlative. Plus, all those hidden extras at the other hotels—health club usage, cabanas at the pool, and so forth—are included in the room rate, which makes it at times even cheaper than the other fancy hotels. And should you get tired of the hush, Mandalay Bay and all its delights are just a hallway away.

3960 Las Vegas Blvd. S., Las Vegas, NV 89119. © **877/632-5000** or 702/632-5000. Fax 702/632-5195. www.fourseasons.com. 424 units. $450 and up double; $630 and up suite. Extra person $30. Children 17 and under stay free in parent's room. AE, DC, DISC, MC, V. Valet parking $18, no self-parking. Pets under 25 lb. accepted. **Amenities:** 2 restaurants; heated outdoor pool; elegant health club (free to guests) & spa; concierge; car-rental desk; courtesy car; business center w/faxing, delivery, and secretarial service open daily during business hours; 24-hr. room service; in-room massage; overnight laundry service; overnight dry cleaning; executive-level rooms. *In room:* A/C, TV/DVD w/pay movies, Wi-Fi (for a fee), minibar, fridge on request, coffeemaker, hair dryer, iron/ironing board, safe.

Mandalay Bay ✦✦   Of all the true Strip casino hotels, this may be the one best suited for non-gamblers. Alone of all the Strip casino-hotels, here guests do not have to enter the casino to reach the guest elevators, though the casino lies between them and all the good clubs and restaurants. There are an awful lot of the latter, and within them are some of the most fanciful interiors in a town lousy with bland dining settings. The rooms are large, handsome, and forgettable, but the bathrooms are the largest on the Strip in this price range.

The pool area is superb: The 11-acre pool zone has a large lazy river, a regular pool, and a wave pool that sends junior-size tubes out at regular intervals for wannabe Surfer Joes (boogie board rentals extra). For an extra (and exorbitant) fee, you can stroll through the

Accommodations on the Strip

SOUTH STRIP
Excalibur **21**
Four Seasons Las Vegas **23**
Luxor **22**
Mandalay Bay **23**
MGM Grand Hotel & Casino **19**
Monte Carlo Resort & Casino **18**
New York–New York Hotel
  & Casino **20**
Planet Hollywood Resort
  & Casino **17**
South Point **24**
THEhotel at Mandalay Bay **23**

CENTER STRIP
Bally's Las Vegas **15**
Bellagio **14**
Caesars Palace **11**
The Flamingo Las Vegas **10**
Harrah's Las Vegas **9**
The Mirage **8**
Palazzo **6**
Palms Casino Resort **13**
Paris Las Vegas **16**
Rio All-Suite Hotel & Casino **12**
TI–Treasure Island Las Vegas **5**
The Venetian **7**
Wynn Las Vegas **4**

NORTH STRIP
Circus Circus **2**
Las Vegas Hilton **3**
Stratosphere Casino Hotel
  & Tower **1**

soothing Shark Bay Reef. Between the hot scenes at rumjungle and the House of Blues, nightlife is well served. While we do know some families who have stayed here happily, note that an extra person over the age of 14 costs an additional $35.

3950 Las Vegas Blvd. S. (at Hacienda Ave.), Las Vegas, NV 89119. © **877/632-7800** or 702/632-7777. Fax 702/632-7228. www.mandalaybay.com. 3,309 units (including THEhotel). From $99 double; $149 and up suite; $149 and up House of Blues Signature Rooms. AE, DC, DISC, MC, V. Free self- and valet parking. **Amenities:** Casino; 12,000-seat events center; 1,700-seat performing arts theater; aquarium; wedding chapels; 22 restaurants; 4 outdoor pools w/lazy river and wave pool; health club; spa; Jacuzzi; sauna; watersports equipment/rentals; concierge; tour desk; business center; 24-hr. room service; in-room massage; babysitting; laundry service; dry cleaning; executive-level rooms. *In room:* A/C, TV w/pay movies, dataport, high-speed Internet access (for a fee), Wi-Fi (for a fee), hair dryer, iron/ironing board, safe.

THEhotel at Mandalay Bay ✦✦✦

A smashing, sophisticated "wow" of a hotel, contemporary and classy; the only thing that keeps it from being our no. 1 choice for the non-gambler—or possibly anyone—is that, unlike the Four Seasons or the Ritz, this is still Vegas-size. Which means that even though it *looks* like a boutique hotel and *acts* like a boutique hotel, it simply can't *run* like a boutique hotel. Pare this puppy down and add some of that cosseting service you find at the Ritz or the Four Seasons, and you would have something that could compete with any fancy-pants Manhattan lodgings. And to be fair, with all rooms true one-bedroom suites, containing no fewer than three flatscreen plasma TVs, bathrooms with tubs so deep most can soak up to their chins, robes and slippers, and even decent sheets, the experience is so unlike anything else in Vegas that we aren't even sure we need much else.

THEhotel is set up in an entirely different building than the rest of Mandalay Bay, though they are connected by a long hallway. So you, the non-gambling guest, can stay in a hushed, mature environment, though you are within easy walking of all that traditional Vegas has to offer. Though you might not be all that tempted; for once, these glossy accommodations (separate living room, wet bar, even a half-bathroom), despite an excess of mirrors and some rather dim lighting, are designed to make you want to stay in your room.

Prices are high; the state-of-the-art health club will cost you $30 a day, and the sleek cafes make you pay for their marvelous decor. But still, if this place does anywhere near the business it ought, watch for the rest of Vegas to take a cue—and about time.

3950 Las Vegas Blvd. S. (at Hacienda Ave.), Las Vegas, NV 89119. © **877/632-7800** or 702/632-7777. Fax 702/632-9215. www.thehotelatmandalaybay.com. 1,120 units. $160 and up suite. Extra person $30. Children under 14 stay free in parent's room. AE, DC, DISC, MC, V. Free self- and valet parking. **Amenities:** 2 restaurants; bar; access to Mandalay Bay restaurants/pool/casino; health club; spa; tour desk; car-rental desk; business center; 24-hr. room service; laundry service. *In-room:* A/C, 3 flatscreen plasma TVs w/pay movies, DVD player, CD player, high-speed Internet access (for a fee), Wi-Fi (for a fee), printer/fax, wet bar, hair dryer, iron/ironing board, safe.

EAST OF THE STRIP

Green Valley Ranch Resort ★★★

In a town that persists in boasting that it's now offering "true resort" options in contrast to the traditional view of Vegas being, well, just for gamblers, it's nice to know that at least *one* place isn't exaggerating. Of course, the resort in question is in Henderson, but you can see the Strip from the pool area, and it's only a 15-minute drive, depending on traffic.

So what makes it worth the (really insignificant unless it's rush hour) drive? Green Valley's odd and oddly successful merging of the Ritz-Carlton luxury with W and the Hard Rock Hotel's style. Inside all is posh and stately, a dignified classy lobby, large rooms with the most comfortable beds in town (high-thread-count linens, feather beds, plump down comforters), and luxe marble bathrooms. Outside is the hippest pool area this side of the Hard Rock Hotel and our favorite for sheer relaxation. It's part lagoon, part modern-geometric, with shallow places for reading and canoodling, and your choice of poolside lounging equipment, ranging from teak lounge chairs to thick mattresses strewn with pillows, plus drinks served from the trendy Whiskey Beach. Use of the tiny health club is free, and the charming spa is modern and hip. At night, Whiskey Sky heats up—more mattresses and couches, strewn with pillows and the fittest bodies in Vegas—while DJs spin tunes and poor souls try to get past the velvet rope. You can, because you stay here.

The entirely separate casino area (it's off in another, adjoining building) offers an assortment of restaurants, from a 24-hour cafe, to the Pancake House, to Hank's, with its fine steaks and fried goodies. Add in a multiscreen movie theater, and this is a resort that has something for every demographic.

2300 Paseo Verde Dr. (at I-215), Henderson, NV 89052. © **866/782-9487** or 702/782-9487. Fax 702/617-6885. www.greenvalleyranchresort.com. 200 units. Sun–Thurs $129 and up double; Fri–Sat $189. Extra person $12. Children under 18 stay free in parent's room. Crib/rollaway free. AE, DC, DISC, MC, V. Free self- and valet parking. **Amenities:** Casino; nightclub; movie theater; 10 restaurants plus a food court; outdoor pool; health club; spa; Jacuzzi; sauna; concierge; free shuttle to the Strip and the airport; business center; shopping arcade; 24-hr. room service; in-room massage; laundry service; dry cleaning; executive-level rooms. *In room:* A/C, TV w/pay movies, dataport, high-speed Internet access (for a fee), Wi-Fi (for a fee), coffeemaker, hair dryer, iron/ironing board, safe.

Ritz-Carlton, Lake Las Vegas ✸✸✸ (Kids)   Say you are coming to Vegas not for a convention or to visit relatives, both of which may require a stay in town, but for a genuine getaway. Consider this: Don't stay in Vegas. Stay outside of town. About a half-hour and a whole different attitude away is the man-made but still comely Lake Las Vegas, bridged at one end by this striking hotel, modeled after the Ponte Vecchio in Florence, Italy. It's our hands-down favorite in the area. There is very little incentive to leave the premises. Ever. The setting—fire-blue lake, ring of austere mountains, all serenity—is the polar opposite of the usual hectic, overwhelming Vegas. The result is a true resort of great appeal. It's not a bit snobby, as the well-trained and solicitous staff coddle every guest, regardless of their dress or wallet.

With a swimming pool and shady beach pool (both with cabanas as well as umbrellas), free yoga and aerobics classes, hikes, bike rides, stargazing, watersports and other activities for additional fees, and a nice gym and even nicer spa, this is an excellent choice for couples looking for romance or friends on a bonding weekend. All kinds of wholesome activities (albeit usually for an extra fee) and the distance from Vegas mayhem make this a fine choice for families as well. Rooms are well-sized, done in pleasing muted pastels with nicely squishy beds, and all have lake or mountain views. Consider the extra nightly fee for the Club Level (about $100), which will be more than worth it for the four daily food services and unlimited drinks. The adjacent village offers some adequate dining options, but the food at the Ritz is (if pricey) superior. The casino in that same complex is so-so, so if gambling urges overwhelm, you may prefer to drive to Vegas or take the regular shuttles to the Strip (they run roughly 9am–9pm and cost $35).

1610 Lake Las Vegas Pkwy., Henderson, NV 89011. (C) **800/241-3333** or 702/567-4700. Fax 702/567-4777. www.ritzcarlton.com. 349 units. $179 and up. Children stay free in parent's room. Additional charge for rollaway bed. AE, DC, DISC, MC, V. Free self-parking. Pets accepted. **Amenities:** Restaurant; bar; 2 pools; health club; spa; some free exercise classes; concierge; shuttle to Strip; water taxis to nearby attractions; business center; 24-hr. room service; in-room massage; babysitting; laundry service; dry cleaning; executive-level rooms. *In room:* A/C, TV w/pay movies, Nintendo, dataport, high-speed Internet access (for a fee), Wi-Fi (included in resort fee), minibar, hair dryer, iron/ironing board, safe.

WEST OF THE STRIP

Red Rock Resort ✸✸✸   Costing a mere $1 billion—a pittance compared to other new resorts until you notice how relatively few rooms this one has—this is one of the newest and highfalutin-est

Tips So Your Trip Goes Swimmingly . . .

Part of the delight of the Vegas resort complexes is the gorgeous pools—what could be better for beating the summer heat? But there are pools and there are *pools,* so you'll need to keep several things in mind when searching for the right one.

During the winter, it's often too cold or windy to do much lounging, and even if the weather is amenable, the hotels often close part of their pool areas during winter and early spring. The pools are also not heated for the most part, but they largely don't need to be.

Most hotel pools are shallow, chest-high at best (the hotels want you gambling, not swimming). Diving is impossible—not that a single pool allows it anyway. Some resorts, such as Mirage, Venetian, and MGM Grand, offer adults-only pool areas, where you can find nightclub-style party-hearty action—and occasionally topless sun-bathing—during the day (for a fee running $20–$40 per person).

And finally, during those hot days, be warned that sitting by pools next to heavily windowed buildings such as The Mirage and Treasure Island will allow you to experience the same thing a bug does under a magnifying glass with a sun ray directed on it. Regardless of time of year, be sure to slather on the sunscreen; there's a reason you see so many lobster-red people roaming the streets. Many pool areas don't offer much in the way of shade.

At any of the pools, you can rent cabanas (which often include TVs, special lounge chairs, and special poolside service), but these should be reserved as far in advance as possible, and with the exception of the Four Seasons and the Ritz, where they are complimentary, most cost a hefty fee. If you are staying at a chain hotel, you will most likely find an average pool, but if you want to spend some time at a better one, be aware that most of the casino-hotel pool attendants will ask to see your room key. If they are busy, you might be able to sneak in or at least blend in with a group.

places around. Perched right on the edge of the Red Rock National Conservation Area (p. 192), a stunning natural wonderland of red-hued rock formations and desert landscape, like the Ritz, it's a drive from the Strip, but also like the Ritz, it's a true resort escape. Even you non-gamblers will want to goggle at the casino, an 80,000-square-foot monster that meanders through the building wrapped in natural woods, stonework, glass sculptures, and stunning amber-hued chandeliers. The rooms are impressive, modern wonders with high-end furnishings and linens, 42-inch plasma TVs, iPod sound systems, giant bathrooms, and more all wrapped up in clean, sleek lines and vibrant earth tones.

Eight restaurants serve up a wide variety of food selections including a buffet and a branch of the famed Salt Lick BBQ, out of Austin, Texas. Even the food court knocks it up a notch with a Capriotti's outlet offering some of the best submarine sandwiches we've ever tasted. Throw in a 16-screen movie theater, a daycare center, night-clubs and bars (including two from Rande Gerber of Whiskey Sky renown), a sumptuous spa and health club, and a 3-acre circular "backyard" area with a sandy beach, swimming and wading pools (eagle-eyed sunbathers caught a pre-second-pregnancy-announcement Britney Spears wandering around here after a spousal tiff, so you know this is an instant celeb hot spot and getaway), Jacuzzis, private cabanas, and a stage where big-name entertainers perform and—what could they have left out? Possibly economy; the listed price below notwithstanding, look to be charged as much as $300 or $400 a night, not to mention all kinds of hidden extra charges.

10973 W. Charleston Rd., Las Vegas, NV 89135. ℂ **866/767-7773** or 702/797-7625. Fax 702/797-7745. www.redrockstation.com. 800 units. $160 and up (up to 4 people). AE, DC, DISC, MC, V. **Amenities:** Casino; bars, lounges, and night-club; 16-screen movie theater; 8 restaurants; food court; outdoor pools and beach area; health club; spa; concierge; business center; 24-hr. room service; in-room massage; babysitting; laundry service; dry cleaning; nonsmoking rooms; *In room:* A/C, TV w/pay movies, dataport, high-speed Internet access (for a fee), Wi-Fi (for a fee), mini-bar, hair dryer, iron/ironing board, safe.

2 Best Casino Hotels

Each of the following has something to recommend it, whether it's a preponderance of non-gambling activities, or an easy-to-handle lay-out, or just a particularly swell Vegas motif. They each have their own drawbacks as well. Choose based on your own needs.

SOUTH STRIP

Excalibur   You may be tempted to stay here because it's shaped like a big castle and you have King Arthur fantasies. Good enough, but be warned that it's huge, sprawling, and they've taken out much of the charming kitsch and replaced it with nothing much. Kids swarm the place, hoping to run into Merlin; grown-ups who left their families at home are there because they got a comfortable but unassuming room for under $60, thus saving some cash for the slots. Note that none of the bathrooms have tubs, just showers. In addition to finding the smoky casino area hard to avoid, you aren't going to find much in the way of interesting shopping or eating, though they do have a Krispy Kreme on-site. The pool area is getting a facelift to add in better landscaping, fancy cabanas, and the like which will hopefully improve on its blandness. On the other hand, if you want a fantasy Camelot wedding, they rent the costumes needed to properly dress such an event.

3850 Las Vegas Blvd. S. (at Tropicana Ave.), Las Vegas, NV 89109. ℭ **800/937-7777** or 702/597-7700. Fax 702/597-7163. www.excalibur.com. 4,008 units. $59 and up double. Extra person $20. Children under 13 stay free in parent's room. AE, DC, DISC, MC, V. Free self- and valet parking. **Amenities:** Casino; showrooms; wedding chapel; 5 restaurants; food court; outdoor pool; video arcade; concierge; tour desk; car-rental desk; shopping arcade; 24-hr. room service; laundry service; dry cleaning. *In room:* A/C, TV w/pay movies, dataport, high-speed Internet access (for a fee), hair dryer, iron/ironing board.

Luxor ✯   Once one of the most melothematic hotels on the Strip, the minds behind Luxor inexplicably decided that this Egyptian extravaganza should look like a generic luxury hotel, albeit one set in a glass pyramid. Kitsch fans everywhere have been in deep mourning. But staying in a glass pyramid may be enough joy for you, and so we still recommend it.

The Pyramid rooms, accessible by a slanting elevator known as an "inclinator", have those slanted outside walls, plus shower-only bathrooms, so guests with space issues may have problems. On the other hand, corner Pyramid rooms are larger and have a Jacuzzi tub tucked into the nook of the walls, a nice tip for romance-seekers. Pyramid rooms are also arranged around the perimeter of the casino, though, of course, that will be many floors below unless you get a room on the first floor or two. Tower rooms are more spacious and away from all the hustle and bustle (you can pretty much avoid the casino if you stay in these rooms), and they have better bathrooms. Be careful, however, that you don't get one on a low floor because your view might be of a wall.

The buffet here is the best in its price range. The pool area offers five pools but is still kind of shabby; the health club is small but well-stocked.

3900 Las Vegas Blvd. S. (btw. Reno and Hacienda aves.), Las Vegas, NV 81119. ⓒ 800/777-0188 or 702/262-4000. Fax 702/262-4478. www.luxor.com. 4,400 units. $69 and up double; $149 and up whirlpool suite; $249–$800 other suites. Extra person $30. Children under 12 stay free in parent's room. Crib $15; rollaway $25. AE, DC, DISC, MC, V. Free self- and valet parking. **Amenities:** Casino; show-rooms; 8 restaurants; food court; 5 outdoor pools; health club; spa; 18,000-sq.-ft. video arcade; concierge; tour desk; car-rental desk; business center; shopping arcade; 24-hr. room service; dry cleaning; executive-level rooms. *In room:* A/C, TV w/pay movies, dataport, high-speed Internet access (for a fee), hair dryer, iron/iron-ing board.

MGM Grand Hotel & Casino ⓕ   We've grown very fond of this hotel, as it has gradually shed its "family fun" skin for something more mature. This mostly translates into several naughty shows, clubs, and bars, which in turn translates into a clientele that is a mix between giggly woo!-gals who find Paris and Britney superior role models and middle-age Jimmy Buffett fans in town for a concert. The hotel can be a horror for anyone not interested in gaming; between you and the outside world stands the largest casino in Vegas, and navigating it would make Magellan cry. Having said that, should you find yourself here, you will unearth some comforts: The rooms are a delight—pale pastels or earth tones evoking '30s Hollywood curvy elegance, with black-and-white matinee-idol photos on the walls. It's the best style and floor space for the price, for sure.

The pool area is also marvelous in the summer months—five large pools, plus a lazy river—but is likely to be shut down otherwise. If you're sans kids and care to avoid those belonging to others, be advised that packs of children are always likely to be present in the pool area. The spa is a Zen-Asian retreat dripping with ambience, complete with a decent-size workout room. The restaurant section has a better variety than many of the other hotels, and there is Stu-dio 54, which still isn't the nightclub we hoped it to be. The glass Lion Exhibit is pretty swell; different lions lounge about within for a few hours a day. Shows include the racy *La Femme* and a stunning Cirque du Soleil production, *KÀ*.

3799 Las Vegas Blvd. S. (at Tropicana Ave.), Las Vegas, NV 89109. ⓒ 800/929-1111 or 702/891-7777. Fax 702/891-1030. www.mgmgrand.com. 5,034 units. $99 and up double; $159 and up suite. Extra person $30. Children under 13 stay free in parent's room. Crib free; rollaway $30 per night. AE, DC, DISC, MC, V. Free self- and valet parking. **Amenities:** Casino; events arena; showroom; cabaret theater; 2 wedding chapels; 15 restaurants; 5 outdoor pools w/lazy river; health club; spa; Jacuzzi; sauna; game room/video arcade; concierge; tour desk; car-rental desk; business center; shopping arcade; salon; 24-hr. room service; in-room massage; babysitting; laundry service; dry cleaning; executive-level rooms. *In room:* A/C, TV w/pay movies, dataport, high-speed Internet access (for a fee), hair dryer, iron/ironing board, safe.

Monte Carlo Resort & Casino   Once meant to evoke the grand style of the real Monte Carlo, it still does, sort of, with its gleaming marble lobby, nicely separated from the James Bond–style casino. The rooms are getting a much needed makeover (little can be done for the dinky bathrooms) as we write this, and are accessible without going through the casino. The pool area features a couple desultory pools plus an itty wee lazy river—and you have to pay $10 for an inner tube. Kids run rampant in the pool area, which ends up look- ing rather dirty. The health club is nothing to speak of. There are, however, some good-value restaurants and a wonderful food court. And Lance Burton is one of the best shows in town.

3770 Las Vegas Blvd. S. (btw. Flamingo Rd. and Tropicana Ave.), Las Vegas, NV 89109. ℭ **800/311-8999** or 702/730-7777. Fax 702/730-7250. www.montecarlo.com. 3,002 units. $99 and up double; $149 and up suite. Extra per- son $25. AE, DC, DISC, MC, V. Free self- and valet parking. **Amenities:** Casino; show- room; wedding chapel; 7 restaurants; food court; outdoor pool; wave pool, lazy river; health club; spa; Jacuzzi; sauna; watersports equipment/rentals; video arcade; concierge; tour desk; business center; shopping arcade; 24-hr. room service; in-room massage; babysitting; laundry service; dry cleaning; executive-level rooms. *In room:* A/C, TV w/pay movies, dataport, high-speed Internet access (for a fee), hair dryer, iron/ironing board.

New York–New York Hotel & Casino ℱ   If you are in Vegas for the hoot value, you could do far worse than this hilarious theme hotel. But if you really want to stay away from gaming, this is not for you; it's another maze-trap, where utility is subverted in the name of over-the-top style. Sure, the casino is funny at first, with sections bordering it modeled after an iconic part of New York (for example Greenwich Village, complete with faux brownstones), but it's smoky, crowded, large, and meandering. Walking anywhere here is a navi- gational nightmare. (They seem to have forgotten the lesson of the real Manhattan's user-friendly grid.)

The restyled rooms are no longer as striking as they once were (and, yes, they are housed in the towers that make up the faux sky- line, and no, that skyline never did include the World Trade Center), though they remain comfortable. But some can be quite cramped and, oddly, the style goes down the larger the room gets. The roller coaster (oh, yeah) passes right over the pool area, which borders the parking garage, so you wouldn't catch us swimming there. The health club has been recently upgraded, and there are lots of quite decent restaurants (including reliable chains such as Il Fornaio and

Chin Chin), though breakfast anywhere comes at a dear price, and there is no excuse for a hotel modeled on the city that never sleeps to have no food available at midnight. There is a fabulous arcade area for the kids, while grown-up children won't find a more fun bar than Coyote Ugly.

3790 Las Vegas Blvd. S. (at Tropicana Ave.), Las Vegas, NV 89109. ℂ **800/693-6763** or 702/740-6969. Fax 702/740-6920. www.nynyhotelcasino.com. 2,023 units. $79 and up double. Extra person $30. AE, DC, DISC, MC, V. Free self- and valet parking. **Amenities:** Casino; showrooms; roller coaster; 9 restaurants; food court; outdoor pool; small health club; spa; Jacuzzi; sauna; video arcade w/carnival midway games; concierge; tour desk; business center, 24-hr. room service; laundry service; dry cleaning; executive-level rooms. *In room:* A/C, TV w/pay movies, dataport, high-speed Internet (for a fee), hair dryer, safe.

Planet Hollywood Resort & Casino 𝓰𝓰 Walking a line between the current generic resort hotel look—all sleek this and gleaming that—and gimmick, Planet Hollywood should certainly be considered if you are looking for a playful vibe. Each room is slightly thematic, based around a piece of Hollywood memorabilia (a dress Judy Garland wore in a musical, a blade from the Wesley Snipes pic *Blade*), it means your room stands out among the cookie cutter ones found elsewhere on the Strip. Add in an excellent and egalitarian nightclub, Prive, one of the best shopping malls in town, and some good mid-priced dining options and this is a fine Vegas hotel for the non-gambler. But be aware that it's not kid-friendly, despite the Hollywood angle, and not mobility friendly; the self-parking requires a ridiculously long schlep through the aforementioned, very very long shopping mall, while the rest of the place is the usual Vegas confusing noisy maze.

3667 Las Vegas Blvd. S., Las Vegas, NV 89109. ℂ **877/333-9474** or 702/785-5555. Fax 702/785-5558. www.planethollywoodresort.com. 2,600 units. $99 and up double. Extra person $30. No discount for children. AE, DC, DISC, MC, V. Free self- and valet parking. **Amenities:** Casino; performing-arts center; showroom; chapel; 19 restaurants; 7 bars/lounges; 2 outdoor pools; health club and spa; 2 Jacuzzis; concierge; tour desk; car-rental desk; business center; extensive shopping arcade; 24-hr. room service; in-room massage; laundry service; dry cleaning; executive-level rooms. *In room:* A/C, TV w/pay movies, dataport, high-speed Internet access (for a fee), Wi-Fi (for a fee), hair dryer, iron/ironing board, safe.

South Point 𝓰𝓰 Waaaaay south on the Strip, we include this because it's a model of what a modern Vegas hotel ought to be, to wit, comfortable, all-mod-cons, and yet not bankbook-busting. Rooms are spacious, with appealing streamlined decor and flatscreen TVs, and there are all sorts of entertainment options (movie theaters, bowling alley, even an Equestrian Center, though you have to bring your own hoofed animal), plenty of budget food options, and so forth. Not mind-boggling like some of the options here, but then again, neither are the prices. A great deal if you have a car; it's just a fast zoom up the Strip to plenty of free parking and other action, if that's what you require.

9777 Las Vegas Blvd. S., Las Vegas, NV 89123. ⓒ **866/796-7111** or 702/796-7111. Fax 702/365-7505. www.southpointcasino.com. 650 units. $59 and up double. Extra person $15. Children under 15 stay free in parent's room. AE, DC, DISC, MC, V. Free self- and valet parking. **Amenities:** Casino; 4,400-seat equestrian and events center; 16-screen movie theater; 64-lane bowling center; 6 restaurants; outdoor pool; spa; concierge; free shuttle to the Strip; 24-hr. room service; laundry service; dry cleaning; nonsmoking rooms. *In room:* A/C, TV w/pay movies, dataport, high-speed and wireless Internet access (for a fee), hair dryer, iron/ironing board.

MID-STRIP

Bellagio ⓖⓖ   Recalling that no place with more than 3,000 rooms can be as chic and pampering as the image Bellagio wants to present, this is decidedly the place where the grown-ups stay in town. It's still mostly about the gambling—it's hard to avoid the massive casino, but routes through the hotel are plainly marked and mostly accessible around the perimeter—but there are still enough genuine resort elements here, and the superlatives just pile up. Rooms are the poshest of the bigger casino hotels; take a basic room at The Mirage, but jump everything up a notch or two in quality and size—linens are nicer, beds softer, and bathrooms are larger, gleaming with marble and glass. The newish Spa Tower has rooms styled in handsome hunter tones, and are close to the pool and spa, though their view of the dancing fountains is somewhat obscured.

The pool area is the most sophisticated on the Strip, with a trio of elegant Roman villa-esque pools (we ruin our own pretensions of cool by standing underneath the fountains in the center of each pool). The spa and health club are marvelous but pricey. You'll find one of the better collections of restaurants in town, run by such celebrity chefs as Julian Serrano and Jean-Georges. The show is Cirque du Soleil's *O*, an expensive ticket that is worth the money. The nightclub, Light, is grown-up but not stodgy, while Petrossian has the most knowledgeable bartenders in town. And the Conservatory right off the lobby is full of seasonal flowers and plants—the best hotel-based antidote to the artificial Vegas you are likely to find.

3600 Las Vegas Blvd. S. (at the corner of Flamingo Rd.), Las Vegas, NV 89109. ⓒ **888/987-6667** or 702/693-7111. Fax 702/693-8546. www.bellagio.com. 3,933 units. $169 and up double; $450 and up suites. Extra person $35. AE, DC, DISC, MC, V. Free self- and valet parking. **Amenities:** Casino; showrooms; art gallery; wedding chapel; 14 restaurants; 6 outdoor pools; health club; spa; concierge; tour desk; car-rental desk; business center; shopping arcade; 24-hr. room service; in-room massage; laundry service; dry cleaning; executive-level rooms. *In room:* A/C, TV w/pay movies, dataport, high-speed Internet access (for a fee), hair dryer, iron/ironing board, safe.

Caesars Palace ⭐   Once the sine qua non of romantic but schlocky Vegas, Caesars still has a great deal going for it, but easy it's not in the maneuvering department. One of the most sprawling hotel complexes, you'll need a compass to navigate it, and once you get outside, it's set so far back from the street—and by then you are so exhausted—you may rethink the whole "leaving" idea. Having said that, there is ample reason to stay here, most of it found in the Forum Shops (recently expanded yet again), where a number of fine restaurants, snack places (still more in the food court, though you have to navigate the tortuous casino yet again to get there), rides, and stores, plus ridiculous animatronic statues, are there to amuse you.

The rooms are no longer the over-the-top, glorious whacked-out orgies of "Roman" statues, but the ones in the main complex still have bits of silliness, while rooms in the newer towers feature nearly floor-to-ceiling windows and lots of regular hotel room space. The Greco-Roman pool area is so grown-up, it even has a topless pool (protected with walls) so you can avoid tan lines. The spa is small, but we've had some of the best facials, massages, and eyebrow waxes of our lives there. Caesars is an excellent choice for someone wanting to experience the Vegasness of Vegas, but you'll need to bring sturdy walking shoes.

3570 Las Vegas Blvd. S. (just north of Flamingo Rd.), Las Vegas, NV 89109. 📞 **877/427-7243** or 702/731-7110. Fax 702/697-5706. www.caesars.com. 3,348 units. $129 and up standard double; $149 "run of house deluxe" double; $549 and up suite. Extra person $30.No discount for children. Crib free; rollaway $20. AE, DC, DISC, MC, V. Free self- and valet parking. **Amenities:** Casino; nightclub; wedding chapel; 24 restaurants; 4 outdoor pools; health club; spa; concierge; tour desk; car-rental desk; business center; shopping arcade; salon; 24-hr. room service; laundry service; dry cleaning; executive-level rooms. *In room:* A/C, TV w/pay movies, dataport, high-speed Internet access (for a fee), Wi-Fi (for a fee), hair dryer, iron/ironing board, safe.

The Mirage ⭐   There is lots to like here, but all of it is arranged so that, at all times, you must navigate the most twisting casino in Vegas. While it's not the largest (the MGM Grand is), it is so exhausting that it might as well be. But the redone rooms can finally start to compete with newer ones around town, though the bathrooms remain cramped. One of the best pools in Vegas is here, a tropical, curvy monster complete with slides and waterfalls. The health club features attendants handing you iced towels and smoothies, while the spa is pretty in the same neutral-heavy way the guest rooms are. An extra fee gets you into one of the best attractions in Vegas, the Siegfried & Roy's Secret Garden and the Dolphin Habitat (p. 120). Restaurant row has several high-priced basics, plus the recently renovated buffet, looking quite snazzy. Two major production shows, Cirque du Soleil's Beatles homage *LOVE* and impressionist Danny Gans, are here, but "major" comes with an indefensible price tag. And don't forget that volcano out front, with its regular explosions, the soothing front-desk aquarium, and the vanilla-smelling rainforest at the opening to the casino. Now, about that casino . . .

3400 Las Vegas Blvd. S. (btw. Flamingo Rd. and Spring Mountain Rd.), Las Vegas, NV 89109. ℂ 800/374-9000 or 702/791-7111. Fax 702/791-7446. www.mirage.com. 3,044 units. $109 and up double; $275 and up suite. Extra person $30. No discount for children. AE, DC, DISC, MC, V. Free self- and valet parking. **Amenities:** Casino; showrooms; 11 restaurants; beautiful outdoor pool; health club and spa; concierge; tour desk; car-rental desk; business center; shopping arcade; salon; 24-hr. room service; laundry service; dry cleaning; executive-level rooms. *In room:* A/C, TV w/pay movies, dataport, high-speed Internet access (for a fee), Wi-Fi (for a fee), hair dryer, iron/ironing board, safe.

Palazzo ✰✰   Not to be lazy, but just go read the description below of the Venetian, except the parts about it being like Venice. No, really. This sister property/expansion is the same idea, but without the thematic fun out front—but everything is even bigger! And more of it! It's *elegant,* darn it, and if elegance is good, elegance on steroids must be even better.

Okay, calming down now. It's really nice, but it's definitely the hotel you go to if you don't want to leave the hotel. Your room will be a mini-suite, with a plush bedroom area giving way to a sunken, party-pit living space. The bathrooms are grand, the TVs (three!) are flatscreen. The restaurants have celebrity chefs backing them, and there is a Barney's New York anchoring the shopping area. But it's costly, and it is the usual problem with luxury on a gigantic scale; little bits are already looking worn, because you can't keep close track on tiny details when there are tens of thousands of them.

3325 Las Vegas Blvd. S., Las Vegas, NV 89109. ℂ 877/883-6423 or 702/607-7777. Fax 702/414-4805. www.palazzolasvegas.com. 4,027 units. $199 and up double; $229 and up suite. Extra person $35. Children under 13 stay free in parent's room. AE, DC, DISC, MC, V. Free self- and valet parking. **Amenities:** Casino; showroom; 15 restaurants; 7 outdoor pools shared with Venetian; health club and spa shared w/Venetian; concierge; tour desk; car-rental desk; business center; extensive shopping arcade; 24-hr. room service; laundry service; dry cleaning; executive-level rooms. *In room:* A/C, TV w/pay movies, fax, high-speed Internet access (for a fee), Wi-Fi (for a fee), fridge on request, hair dryer, iron/ironing board, safe.

Palms Casino Resort 𝒦𝒦

The hip and the happening wouldn't dream of staying anywhere else—unless they're at the Hard Rock or Red Rock, that is—and so if you are one of them, fancy you are one of them, want to be one of them, or want to hang out with them, you should stay here, too. It's Hard Rock hip with the sort of nebulous architecture/design only found in Vegas—swoops and circles on the ceiling that are not quite Miami, not quite Jetsons–space age. Not everyone here is as aggressively young as the target demographic, and good for them. Rooms have the second-nicest beds in town (the first are over at Green Valley Ranch), with high-quality linens and soft mattresses. Some of the best views in town are from the windows here because there are no other tall buildings near enough to obstruct said view. The elevators are watched constantly, lest the Wrong Sort board them and get into the wonderful (one of the best in town) restaurant Alizé or the ultratrendy ghostbar or Playboy Club, which is so beyond-ultratrendy that we don't have a phrase to describe it. That sort of diligence in black Armani can feel intimidating. The Palm Springs–influenced pool area—with an above-ground glass pool and hammocks—is also a place to see and be seen, so you might seek refuge across the casino at either the surprisingly good buffet or the food court, where regular-folk places such as McDonald's and the Coffee Bean & Tea Leaf are represented. And who needs ghostbar when you've got actual movie theaters on the premises?

4321 W. Flamingo Rd. (at I-15), Las Vegas, NV 89103. ⟨ℂ⟩ **866/942-7777** or 702/942-7777. Fax 702/942-6859. www.palms.com. 664 units. Sun–Thurs $99 and up double; Fri–Sat $229 and up double. Extra person $30. AE, DC, DISC, MC, V. Free self- and valet parking. **Amenities:** Casino; nightclub/showroom; movie theater; 7 restaurants; food court; outdoor pool; health club; spa; Jacuzzi; sauna; concierge; business center; 24-hr. room service; in-room massage; laundry service; dry cleaning; executive-level rooms. *In room:* A/C, TV w/pay movies, dataport, high-speed Internet access (for a fee), Wi-Fi (for a fee), coffeemaker, hair dryer, iron/ironing board, safe.

Paris Las Vegas 𝒦

An in-between hotel—just right if you're going to feel cheated if your stay in Vegas doesn't include some Vegas theme—but laid out to be user-friendly. The casino is right there, to be sure, in the lobby like a good casino should be, but all paths to all things (registration, concierge, rooms, shops, food) skirt around it, making it an easy place to navigate, if you don't mind signage in

Franglais ("le car rental" indeed!) or employees who will "Bonjour, Madame!" you to death. Of course, you are going to do a lot of neck craning at this Disney version of gay Paree. It's all here, all boiled down to an iconic essence, starting with that half-size replica Eiffel Tower out front with what appears to be the five or six most famous buildings from the City of Light shrunk to play-piece size and all crammed into the courtyard of the Louvre. The fleur-de-lis–bedecked rooms are pretty, if not particularly extraordinary, with deep tubs in the bathrooms. The rooftop pool is small and dull. There are reasonably authentic and terribly overpriced pastries and fresh bread in several locations, plus the charming Mon Ami Gabi restaurant and the terrific buffet. *Viva la France!*

3655 Las Vegas Blvd. S., Las Vegas, NV 89109. $\textcircled{C}$ **888/266-5687** or 702/946-7000. Fax 702/967-3836. www.harrahs.com. 2,916 units. $119 and up double; $350 and up suites. Extra person $30. No discount for children. Crib free; rollaway $10. AE, DC, DISC, MC, V. Free self- and valet parking. **Amenities:** Casino; showrooms; 2 wedding chapels; 12 restaurants; outdoor pool; health club; spa; concierge; tour desk; business center; shopping arcade; 24-hr. room service; laundry service; dry cleaning; executive-level rooms. *In room:* A/C, TV w/pay movies, dataport, high-speed Internet access (for a fee), Wi-Fi (for a fee), hair dryer, iron/ironing board, safe.

TI–Treasure Island Las Vegas $\mathscr{R}\mathscr{R}$

In many ways, this hotel is interchangeable with The Mirage, though each has its own fans. It's easier to navigate the TI (note name alteration, an attempt to give the place a coolness factor like the Palms), thanks to an actual lobby that isn't carved grudgingly out of casino space, and pathways that skirt a square (rather than amorphous) casino. You do have to look hard for any pirate lore these days (apart from the free battle that wages a few times nightly outside), so anxious is the hotel's management to rid itself of all kid-friendly elements. This includes various homages to the scantily clad leggy gals of the *Sirens of TI* "show" that replaced the beloved pirate battle, including a gi-normous bare-breasted ship head's gal that greets you when you walk in from the Strip. Despite this, it still remains a top family choice, and many kids are often running about, which some vacationers may not find desirable and we think was probably poor planning, considering the shift in target demographic.

Rooms are superior to those at The Mirage, with actual signed art on the walls, plus other nice touches, including comfy beds (though not much drawer space) and nice marble bathrooms with deep tubs. Like the one at The Mirage, there are more visually interesting spas in town, but again, the workout room is decent-size and the attendants ready with smoothies. Given how well The Mirage formula has otherwise worked here, it's odd that the TI's pool is so dull and the restaurants not much better. But they do have one of the best shows in town in Cirque du Soleil's *Mystère*.

3300 Las Vegas Blvd. S. (at Spring Mountain Rd.), Las Vegas, NV 89177. © 800/ 944-7444 or 702/894-7111. Fax 702/894-7446. www.treasureisland.com. 2,885 units. $89 and up double; $129 and up suite. Extra person $30. No discount for children. AE, DC, DISC, MC, V. Free self- and valet parking. **Amenities:** Casino; showrooms; 6 restaurants; outdoor pool; health club; spa; very well-equipped game and video arcade; concierge; tour desk; car-rental desk; business center; shopping arcade; 24-hr. room service; laundry service; dry cleaning; executive-level rooms. *In room:* A/C, TV w/pay movies, fax, dataport, high-speed Internet access (for a fee), hair dryer, iron/ironing board, safe.

The Venetian ✦✦ This hotel is a mixed bag for a non-gambler's purposes. The giggle factor for a good Vegas theme hotel actually transforms here into something approaching awe; we hate to admit it, but they did a nice job of replicating the real Venice for the facade, which is the only one you can stroll through in Sin City. Inside you'll find, hands down, the best rooms on the Strip (except perhaps for the comfort level offered over at the Four Seasons)—true "junior" suites complete with a sunken living room and marvelous marble bathrooms. Better still, check into the slightly higher-priced newer tower, the Venezia, where the rooms are even bigger, and the casino-free ambience is more like that at the Ritz—on steroids.

The spa is run by Canyon Ranch, so the health club is better than the one you will find at your gym, the treatments outstanding, and the prices for either so high they undo any good the place might have done for your stress level. (The high health club charge does include a number of daily exercise classes, which is unique among the local health clubs.) The shopping area has its own Venice canal, plus gondoliers and strolling costumed actors. There is a collaboration between the venerable Guggenheim and Hermitage museums, so you can have some actual culture. And the restaurants are a terrific assortment at all prices, from the divine Bouchon to the mammoth-size menu at the Grand Luxe Café, a division of the reliable Cheesecake Factory.

So what's not to love? Well, after you get through that grand colonnade, loaded with marble and preposterous copies of Italian art, you have to endure a mazelike wander through the noisy casino to get to the guest elevators. Signage is poor, so good luck with that. The rooftop pool area is strangely hideous for such an otherwise great hotel, and, like everything else here, it's really hard to find. And you'll feel nickel-and-dimed to death, thanks not just to the health club charges but also to other hidden tricks, such as a minibar that charges you if you so much as touch a bottle within (computer sensors) and the boasted fax machine/printer in each room that also costs dearly. The price-gouging is the one item reminiscent of the real Venice that we could do without.

3355 Las Vegas Blvd. S., Las Vegas, NV 89109. (C) 877/883-6423 or 702/414-1000. Fax 702/414-4805. www.venetian.com. 4,029 units. $149 and up double. Extra person $35. Children under 13 stay free in parent's room. Crib free; no rollaways. AE, DC, DISC, MC, V. Free self- and valet parking. **Amenities:** Casino; showroom; wedding chapels; 18 restaurants; 6 outdoor pools; health club; spa; video arcade; concierge; tour desk; car-rental desk; business center; shopping arcade; 24-hr. room service; laundry service; dry cleaning; executive-level rooms. *In room:* A/C, TV w/pay movies, fax (for a fee), dataport, high-speed Internet access (for a fee), fridge, hair dryer, iron/ironing board, safe.

Wynn Las Vegas (*R*)(*R*)   This only barely missed the cut of "Best Hotels" above, and only because, for all the hype (it cost billions to build), overall it's not that much more impressive, and certainly no more innovative, than any other entry in this section. It certainly has some of the best non-suite rooms on the Strip: particularly large (it's kind of ruined us for even the more spacious of other resorts' rooms), with much-appreciated floor-to-ceiling views, deeply comfortable beds with high-thread-count sheets and feather beds atop good-quality mattresses plus down comforters, a flatscreen TV, and excellent up-to-the-minute bathrooms complete with quite long and deep tubs, a second flatscreen TV, and silky lemony amenities. Love those Warhol flower prints. The rest of the place certainly offers resort options (some of the most excellent restaurants in town, all with their often-name-brand chefs in the kitchen; a thoroughly stuffed gym; a serene and pretty spa; four pools; clubs; a "show" that utilizes the faux mountain that is visible only from the property's interior; fancy shopping), but generally at great extra cost. It's spectacular, but it also looks suspiciously like the Bellagio, Wynn's last project. And since it sticks to the typical Vegas hotel floor plan—that is, the casino is between you and most everywhere you want to go—it's grown-up, but it's not particularly relaxing.

3131 Las Vegas Blvd. S. (at the corner of Sands Dr.), Las Vegas, NV 89109. (C) 888/320-9966 or 702/770-7100. Fax 702/770-1571. www.wynnlasvegas.com. 3,933 units. $249 and up double. Extra person $50. No discount for children. AE, DC, DISC, MC, V. Free self- and valet parking. **Amenities:** Casino; showrooms; 2 wedding chapels; 13 restaurants; 5 outdoor pools; fitness center; spa; concierge; tour desk; car-rental desk; business center; salon; 24-hr. room service; in-room massage; laundry service; dry cleaning; nonsmoking rooms; executive-level rooms. *In room:* A/C, TV w/pay movies, dataport, high-speed Internet access (for a fee), Wi-Fi (for a fee), hair dryer, iron/ironing board, safe.

EAST OF THE STRIP

Hard Rock Hotel & Casino ✸   *Note:* At press time, the hotel's new owners had announced plans for $750 million worth of new hotel towers, including one that is all suites for VIPs. The parking lot in front will become meeting and convention space plus a new, larger version of The Joint, while the old Joint is being removed and turned into additional casino area. All existing rooms and public spaces will get makeovers, so some of what you read below may have changed.

Now, you're thinking, "I'm a rock fan, I oughta stay here," and we're saying, "Yes, probably, BUT." Not a lot of buts, actually—more like caveats. As with many a Vegas hotel, this one is a bit more interested in the high rollers and the highly recognizable than it is in tourists with basic budgets; it just may be a bit more obvious here because of its smaller size, which means it's clear that they are ignoring you in favor of Britney (or someone who looks an awful lot like her) over there.

The smaller size works in your favor, too, as this is an easy property to navigate, if a noisy one. For a small casino, the Hard Rock's is the loudest, thanks to the constant (if catchy) music, and it is plopped down in the middle of the hotel, though all your activity will skirt it on a raised walkway. The hopping restaurants and bars teem with noise and activity, and then there is the pool area—a beach blanket bikini bonanza (yeah, it's got sand), with a constant surfin' soundtrack and loads of women inspired by the tasteful looks of Pamela Anderson. Rooms are a mix of some odd attempts at no-tell motel and more primary-color-based styles, with bathrooms that use stainless steel like other places in town use marble. Truth be told, while certainly standing out more than the usual generic Vegas hotel, the rooms aren't that comfortable. But why be in your room when you could be standing on the edge of the casino/pool/nightclub, trying to see if that really *was* Britney after all?

4455 Paradise Rd. (at Harmon Ave.), Las Vegas, NV 89109. ℰ **800/473-ROCK** (473-7625) or 702/693-5000. Fax 702/693-5588. www.hardrockhotel.com. 657 units. $109 and up double; $250 and up suite. Extra person $50. Children under 12 stay free in parent's room. AE, DC, MC, V. Free self- and valet parking. **Amenities:** Casino; showroom; 6 restaurants; 2 outdoor pools w/lazy river and sandy-beach bottom; small health club and spa; concierge; tour desk; salon; 24-hr. room service; laundry service; dry cleaning; executive-level rooms. *In room:* A/C, TV w/pay movies, Wi-Fi (for a fee), hair dryer, iron/ironing board.

Las Vegas Hilton ✸✸   The LV Hilton (as it's known locally) is largely preferred by businesspeople, thanks to its proximity to the behemoth Convention Center. It doesn't quite have the same savoir-faire elegance it once did, but you may be pleased by the sunken, and thus out-of-the-way (and rather petite), casino. Rooms are standard business—pun intended—with touches of marble that aren't as swell-elegant as those found at, say, The Mirage. The restaurants are all reliable and forgettable (unless you've never experienced the knife shows at a Benihana), the rooftop pool and health club are similarly businesslike, and the shows are often better than the larger extravaganzas on the Strip (perhaps one faint reminder of Elvis, who called the Hilton his Vegas home for so many years).

3000 Paradise Rd. (at Riviera Blvd.), Las Vegas, NV 89109. ℂ 888/732-7117 or 702/732-5111. Fax 702/732-5805. www.lvhilton.com. 3,174 units. $49 and up double. Extra person $35. Children under 18 stay free in parent's room. Crib free; rollaway $35 if you are not paying the extra-person charge. AE, DC, DISC, MC, V. Free self- and valet parking. **Amenities:** Casino; showrooms; 8 restaurants; outdoor pool; golf course adjacent; 6 night-lit tennis courts; health club; spa; Jacuzzi; video arcade; car-rental desk; business center; shopping arcade; salon; 24-hr. room service; laundry service; dry cleaning; executive-level rooms. *In room:* A/C, TV w/pay movies, dataport, high-speed Internet access (for a fee), Wi-Fi (for a fee), hair dryer, iron/ironing board.

The Westin Casuarina Las Vegas Hotel and Spa ✦ While not the kicky Vegas boutique hotel we dream of, this transformation of the seedy and unlamented Maxim nonetheless is perfect for the business traveler who wants a little panache on top of the basic needs. The rooms are in good, subdued taste, nothing compared to the overwhelming flash found at, say, THEhotel, but considerably more pleasant than the generic bores found in many high-profile chains elsewhere in Vegas. The Westin boasts about its "Heavenly Beds," to which we shrug and say, "Eh. The ones at the Palms, Green Valley Ranch, Ritz, Four Seasons, and THEhotel are better." But then again, we are mattress and thread-count snobs. Bathrooms are small but sparkling, and there is a small but serviceable (and free!) gym. The casino area is tiny and feels dated. Boring by Vegas standards, nonetheless it's professional yet personal.

160 E. Flamingo Rd., Las Vegas, NV 89109. ℂ 866/837-4125 or 702/836-9775. Fax 702/836-9776. www.starwood.com. 825 units. $139 and up double. Extra person $30. Children under 18 stay free in parent's room. Cribs free. AE, DC, DISC, MC, V. Free self- and valet parking. Pets accepted. **Amenities:** Casino; showroom; restaurant; bar; coffee shop; small outdoor heated pool; small health club; concierge; tour desk; business center; meeting rooms; 24-hr. room service; in-room massage; babysitting; laundry service; dry cleaning. *In-room:* A/C, TV w/pay movies, dataport, high-speed Internet access (for a fee), minibar, hair dryer, iron/ironing board, safe.

3 Best Casino-Free Hotels

Despite the preponderance of hotels in Vegas, there is one accommodations area where the city is sorely lacking—regular hotels. Not that there aren't any, but every single one of them is a chain hotel. If you earn points in a chain or if you are fond of the various ways a Marriott can be configured, you're in luck. But if you are looking for quirky lodgings with distinct character, or a bed-and-breakfast, or anything other than a hotel identical to the one with the same name in Phoenix or Boston, you are in for a disappointment. And if you want a room with flavor, you simply must go back to the theme hotels.

Normally, this doesn't matter. A large part of the fun of coming to Vegas is for the hotels that are Vegas-specific. But, in glancing over the above listings, you may discover that they don't suit your purposes at all. At least with a non-casino hotel, you've eliminated a lot of noise, and possibly a great deal of rowdy drunks (if they are staying at one of the following, then surely by the time they've stumbled home, they are nearly done for the night). But don't expect much that is particularly special, though some chains and styles are better than others. And in a quirk particular to Vegas, it may not be much cheaper (or cheaper at all) to stay at one of the following than it would be to stay on the Strip in a high-profile destination.

Note: All hotels in this section are located east of the Strip and can be found on the map on p. 33.

Courtyard by Marriott ⊛   Right across the street from the Convention Center, this is precisely the sort of chain hotel that shows you what chain hotels can be: nicely landscaped (yep, arranged around outdoor courtyards), spic-and-span public areas and rooms, a sparkling pool, and just enough style (even if it was ordered up) to make you feel like you are Someplace, rather than Anyplace. Most rooms were designed with the business traveler in mind and have king-size beds; all rooms have balconies or patios.

3275 Paradise Rd. (btw. Convention Center Dr. and Desert Inn Rd.), Las Vegas, NV 89109. © **800/321-2211** or 702/791-3600. Fax 702/796-7981. www.courtyard. com. 149 units. $149 and up double; $179 and up suite. No charge for extra person above double occupancy, max 4 in a room. Crib/rollaway free. AE, DC, DISC, MC, V. Free self-parking at your room door. **Amenities:** Restaurant; outdoor pool; small exercise room; Jacuzzi; business center; limited room service; laundry service; dry cleaning; coin-op washers and dryers; free Wi-Fi in lobby. *In room:* A/C, TV w/pay movies, dataport, free high-speed Internet access, coffeemaker, hair dryer, iron/ironing board.

Desert Rose Resort 🎃🎃 *Kids*   Another of the "all-suite" chain hotels, but one that offers just a little bit more than the others and just the right kinds of "little bit more." The suites themselves (creamy and boring) come not only with full kitchens but also with actual balconies (once you've experienced a stuffy Vegas hotel room with a window that does not open, this becomes a big deal). There is a free continental breakfast buffet and an evening happy hour/manager's reception with snacks. The pool is large! All this, just a block from the corner of the Strip and the Trop! This is really a life-saver for families looking for a nice place not too far off the beaten path—and think of the savings with the free breakfast, the snacks, and that full kitchen for other meals!

5051 Duke Ellington Way, Las Vegas, NV 89119. ℂ 888/732-8099 or 702/739-7000. Fax 702/739-9350. www.shellhospitality.com. 280 units. $99 and up 1-bedroom suite (up to 4 people); $139 and up 2-bedroom suite (up to 6 people). Rates include breakfast and evening snacks. Crib free; no rollaways. AE, DC, DISC, MC, V. Free self-parking. **Amenities:** Large outdoor pool; small exercise room; Jacuzzi; laundry service; dry cleaning; coin-op washers. *In room:* A/C, TV w/pay movies, dataport, high-speed Internet access (for a fee), full kitchen, hair dryer, iron/ironing board.

Hyatt Place 🎃   Well-proportioned but totally bland suites. Still, this hotel offers special rates, a free large buffet breakfast, and a weekly manager's reception with snacks and all for prices that are more attractive than the rooms. If you want to cut up your heels more, the Hard Rock is across the street, ready to take care of more frivolous needs.

4520 Paradise Rd., Las Vegas, NV 89109. ℂ 877/877-8886 or 702/369-3366. Fax 702/369-0009. www.hyatt.com. 202 units. $79 and up double. Extra person $10. Children under 18 stay free in parent's room. Crib free; no rollaways. Rates include breakfast buffet. AE, DC, DISC, MC, V. Free self-parking. **Amenities:** Outdoor pool; fitness room; concierge; tour desk; free airport shuttle; laundry service. *In room:* A/C, TV w/pay movies, dataport, high-speed Internet access (free), kitchenette, hair dryer, iron/ironing board, safe.

La Quinta 🎃   La Quinta happens to be on our own private list of "reliable and surprisingly nice" chains, and this branch justifies our expectations. Not that it's anything but prefab, but it's that increasingly popular, slightly Spanish, slightly mission-style prefab that immediately puts us at our ease. Rooms are decent size (though we would spend the extra few dollars for the executive queen for the larger beds, the fridge, and the microwave), and all come with whirlpool tubs and new pillow top mattresses. Note that ground-level rooms have patios. Outside, on the oddly relaxing grounds (little pools and benches and whatnot), you can find barbecue grills and picnic tables, which are unusual options in a town that assumes everyone is eating at some cheap buffet. The staff is generally particularly nice. Note also that the hotel takes pets under 25 pounds.

3970 Paradise Rd. (btw. Twain Ave. and Flamingo Rd.), Las Vegas, NV 89109. ℂ 800/531-5900 or 702/796-9000. Fax 702/796-3537. www.laquinta.com. 251 units. $89 and up double; $99 and up executive queen; $119 and up suite. Rates include continental breakfast. AE, DC, DISC, MC, V. Free self-parking. Up to 2 pets per room accepted, free of charge with a security deposit. **Amenities:** Outdoor pool; Jacuzzi; tour desk; car-rental desk; free airport/Strip shuttle; coin-op laundry. *In room:* A/C, TV w/pay movies, dataport, high-speed Internet access (free), Wi-Fi (for a fee), kitchens in executive rooms and suites, coffeemaker, hair dryer, iron/ironing board.

Las Vegas Marriott Suites ⍟   The price is probably too much for a chain hotel, though this is a nice one. All the rooms are suites (which makes them extra large), are comfortable, and have unexpected touches, such as French doors separating the bedroom from the sitting area, and surprisingly good art on the walls. The on-site coffee shop, Windows, serves quite good Southwestern-style food. Note that it's a bit of a walk from here to the Strip (10 min., which gets longer and longer with every additional 10°).

325 Convention Center Dr., Las Vegas, NV 89109. ℂ 800/228-9290 or 702/650-2000. Fax 702/650-9466. www.marriott.com. 278 units. $159 and up suite (up to 4 people). AE, DC, DISC, MC, V. Free outdoor parking. **Amenities:** Restaurant; outdoor pool; small exercise room; Jacuzzi; tour desk; business center; free Wi-Fi in business center; limited room service; laundry service; dry cleaning; coin-op laundry available at Residence Inn next door; executive-level rooms. *In room:* A/C, TV w/pay movies, dataport, high-speed Internet access (for a fee), Wi-Fi (for a fee), fridge, coffeemaker, hair dryer, iron/ironing board, safe.

Residence Inn ⍟⍟   Our favorite among the Marriotts, in part because of the actual accommodations, in part because of the attitude—by and large it is run by people who actually seem involved with the property rather than just earning wages at it. Rooms are like small apartments, each with a separate bedroom, a living room (all with VCRs, some with working fireplaces—the desert gets chilly in the winter), and a kitchen fully loaded with dishes and cookware, which makes the whole thing perfect for extended stays. Rooms are distributed throughout the complex in little condo buildings; each section has its own little garden (the entire facility is set on 7 nicely manicured acres), while each room has its own balcony or patio. Guests receive a welcome basket of microwave popcorn and coffee at check-in. There is a generous free breakfast buffet, the pool received a much-needed makeover in 2006, and the gym is located next door at another Marriott.

3225 Paradise Rd. (btw. Desert Inn Rd. and Convention Center Dr.), Las Vegas, NV 89109. (800/331-3131 or 702/796-9300. Fax 702/796-9562. www.marriott.com. 192 units. $119 and up studio; $149 and up penthouse. Rates include continental or buffet breakfast. Children stay free in parent's room. Crib free. AE, DC, DISC, MC, V. Free self-parking. Pets accepted, for a fee. **Amenities:** Outdoor pool; guests have access to small exercise room next door at the Marriott Suites; Jacuzzi; coin-op washers and dryers. *In room:* A/C, TV w/pay movies, dataport, complimentary high-speed Internet access, kitchenette, hair dryer, iron/ironing board.

4 When the Others Are Booked . . .

There are quite a few other hotels in town, of course, but we don't give them full-on listings because they aren't worth your time—unless everything else is booked up, of course. The following are hotels that are perfect for gamblers seeking a cheap bed near the slots, which makes them dandy in many ways—it just probably isn't your way.

THE BEST . . .
MID-STRIP
The Flamingo Las Vegas   Not the home of Bugsy Siegel anymore, just a place that tries hard to keep pace with the bigger boys around it. Still, the pool area is fabulous, a tropical wonderland that ranks with Mandalay Bay's and The Mirage's among the best in the city. For sure get one of the newly redone rooms, with hot pink, '60s swinging bachelor touches that make them some of the more interesting and fun in town. It's centrally located, right in the heart of the Strip, so the location is ideal as a jumping-off point for wandering. Otherwise, plan on sticking to the pool because this is another maze-like setup, and getting outside can be tricky.

3555 Las Vegas Blvd. S. (btw. Sands Ave. and Flamingo Rd.), Las Vegas, NV 89109. (800/732-2111 or 702/733-3111. Fax 702/733-3353. www.flamingolv.com. 3,999 units. $85 and up double; $350 and up suite. Extra person $30. AE, DC, DISC, MC, V. Free self- and valet parking. **Amenities:** Casino; showrooms; 8 restaurants; 5 outdoor pools; 4 night-lit tennis courts; health club; spa; small video arcade; tour desk; car-rental desk; business center; shopping arcade; 24-hr. room service; in-room massage; babysitting; laundry service; dry cleaning; executive-level rooms. *In room:* A/C, TV w/pay movies, dataport, high-speed Internet access (for a fee), hair dryer, iron/ironing board, safe.

NORTH STRIP
Stratosphere Casino Hotel & Tower   Our other "if all else fails" choice, this is the tallest structure west of the Mississippi, though the rooms themselves are not in the Tower, darn it. The rooms are essentially really, really nice motel rooms, and they can often be had for

Tips **Spa Life**

Another element of the "Vegas as luxury resort" theme is the addition of particularly nice spas. But it's also another example of Vegas bait-and-switch; the spas are uniformly expensive—just a pedicure will set you back an absurd $50. And for those of us who want to work off all the nice meals we are eating, that costs even more. On p. 59 is a chart with the daily—yes, daily—fees charged to use the gyms at the major Vegas hotels. (The chain hotels don't charge, but their workout rooms are usually no more than basic.) The fee includes daylong use of equipment, plus saunas, steam rooms, and such. The **Canyon Ranch Spa** at **The Venetian** charges the most, but their workout room is the best, and the fee allows you to take advantage of nearly a dozen daily classes like yoga, aerobics, and Pilates. Not far behind in the fabulousness and price department is the unfortunately named **Bathhouse** at **THEhotel Mandalay Bay,** a gorgeous, spare-no-cost facility that is nearly alone in charging a lesser (but still up-there) price if all you want is to work out and not have spa access. They also have the longest hours. For sheer aesthetics, the nicest spa in town is **Mandara Spa** at **Planet Hollywood;** the architects were sent to Morocco for design inspiration, and the results are drop-dead gorgeous. Mandara Spa and Canyon Ranch have the widest range of exotic and pampering treatments, but we are highly intrigued by the Passion Dip at the **Dolphin Spa** at **Green Valley,** which leaves a guest smelling like dessert. We've had wonderful facials, waxes, and massages at **Caesars,** but the staff treat you the best at **The Mirage** and **Treasure Island,** keeping you refreshed with iced towels during your workout and smoothies after.

as little as $49. That and the genuinely nice staff are the only reasons for you to stay here; the hotel is located at the far north end of the Strip—much too far to walk anywhere useful. Inside is little of great interest, apart from the revolving Top of the World restaurant and bar, which is located, yes, at the top of the Tower, and the views there are smashing. The thrill rides on top of the building will test even the sturdiest of stomachs—don't get us started on the madness that is the rooftop (!) over-the-edge teeter-totter (!!).

2000 Las Vegas Blvd. S. (btw. St. Louis and Baltimore aves.), Las Vegas, NV 89104. (C) 800/99-TOWER (998-6937) or 702/380-7777. Fax 702/383-5334. www.strato sphere hotel.com. 2,444 units. $49 and up double; $109 and up suite. Extra person $20. Children under 13 stay free in parent's room. AE, DC, DISC, MC, V. Free self- and valet parking. **Amenities:** Casino; showrooms; wedding chapel; 9 restaurants plus several fast-food outlets; large pool area w/great views of the Strip; children's rides and games; concierge; tour desk; car-rental desk; shopping arcade; 24-hr. room service; laundry service; executive-level rooms. *In room:* A/C, TV w/pay movies, dataport, high-speed Internet access (for a fee), Wi-Fi (for a fee), hair dryer, iron/ironing board, safe.

. . . & THE REST
MID-STRIP

Bally's Las Vegas   Adjacent to Paris Las Vegas, and accessible by a tunnel that changes from fairy-tale Parisian cobblestones to, well, we can't remember what—which, by the way, pretty much sums up this entire, forgettable hotel. It did get a kind of nice room makeover, and for the price, we sort of love it. When we can remember it. On the plus side, you can avoid the casino floor if you navigate correctly.

3645 Las Vegas Blvd. S. (at Flamingo Rd.), Las Vegas, NV 89109. (C) **800/634-3434** or 702/739-4111. Fax 702/967-3890. www.ballyslv.com. 2,814 units. $99 and up double; $35–$60 extra for concierge floor (including breakfast); $300 and up suite. Extra person $30. No discount for children. AE, DC, MC, V. Free self- and valet parking. **Amenities:** Casino; showrooms; 12 restaurants; outdoor pool; 8 night-lit tennis courts; health club; spa; video arcade; concierge; tour desk; car-rental desk; business center; shopping arcade; 24-hr. room service; laundry service; dry cleaning; executive-level rooms. *In room:* A/C, TV w/pay movies, dataport, high-speed Internet access (for a fee), hair dryer, iron/ironing board, safe.

Harrah's Las Vegas   Yes, you can get to your room without heading into the casino—if you go through the back door, which should indicate what the hotel thinks of non-gamblers. Actually, the Carnaval Court, the outdoor shopping and dining area, is a lot of fun, thanks to the Ghirardelli Ice Cream Parlor and the regular performing presence of Mr. Cook E. Jarr, the best worst lounge act in Vegas. And Mac King, one of the best bargains in town, plays here in the afternoons.

3475 Las Vegas Blvd. S. (btw. Flamingo and Spring Mountain roads), Las Vegas, NV 89109. (C) **800/427-7247** or 702/369-5000. Fax 702/369-5283. www.harrahs.com. 2,579 units. $99 and up "deluxe" double; $109 and up "superior" double; $199 and up suite. Extra person $30. AE, DC, DISC, MC, V. Free self- and valet parking. **Amenities:** Casino; showrooms; 9 restaurants; outdoor pool; health club; spa; concierge; tour desk; car-rental desk; business center; shopping arcade; salon; 24-hr. room service; laundry service; dry cleaning; executive-level rooms. *In room:* A/C, TV w/pay movies, fax, dataport, high-speed Internet access (for a fee), minibar, coffeemaker, hair dryer, iron/ironing board, safe.

Rio All-Suite Hotel & Casino This hotel, located a block off the Strip, is Frat Boy Party Hearty central; come here for the nightlife or if you love large rooms (they do have spacious, if dull, quarters). Definitely leave the kids at home—the fun's aimed at adults only, and the hotel actively discourages parents from bringing kids. If you prefer to make your wagers on the golf course, this one's for you; the 18-hole championship **Rio Secco golf course** (located off property in Henderson) was designed by Rees Jones.

3700 W. Flamingo Rd. (at I-15), Las Vegas, NV 89103. ⓒ **888/752-9746** or 702/777-7777. Fax 702/777-7611. www.playrio.com. 2,582 units. $99 and up suite. Extra person $30. AE, DC, MC, V. Free self- and valet parking. **Amenities:** Casino; showrooms; 12 restaurants; 4 outdoor pools; golf course; health club; spa; Jacuzzi; sauna; concierge; car-rental desk; business center; shopping arcade; 24-hr. room service; in-room massage; laundry service; dry cleaning; executive-level rooms. *In room:* A/C, TV w/pay movies, high-speed Internet access (for a fee), Wi-Fi (for a fee), fridge, coffeemaker, hair dryer, iron/ironing board, safe.

NORTH STRIP

Circus Circus *(Kids)* If you love clowns, you might want to consider this venerable establishment, but if you are a clown-a-phobe, for the love of everything that is holy, stay far away. But they still do have the circus acts high-flyin' over the casino, which is pretty cool, and the theme park is air-conditioned, thanks to the large dome. And, best of all, it is cheap. What with the clown theme, the circus acts, and the pretty good amusement park, this remains a relatively child-friendly place, though lately less by design than by default.

2880 Las Vegas Blvd. S. (btw. Circus Circus and Convention Center drives), Las Vegas, NV 89109. ⓒ **877/434-9175** or 702/734-0410. Fax 702/734-5897. www.circus circus.com. 3,774 units. $59 and up double. Extra person $12. Children under 17 stay free in parent's room. AE, DC, DISC, MC, V. Free self- and valet parking. **Amenities:** Casino; circus acts; wedding chapel; 7 restaurants; several fast-food outlets; 2 outdoor pools; video arcade; midway-style carnival games; tour desk; car-rental desk; shopping arcade; 24-hr. room service; laundry service; dry cleaning; executive-level rooms. *In room:* A/C, TV w/pay movies, high-speed Internet access (for a fee), hair dryer, safe.

Las Vegas Hotel Spas & Gyms

Hotel	Phone	Gym Hours	Gym/Workout Room Fee	Min. Age	Spa Hours	Name	Notes
Bally's	702/967-4366	6am–8pm	$22	18	8am–7pm	The Spa at	Non-hotel guests may get services, no use of spa unless getting service. No gym use.
Bellagio	702/693-7472	6am–8pm	$25	18	7am–6:30pm	Spa Bellagio	Spa open to non-registered guests Mon–Thurs only; no use of gym.
Caesars Palace	866/782-0655	6am–8pm	$25	18	6am–8pm	Qua Baths & Spa	Non-hotel guests $25 per day gym fee (waived if spa service is booked).
Flamingo Las Vegas	702/733-3535	6am–8pm	$10 for gym, $20 for gym and spa	18	6am–7:30pm	The Spa at Flamingo	Non-hotel guests same rates per day.
Four Seasons	702/632-5000	6am–9pm	comp.		8am–7pm	The Spa at	Gym is complimentary to hotel guests with spa service appt.; non-hotel guests can use the gym with spa service appt. Day passes for gym $30 for non guests available depending on space available.
Green Valley Resort	702/617-7777	6am–8pm	comp.	18	8am–8pm	The Spa at	Non-hotel guests $50 per day to use gym Mon–Thurs.
Hard Rock	702/693-5554	6am–10pm	$20	18	9am–9pm	Rock Spa	Non-hotel guests $30 per day.

Hotel	Phone	Gym Hours	Gym/Workout Room Fee	Min. Age	Spa Hours	Name	Notes
Harrah's	☎ 702/369-5000	6am–8pm	$20	18	8am–7pm	The Spa at	$50 for 3 days; same fees for non-hotel guests; gym usage complimentary with spa service.
Las Vegas Hilton	☎ 702/732-5648	6am–8pm	$20	16	7am–7:30pm	The Spa at	2 days/$36, 3/$51, 4/$64, 5/$75; same fees for non-hotel guests.
Luxor	☎ 800/258-9308	6am–8pm	$25	18	6am–8pm	Nurture	Discounted multiple day passes available. Gym only $10. Non-hotel guests $30 per day. Spa pass fee waived with service to $70 or more.
Mandalay Bay	☎ 877/632-7800	6am–8:30pm	$30	18	6am–8:30pm	Spa Mandalay	Non-hotel guests $35 per day.
MGM Grand	☎ 702/891-3077	6am–8pm	$25 Mon–Thurs, Fri–Sun $35	18	6am–8pm	Grand Spa	Open to public Mon–Thurs, same fees. Gym only $10.
The Mirage	☎ 702/791-7472	5:30am–7:30pm	$25	18	8am–5:30pm	The Spa	Open to public Mon–Thurs; non-hotel guests $25 per day.
Monte Carlo	☎ 702/730-7777	6am–8pm	$19	18	8am–7pm	The Spa at	$19 for gym; $22 for gym and spa; open to non-hotel guests daily, $25 gym and spa.
New York–New York	☎ 702/740-6955	6:30am–7pm	$20	16	8am–6pm	Spa	Multiple-day and evening rates available.
Palms	☎ 702/942-6937	6am–8pm	$20	18	6am–8pm	Spa & Salon	Non-hotel guests $25 per day.

Hotel	Phone	Gym Hours	Gym/Workout Room Fee	Min. Age	Spa Hours	Name	Notes
Paris	☎ 702/946-4366	6am–7pm	$25	18	6am–7pm	Spa by Mandara	Non-hotel guests $25 per day; service of $100 or more includes complimentary use of gym.
Planet Hollywood	☎ 866/935-3647	6am–7pm	$25	18	8am–6pm	Mandara Spa	Non-hotel guests $35 per day; multiple-day discount passes available.
Rio	☎ 702/777-7779	6am–8pm	$22	18	8am–7pm	Spa & Salon	$55 for 3 consecutive days; non-hotel guests same fees.
THEhotel	☎ 877/632-9636	6am–8:30pm	$30	18	6am–8pm	Bathhouse	Non-hotel guests must have a treatment of $60 or more, then fee will be waived.
TI-Treasure Island	☎ 702/894-7474	6am–8 or 10pm	$22	18	7am–6 or 8pm	Wet	Non-hotel guests $22 per day. Fee waived with spa service. Multiple day rate available. Separate "exclusive services for men" on the 3rd floor.
The Venetian	☎ 877/220-2688	5:30am–10pm	$40	18	8am–8pm	Canyon Ranch Spa Club	Non-hotel guests $45 for gym. Gym passes for both guests and non-hotel guests are $15 with spa service appt. Multiple day rates available.

4

Where to Dine

You may have heard that a great part of the fun in Vegas these days is the eating. This is true. Where once Vegas was, at best, ignored by anyone with a palate and, at worst, openly mocked, it is now considered one of the best dining towns in the country. All sorts of celebrity chefs have set up shop here, from the ubiquitous Emeril to Julian Serrano to even Michelin star culinary hero Joël Robuchon. Branches of a number of significant restaurants (**L'Atlier, Bouchon, Fleur de Lys, Commander's Palace, Michael Mina, Aureole, Le Cirque**) can be found here, though of course, rare is the day you are going to find the signature chef in the kitchen. But the city boasts a few Vegas-based master chefs who can compete with any of those dudes on the Food Network.

On the other hand, the town of the great meal deal—the 99¢ shrimp cocktail or $4.99 all-you-can-eat buffet!—has now reversed itself. For the most part, if you want to eat well, you need to be well-heeled. But you, the non-gambler, with all that money you've saved from the clutches of the craps table, may well be able to take full advantage of the haute cuisine currently offered. And while little hole-in-the-wall ethnic places aren't nearly as abundant as we would like, there are a few noteworthy spots—including perhaps the best Thai restaurant on the continent—and we will help you find your way to them. We may make you drive to certain finds, but don't worry; we've included even a few hotel-based mid-price restaurants worth your patronage as well, plus we've picked our favorites among the many buffets around—after all, it's not a trip to Vegas unless you've piled your plates with a mound of shrimp and endless helpings of prime rib.

Note: A new smoking ban was recently enacted prohibiting smoking in restaurants. For more information, see p. 196.

1 South Strip

VERY EXPENSIVE

Aureole ✸✸✸ NOUVELLE AMERICAN   This branch of a New York City fave (it's pronounced are-ree-*all*) run by Charlie Palmer is

Dining on the Strip

BUFFETS

Bally's Sterling
  Sunday Brunch **22**
Bellagio's Buffet **21**
Golden Nugget's Buffet **2**
Main Street Station's
  Garden Court **1**
Mandalay Bay's Bay
  Side Buffet **31**
MGM Grand Buffet **26**
Mirage's Cravings **16**
Monte Carlo's Buffet **25**
MORE, The Buffet at Luxor **30**
Palms Fantasy
  Market Buffet **20**
Paris Las Vegas's
  Le Village Buffet **23**
Rio's Carnival World Buffet **19**
Wynn Las Vegas Buffet **12**

DOWNTOWN

El Sombrero Cafe **5**
Hugo's Cellar **3**
Ice House Lounge **4**
M&M Soul Food **6**

SOUTH STRIP

Aureole **31**
Border Grill **31**
Burger Bar **31**
Charlie Palmer Steak **31**
Dick's Last Resort **29**
Dragon Noodle Co. **25**
Earl of Sandwich **24**
Emeril's New Orleans
  Fish House **26**
ESPN Zone **27**
Fleur de Lys **31**
Grand Wok and
  Sushi Bar **26**
House of Blues **31**
Jody Maroni's
  Sausage Kingdom **27**
Joël Robuchon at
  the Mansion **26**
L'Atelier de
  Joël Robuchon **26**
Monte Carlo Pub
  & Brewery **25**
Red Square **31**
Wolfgang Puck Bar
  & Grill **26**

CENTER STRIP

Alizé **20**
B&B Ristorante **15**
Bouchon **15**
Canaletto **15**
Canter's **13**
Circo **21**
Cypress Street
  Marketplace **18**
Delmonico Steakhouse **15**
Eiffel Tower **23**
Fin **16**
Fix **21**
Isla **13**
Le Cirque **21**
Mesa Grill **18**
Mon Ami Gabi **23**
Olives **21**
The Palm **18**
Payard Patisserie
  & Bistro **18**
Petrossian Bar **21**
Picasso **21**
Pinot Brasserie **15**
The Range Steakhouse **17**
Sensi **21**
Spago **18**
Table 10 **14**
Valentino **15**
The Wine Cellar &
  Tasting Room **19**

NORTH STRIP

Alex **12**
Bartolotta Ristorante
  di Mare **12**
Cafe Heidelberg
  German Deli
  and Restaurant **10**
Capriotti's **11**
Doña María Tamales **7**
Fellini's **9**
Tiffany's at the White
  Cross Pharmacy **8**
Top of the World **9**

noted for its glass wine tower. Four stories of carefully chosen bottles (including the largest collection of Austrian wines outside that country—well worth trying) are plucked from their perches by comely, cat-suited lasses who fly up and down via pulleys. It's quite the show, and folks come in just to watch.

Should you come for the food? You bet. The current chef is a wonder, serving a seasonal three-course prix-fixe menu, though flirting with your waiter might earn you luxurious extras like pâté on brioche topped with shaved truffles or an espresso cup of cold yellow pepper soup with crab. Expect other marvels like a tender roasted lamb loin and braised shoulder, or a rack of venison accompanied by sweet potato purée and chestnut crisp. Everything demonstrates the hand of a true chef in the kitchen, someone paying close attention to his work and to his customers. Service is solicitous, and desserts are playful, including a bittersweet chocolate soufflé with blood orange sorbet and a Bartlett pear crisp with toasted cinnamon brioche and lemon-grass foam. Do try the wine list; it comes on a handheld computer, designed not just to guide you through their vast tower but also to recommend pairings with your meal choices.

In Mandalay Bay, 3950 Las Vegas Blvd. S. ℭ **877/632-7800**. www.aureolelv.com. Reservations required. Fixed-price dinner $75; tasting menu $95. AE, DISC, MC, V. Daily 6–10pm.

Charlie Palmer Steak ☆☆ STEAKHOUSE   There are many, many steakhouses in Vegas, as if there is some natural law that states that any hotel without one will suffer from entropy and eventually collapse into a black hole. Discerning palates know there can be a significant difference among steakhouses; discerning wallets might not care. If you find yourself among the former, do try Charlie Palmer's, probably the best of the costlier Shrines to Beef. Those with the latter can be reassured that with entrees weighing in at around 22 to 45 ounces *each,* diners can legitimately, and in the name of decency ought to, share portions, which makes this a much more affordable experience than it might appear at first glance. And why not? Those enormous slabs o' meat are as tender as anything because with the big bucks, you do get the best cuts. Charlie Palmer, by the way, is the chef mind behind Aureole on the other side of Mandalay Bay; this makes two for two for this one celeb chef.

In Four Seasons Las Vegas, 3960 Las Vegas Blvd. S. ℭ **702/632-5120**. www. charliepalmersteaklv.com. Reservations recommended. Main courses $30–$42. AE, DC, DISC, MC, V. Daily 5–10:30pm.

Emeril's New Orleans Fish House ☆ CONTEMPORARY CREOLE   Chef Emeril Lagasse, a ubiquitous presence on cable's Food Network, probably needs to focus on his name restaurants; the original in New Orleans is just as good as ever, but this one has lost some of its punch. How else to explain that the best dish is Creole-spiced rib-eye? And that the duck on the duck salad is better than the salad itself? But the famous savory lobster cheesecake is still a must-try, and we do love his version of barbecue shrimp, slathered in a garlicky herb-Worcestershire-tinged sauce, paired with a rosemary biscuit. And it all seems worthwhile when you have a slice of the banana cream pie with banana crust and caramel drizzle.

In MGM Grand, 3799 Las Vegas Blvd. S. ⓒ **702/891-7374**. www.emerils.com. Reservations required. Main courses $17–$30 lunch, $28–$45 (more for lobster) dinner. AE, DC, DISC, MC, V. Daily 11:30am–2:30pm and 5:30–10:30pm.

Fleur de Lys ☆☆☆ FRENCH CONTINENTAL   One of the most sophisticated restaurants in Las Vegas, this is an offshoot of a highly regarded San Francisco establishment run by chef Hubert Keller. Continuing the tradition of visually showstopping restaurant spaces in Mandalay Bay, most tables are set in the semicircular two-story interior consisting half of '70s-style stone brick walls, half of billowing drapes, behind which are concealed a few dining booths. It's one of the few places in town where you ought to dress up to dine, but in a good way. At this writing, one orders from a three-, four-, or five-course tasting menu (including a well-thought-out vegetarian option), featuring seasonal choices such as an appetizer of delicate seared ahi tuna with a gelée of chile and garlic, a silly-appearing but hearty ocean "baeckeoffe" (a collection of seafood options including a sort of seafood burger-style crab cake on a brioche), pan-seared diver scallops with parsnip fires served in a cunning mini flower pot, and roasted guinea hen breast and leg confit topped with crispy basil. Our descriptions won't do these playful, sexy dishes justice. It's food as art, certainly, but not so that the point of food—the eating of it, the very taste—is lost. Despite the presence of a perfect white and dark chocolate mousse on the "Chocolate Feast" sampler plate, you owe it to yourself to try the fresh fruit minestrone—basil sorbet, raspberries, mango, and more—for once, a no-fat dessert worth ordering.

In Mandalay Bay, 3950 Las Vegas Blvd. S. ⓒ **877/632-7800**. Reservations recommended. Jacket recommended. 3- to 5-course menu $74–$94. AE, DC, DISC, MC, V. Daily 5:30–10:30pm.

Joël Robuchon at the Mansion ✪✪✪ FRENCH This is listed under "very expensive" only because there is no category for "unbelievably, heart-stoppingly, stratospherically expensive." But it's here because legendary chef Joël Robuchon—the first (and youngest) chef to win three consecutive Michelin stars—who closed his restaurants in France (where he was proclaimed "chef of the century") at the height of his fame, has proven that all the hype is justified. The *Los Angeles Times* gave Robuchon four stars (their highest rating), only the second time they've done so, while the *New York Times* reviewer proclaimed this "some of the very best French food I've eaten on this continent." These are no pushovers. And if you aren't going to blow your money at the tables, why not blow it on what may well be the meal of a lifetime? The menu changes frequently, with many key ingredients flown in daily from France. And service reminds one that Michelin ratings put that into account, too. And then there is always the somewhat less expensive—that's relative, of course—neighbor **L'Atelier de Joël Robuchon,** where the focus is on counter seating, an intimate interactive experience between diner, server, and chef.

In MGM Grand, 3799 Las Vegas Blvd. S. ✆ 702/891-7925. Reservations strongly recommended. Jacket required. 6-course tasting menu $250; 16-course tasting menu $385. AE, DC, DISC, MC, V. Sun–Thurs 5:30–10pm; Fri–Sat 5:30–10:30pm.

L'Atelier de Joël Robuchon ✪✪✪ FRENCH Despite the four-star L.A. and N.Y. *Times* reviews for the main establishment reviewed above, trustworthy foodies tipped this place as actually superior. Then it won the James Beard Award for best new restaurant in 2007, which only adds to the debate. You won't go wrong either way. Certainly, it's relatively cheaper here, but the casual, almost entirely counter seating (it's like an extremely high-style diner) might dismay those looking for a different sort of atmospheric experience. But food is supposed to be fun, and interacting with the charming (and often handsome and French) staff on the other side only adds to the great good pleasure.

Portions are small but exquisitely conceived and constructed. The tasting menu, which will likely change seasonally, is probably your best way to go, but consider coming just to treat yourself to a couple of dishes, such as the wee, perfect burgers topped with foie gras, or the Maine lobster with curry scent and fennel foam, a dish that sent us into a fit of uncontrollable giggles of delight. La Pied de Cochon is pâté made of pig feet, a robust and yet unctuous pork topped with shaved truffle and parmesan on toast. An amuse-bouche of foie gras parfait with port wine and parmesan foam comes layered in a teeny parfait glass with all three flavors clear and distinct and yet harmonizing into a powerful whole. The artistry only continues with dessert. A marvelous culinary experience.

In MGM Grand, 3799 Las Vegas Blvd. S. ✆ 702/891-7925. Reservations strongly recommended. 8-course discovery menu $135; small plates $16–$32; main courses $38–$70. AE, DC, DISC, MC, V. Sun–Thurs 5:30–10:30pm; Fri–Sat 5–11pm.

Red Square ✶✶ CONTINENTAL/RUSSIAN   It's the restaurant with the giant beheaded statue of Lenin out front and the bar made of ice (all the better to keep your drinks chilled) inside. It's the place for vodka and blow-your-expense-account Beluga (we prefer Osetra, in case you are treating us), along with Roquefort-crusted, tender filet mignon—one of the best filets in a town full of red meat. Silly theme drinks keep up the goofy quotient (the "Cuban Missile Crisis," for example, features Rain Vodka, dark rum, sugar-cane syrup, and lime juice), but do consider trying a vodka flight. Dessert is not so clever but is worth saving room for; we liked the Chocolate Trilogy, a white-chocolate cake tower topped with chocolate mousse and wrapped in chocolate.

In Mandalay Bay, 3950 Las Vegas Blvd. S. ✆ 702/632-7407. Reservations recommended. Main courses $22–$46. AE, DC, MC, V. Daily 4–10:30pm.

EXPENSIVE

Border Grill ✶✶✶ MEXICAN   More entries from Food Network denizens—in this case, the "Two Hot Tamales," Mary Sue Milliken and Susan Feniger. In a riotous-colored venue (the highly popular original is in Los Angeles), you will find truly authentic Mexican home-cooking—the Tamales learned their craft from the real McCoy south of the border—but with a nuevo twist. So don't expect precisely the same dishes you'd encounter in your favorite corner joint, but do expect fresh and fabulous food, arranged as brightly on the plates as the decor on the walls. It might be hard to get kids interested in anything other than tacos and enchiladas, but you should try the *cochinita pibil* (marinated shredded pork) or some of their excellent tamales. Stay away from the occasionally bland fish and head right toward rich and cheesy dishes such as the chiles rellenos (with perfect black beans), or try the mushroom empanadas. Don't miss the dense but fluffy Mexican chocolate cream pie (with a meringue crust).

In Mandalay Bay, 3950 Las Vegas Blvd. S. ✆ 702/632-7403. www.bordergrill.com. Reservations recommended. Main courses $15–$24 lunch, $21–$34 dinner. AE, DC, DISC, MC, V. Sat–Sun 10am–10pm; Mon–Fri 11:30am–11pm.

Table 10 ☆☆☆ AMERICAN   The natural conclusion to draw about celebrity chefs with multiple restaurants is that they are spreading themselves too thin. That may or may not be true as a whole, but this latest venture by New Orleans-based and TV-ubiquitous Emeril belies conventional wisdom. Not a copy of another holding in the Emeril empire (as are the excellent Delmonico and the hit-and-miss Emeril's Seafood) but a new endeavor with its own personality—albeit one that clearly benefits from its Emeril origins. Named after a special seating spot in Emeril's flagship New Orleans restaurant, the food at this locale hits a high note on a level with that standout eatery. Further, at this writing, while not cheap, meals here come off as a bargain in comparison to comparable fine dining options in town. (As is often the case, you may want to consider dropping by for an even more affordable lunch.) The menu will likely change regularly, but look for appetizers such as oyster fritters with Rockefeller sauce and Bibb salad with housemade bacon, and entrees such as tender roasted lamb with black truffle reduction, and sides including a sumptuous lobster macaroni and cheese. Desserts are clever, while standout is the malassadas, deep-fried dough balls filled with white chocolate.

In the Palazzo, 3328 Las Vegas Blvd. S. ✆ **702/607-6363.** www.emerils.com. Reservations recommended. Main courses $11–$29 lunch, $25–$38 dinner. AE, MC, V. Sun–Thurs 11am–11pm; Fri-Sat 11am–midnight.

MODERATE

Burger Bar ☆ DINER   What to do, what to do? We get exhausted by the relentless Vegas high-concept that takes a simple idea like a hamburger and gives it an entire restaurant, an entire menu designed so you can "build" your own burger with dozens of options available—People, cheese! Ketchup! Onions! Why do you need more? Why, why, why?—so that the naive could suddenly turn their affordable lunch into something approaching $20 a person. Assuming, of course, that you didn't fall for pricey gimmicks like Kobe beef (too soft for a good burger) and foie gras, in which case you would be looking at more like $50 a person. But then again, we love gimmicks. We also see the point of avocado bacon burgers. Plus, they make excellent shakes here, and there is that "sweet burger" (a donut "bun" with a chocolate pâté patty and fruit!), which is so charming we are disarmed. And the burgers are good. So. Order carefully, don't show off, and don't forget about the genuine (and appropriately priced) hamburgers sold at the Tiffany's coffee shop near the Strat.

In Mandalay Place in Mandalay Bay, 3950 Las Vegas Blvd. S. ✆ **877/632-7800.** Burgers $8–$20. AE, DISC, MC, V. Sun–Thurs 10am–11pm; Fri-Sat 10am–2am.

Dick's Last Resort 🏵🏵 DINER Boy food for the boisterous. This is not the place to go for a relaxing or dainty meal. The gimmick is customer abuse—yes, you pay for the privilege of having a wait staff hurl napkins and cheerful invective at you. But they mean it with love. Sounds a bit strange, but it works, in a party-hearty way. Speaking of, the food itself is hearty indeed, with house specialties (BBQ ribs, honey-glazed chicken) arriving in buckets. Entrees are substantial, both in quantity and construction—look for chicken fried steak, fried chicken, meats or pastas covered in cream sauces. The most successful item could well be their burger, a juicy mammoth. Probably best for rowdy teenagers or stag parties, but both attitude and grub might be a relief after all those houses of reverent culinary worship.

In Excalibur, 3850 Las Vegas Blvd. S. ℂ **702/597-7991**. Main courses $13–$24. AE, MC, V. Daily 11am until "late."

Dragon Noodle Co. 🏵🏵 ASIAN FUSION A strong choice for a reasonably priced meal, Dragon Noodle is one of the better Chinese restaurants in town. We were glad to see that in addition to the usual suspects, there are some other interesting (if not radically less safe) choices on the menu. Note also the many Asian clients (part of our criteria for the authenticity of a place) and that the restaurant can handle large groups. Food is served family-style and prepared in an open kitchen, so you know it's fresh. Be sure to try the very smooth house green tea. You might let your waiter choose your meal for you, but try the crispy Peking pork, the sweet pungent shrimp, the pot stickers, and perhaps the generous seafood soup. We were a little disappointed by the popular sizzling black-pepper chicken, but you may not be, so don't let us stop you. And they now have a sushi bar!

In Monte Carlo Resort & Casino, 3770 Las Vegas Blvd. S. (btw. Flamingo Rd. and Tropicana Ave.). ℂ **702/730-7965**. www.dragonnoodleco.com. Main courses $5.50–$17 (many under $10). AE, DC, DISC, MC, V. Sun–Thurs 11am–11pm; Fri–Sat 11am–midnight.

Grand Wok and Sushi Bar 🏵🏵 *Value* PAN-ASIAN A pan-Asian restaurant runs the risk of attempting to be a jack-of-all-trades and master of none, but somehow, this new MGM eatery pulls it off. You can choose among Japanese, Chinese, Korean, Vietnamese, and probably more—we just aren't sure what Laotian food looks like (but would love to learn). Sushi is fresh and lovely, and the Vietnamese soups are enormous, full of noodles and different kinds of meat or fish; four people can easily split an order, so this is a great budget option for lunchtime.

In MGM Grand, 3799 Las Vegas Blvd. S. ℂ **702/891-7777**. Reservations not accepted. Main courses $15–$18; sushi rolls and pieces $7–$30. AE, DC, DISC, MC,

You Gotta Have a Theme

It shouldn't be too surprising that a town devoted to themes (what hotel worth its salt doesn't have one, at this point?) has one of virtually every theme restaurant there is. For the most part, these establishments glorify some aspect of pop culture: movies, sports, rock music, and so forth. Almost all have prominent celebrity co-owners and tons of "memorabilia" on the walls, which in virtually every case means throwaway items from blockbuster movies or some article of clothing a celeb wore once (if that) onstage or on the playing field. Almost all have virtually identical menus and have gift shops full of logo items.

This sounds cynical, and it is—but not without reason. Theme restaurants are, for the most part, noisy, cluttered, overpriced tourist traps, and though some have their devotees, if you eat at one of these places, you've eaten at them all. We don't want to be total killjoys. Fans should have a good time checking out the stuff on the walls of the appropriate restaurant. And while the food won't be the most memorable ever, it probably won't be bad. But that's not really what you go for. In any case, here are our two best bets in the theme department:

The **House of Blues** *Ɍ̃Ɍ̃*, in Mandalay Bay, 3950 Las Vegas Blvd. S. (✆ **702/632-7600;** www.hob.com), is, for our money, food, and theme-wise, the best of the theme restaurants. The food is really pretty good (if a little more costly than it ought to be), and the mock Delta/ New Orleans look works well, even if it is unavoidably

V. Restaurant Sun–Thurs 11am–10pm; Fri–Sat 11am–1am. Sushi bar Mon–Thurs 5–10pm; Fri–Sat 11am–1am; Sun 11am–10pm.

Wolfgang Puck Bar & Grill *Ɍ̃Ɍ̃* CALIFORNIA This transformed Puck Café is still a desirable, if slightly less affordable, option in MGM Grand. There is nothing surprising on the menu if you've eaten in any modern cafe in the post-Puck era; it's not his fault his influence has extended so far. There is enough variety that everyone in your party should find something to please them, from crab cakes with basil aioli, to a prime rib sandwich, to homemade veal ravioli, to Puck's pizzas, plus a good wine cellar. The fresh salads (we love the commercial. You can dine here without committing to seeing whatever band is playing since the dining room is separate from the club (note that HOB gets very good bookings from nationally known acts). The gospel brunch might also be worth checking out (the food is good, but there's too much of it), but be warned: It's served inside the actual club, which is miked very loudly, and it can be unbelievably loud, so bring earplugs (we left with splitting headaches). Open Monday through Thursday from 7:30am to midnight and Friday and Saturday from 7:30am to 1am.

Presumably filling the hole left by the demise of the All Star Café, so you sports fans won't feel left out in the theme restaurant race, the gigantic **ESPN Zone** ⭐, in New York–New York, 3790 Las Vegas Blvd. S. (✆ **702/933-3776;** www.espnzone.com), actually has rather wacky and entertaining sports memorabilia (such as Evel Knievel set up as the old Operation game, displaying his many broken bones), plus additions such as a rock-climbing wall/machine. It's pretty fun, actually, and the food, in a couch-potato junk-food-junkie way, is not bad, either, especially when you sit in La-Z-Boy recliners to watch sports and order delights such as three Krispy Kreme donuts topped with ice cream, whipped cream, and syrup. Sadly, we find this entire concept tremendously appealing. It's open Sunday through Thursday 11am to midnight and Friday and Saturday 11am to 1am.

seasonal roasted beet) are better constructed than those at comparable eateries in town where Puck's hand is still on the helm; witness the silly potato chips drizzled with truffle oil and melted bleu cheese. It's all set in an almost entirely open space, a minimalist-art take on a country kitchen, and it's a bit noisy, thanks to proximity to the casino floor. Expect it to be crowded right before and after *KÀ* but possibly quiet during.

In MGM Grand, 3799 Las Vegas Blvd. S. ✆ 702/891-3019. www.wolfgangpuck. com. Reservations accepted for dinner. Main courses $12–$35 lunch, $18–$38 (most under $28) dinner. AE, DISC, DC, MC, V. Sun–Thurs 11:30am–10pm; Fri–Sat 10:30am–11pm.

INEXPENSIVE

Earl of Sandwich ✦✦✦ SANDWICHES It seems credulity-straining, but the sandwich was something that had to be invented, and thus someone got their simple yet ingenious idea named after them. At least, so the story goes, so sufficiently accepted as historical lore that it carries enough weight for the intrepid inventor's descendent, the 11th Earl of Sandwich, to lend their name to a chain of sandwich shops. It's a gimmick, but a good one, and so is the food. The eponymous, and largely excellent, sandwiches are served warm (wraps are cold) on bread made for the shop, and include combos such as grilled Swiss, bleu and brie with applewood smoked bacon; and roast beef with horseradish cream and cheddar cheese. There are also complex if unoriginal salads, smoothies, and breakfast sandwiches. Portions aren't huge, but it's not a problem if you are devoted to Vegas-sized meals; the low prices make it possible to order two of everything if appetites demand.

In Planet Hollywood, 3667 Las Vegas Blvd. S. ✆ 702/463-0259. www.earlof sandwichusa.com. Everything under $6. AE, MC, V.

Jody Maroni's Sausage Kingdom ✦✦✦ (Kids) SAUSAGES There are several worthy fast-food stands in the New York–New York food court, but this one deserves an individual mention. What began as a humble stand on the Venice boardwalk in Los Angeles has expanded into a sausage empire, and we are glad. You will be, too, especially if you take a chance on the menu and don't just stick with the basic hot dog (though they do offer three tempting varieties—and kids love 'em) and instead try something a little more adventurous, like the tequila chicken sausage made with jalapeños, corn, and lime. Maybe some chili fries, too. Our first choice for fast food in the immediate area.

In New York–New York Hotel & Casino, 3790 Las Vegas Blvd. S. ✆ 702/740-6969. www.jodymaroni.com. Everything under $11. AE, DC, MC, V. Daily 11am–6pm.

Monte Carlo Pub & Brewery ✦✦✦ (Finds) (Kids) PUB FARE Lest you think we are big, fat foodie snobs who can't appreciate a meal unless it comes drenched in truffles and caviar, we hasten to direct you to this lively, working microbrewery (with a sort of rustic factory appearance) and its hearty, not-so-highfalutin food (pizza, ribs, shrimp salads, chocolate fudge brownies). No fancy French frills and, best of all, no inflated prices. Combine the general high quality with generous portions—a nachos appetizer could probably feed eight (though it was not the best nachos appetizer ever)—and this may be

> ## *Tips* Quick Bites
>
> Many Vegas hotels have food courts, but the one in the **New York–New York,** 3790 Las Vegas Blvd. S. (✆ **702/740-6969**), deserves a mention for two reasons: It's the nicest setting for this sort of thing on the Strip, sitting in the Greenwich Village section of New York–New York, and the choices, while not surprising (except at Jodi Maroni's Sausage Kingdom, listed above), are superior. Expect Chinese food and pizza (as befitting an ode to New York City) and excellent, if expensive (for this situation), double-decker burgers, plus **Ben & Jerry's** ice cream.
>
> If you head farther down the Strip, to The Grande Canal Shoppes at **The Venetian,** 3355 Las Vegas Blvd. S. (✆ **702/414-1000**), you can find another decent food court, with a Panda Express, a good pizza place (despite the confusing name **LA Pizza Kitchen**), a burrito stand, and a juice joint, and best of all, a **Krispy Kreme,** where they actually make the donuts on the premises. Plus, it's right by the canals of this faux Venice, one of our favorite places in Vegas.

a better deal than most buffets. It's not, however, the place for a quiet rendezvous, with about 40 TVs spread throughout (a sports fan's dream) and music blaring. After 9pm, only pizza is served, and nightly entertainment keeps things hopping late.

In Monte Carlo Resort & Casino, 3770 Las Vegas Blvd. S. ✆ 702/730-7777. Reservations not accepted. Main courses $6–$15. AE, DC, DISC, MC, V. Closed Mon–Tues; Wed–Thurs and Sun 11am–11pm; Fri–Sat 11am–1am.

2 Mid-Strip

VERY EXPENSIVE

Alizé ✸✸✸ CONTINENTAL   Situated at the top of the Palms, this Michelin-starred restaurant's divine dining room has three sides of full-length windows that allow a panoramic view of the night lights of Vegas; it may also have the best chef in town. The menu changes seasonally, but anything you order will be heavenly.

On our last visit, we had perhaps 14 different courses, and not a single one disappointed. In the appetizer department, the marinated jumbo lump crabmeat and avocado salad with heirloom tomato consommé and basil oil was a riot of freshness, while the gnocchi with sautéed wild mushrooms, black truffle, and mushroom emulsion was the kind of dish clearly created by someone thoughtful and clever. Fish can be a little dry here, so we suggest either the stunning New York steak with summer truffle jus and potato herb pancakes, or the meltingly tender lamb chops with some shredded lamb shank wrapped in a crispy fried crepe. Desserts are similarly outstanding, and often of great frivolity, such as sorbet in a case of browned marshmallow, floating in raspberry soup. Yeah, we're going over the top on this one, but we bet you won't think we're wrong.

Note: Obviously, window-side tables here are best, but even seats in the center of the room have a good view, so don't despair if you aren't seated right next to the glass. The romance oozes, regardless of where you are seated.

In Palms Casino Resort, 4321 W. Flamingo Rd. ℂ 702/951-7000. Fax 702/951-7002. www.alizelv.com. Reservations strongly recommended. Entrees $34–$67; 5-course tasting menu $95; 7-course tasting menu $125. AE, DC, DISC, MC, V. Sun–Thurs 5:30–10pm; Fri–Sat 5:30–11pm, last reservation at 10:30pm.

B&B Ristorante ★★ ITALIAN

Long time Food Network staple Mario Batalli has a couple of Vegas outposts, and this is perhaps the most notable. It looks like an uber-Italian trattoria, full of dark wood, quite inviting and unfortunately very loud. Naturally, the desirable room is in the wine cellar. The menu options are a little too casual for the price, and might be intimidating for those uninitiated in Batalli, but there's probably no one in Vegas doing such interesting Italian food. To that end, you might be best served sticking with the primi, pasta selections, which are cheaper and arguably more interesting than the secondi, though portions are not hearty. Don't miss the beef cheek ravioli with duck liver but other notables are the mint love letters with lamb sausage and the stinging nettle pappardelle with wild boar ragu. Or just do the rather reasonable $75 pasta tasting menu. Meanwhile, if you are lucky, Chef himself might be roaming the place in his famous clogs.

In the Venetian, 3355 Las Vegas Blvd. S. ℂ 702/266-9977. Main courses $21–$49. AE, DISC, MC, V. Daily 5–11pm.

Delmonico Steakhouse ★★ CONTEMPORARY CREOLE/STEAK

This, the latest of Emeril Lagasse's Vegas variations on his Big Easy brand-name eateries, is a steakhouse version of his hardcore classic Creole restaurant; and this ever-so-slight twist is just enough to make it a superior choice over the more disappointing New Orleans locale. You can try both Emeril concoctions and fabulous cuts of red meat. You can't go wrong with most appetizers, especially the superbly rich smoked mushrooms with homemade tasso over pasta—it's enough for a meal in and of itself—any of the specials, or the gumbo. If you want to experiment, definitely do it with the appetizers. You're better off steering clear of complex entrees, no matter how intriguing they sound. The bone-in rib steak is rightly recommended (skip the gummy béarnaise sauce in favor of the fabulous homemade Worcestershire or the A.O.K. sauce). Too full for dessert? No, you aren't. Have a chocolate soufflé, a Bananas Foster cream pie, a chocolate Sheba (a sort of dense chocolate mousse), or the lemon icebox pie, a chunk of curd that blasts tart lemon through your mouth.

In The Venetian, 3355 Las Vegas Blvd. S. ℂ **702/414-3737.** Reservations strongly recommended for dinner. Main courses $12–$40 lunch, $40–$50 dinner. AE, DC, DISC, MC, V. Daily 11:30am–2pm; Sun–Thurs 5:30–10pm; Fri–Sat 5:30–10:30pm.

Fin ⭐ SEAFOOD/CHINESE   Elegant and decorous, perhaps a little higher on style (love the glass ball curtains, evocative of bubbles rising in water) than on substance, though that may just be our reaction to the prices, especially when you see how cheap dim sum is in other (admittedly, much less convenient) parts of town. Still, the quiet flourish of ritual that accompanies course presentation makes for a peaceful break from casino madness. Highlights include the rice cooked in chicken fat; the crispy shiitake mushrooms in a sweet-and-sour sauce that ought to convert even a non-mushroom fan; and the deeply spicy seared black-pepper beef tenderloin.

In The Mirage, 3400 Las Vegas Blvd. S. ℂ **866/339-4566,** or 702/791-7353. Reservations recommended. Main courses $11–$27 lunch, $19–$48 dinner. AE, DC, DISC, MC, V. Daily 11am–3pm and 5–11pm.

Fix ⭐⭐ AMERICAN   A just-right synthesis of gourmet dining, fun dining, and accessible dining, created by the people behind Bellagio's excellent Bank nightclub. Looking, as one visitor described it, like a "giant clam opening up toward the casino," the menu continues this playful vibe. Look for the silly presentation called "Forks," appetizers of smoked salmon and caviar skewed on forks, served tines in the air. Or desserts like "Shake and Cake" (espresso shake and a brownie), a peanut-butter-and-jelly crème brûlée (misconceived? Or an idea whose time has come? You decide!), and delightful banana sugared donuts with chocolate and peanut butter dipping sauce. Best of all are the steaks, which are grilled over cherry wood, giving the meat a smoky yet fruity flavor, reminding you that meat is supposed to have dimensions to its taste. From the trendy "small plates" to hamburgers, this is one complete menu. All in all, a good compromise fancy location for a special occasion or just a treat of a meal. The crowd grows younger and trendier as the night wears on.

In Bellagio, 3600 Las Vegas Blvd. S. ② 702/693-8400. Reservations recommended. Main courses $29–$75. AE, MC, V. Sun–Thurs 5pm–midnight; Fri–Sat 5pm–2am.

Le Cirque ⭐ FRENCH The influx of haute-cuisine, high-profile restaurants in Vegas means there are so many places where you may feel you have to take out a bank loan in order to eat there—and you may wonder why you ought to. Although we always feel free to spend your money, we aren't prepared to suggest you blow it all at Le Cirque. Service is haughty, the food well-prepared, but nothing earthshaking. The menu changes seasonally, but you can expect genuine French cuisine—heavy, with lots of butter, though a recent visit brought a duo of cold cucumber and heirloom tomato soups that were so refreshing, every restaurant in this desert town ought to serve them. The lobster salad is sweet and tender, with a perfect black truffle dressing; risotto is French-style, almost soupy, perfect with fresh morels (in season) and Parmesan. The filet mignon is, oddly, not as good a cut as served elsewhere, but it does come with a generous portion of foie gras. For dessert, we loved the white-chocolate cream, layered with banana and wrapped in phyllo, along with a milk chocolate dome with crème brûlée espresso.

In Bellagio, 3600 Las Vegas Blvd. S. ② 877/234-6358. Reservations required. Jacket preferred; no jeans, shorts, tee shirts, or sneakers. Prix fixe dinner $105 or $145. AE, DC, DISC, MC, V. Daily seating 5:30–10pm.

Mesa Grill ⭐⭐ SOUTHWESTERN Food Network darling Bobby Flay has his fans and his detractors, and we aren't going to mediate that argument here, especially since the man isn't cooking in the kitchen any more often than most celebrity chefs in this town. More significantly, regardless of where you fall in the debate, this is a worthy restaurant, if, like so much in Vegas, a bit overpriced. Just about every well-spiced entree is over $30, and sometimes well over. (A buffalo rib-eye with mustard-habanero sauce and cayenne sour cream onion rings at $38, ancho chile-cumin rubbed rabbit for $33. See what we mean?)

Still, there is so much that is fun here; blue-corn pancakes with barbeque duck, pumpkin soup with pomegranate and pecan relish; even the chicken quesadilla (made in a special dedicated oven) comes with garlic crème fraîche. Presentation is over the top—yes, yes, this is playful food, we get it, now stop it—but those who are a bit on the wimpy side when it comes to spices will appreciate how each entree comes with its own cooling element (the aforementioned crème fraîche, for example). Desserts are equally frivolous, though not particularly theme-intensive (unless you consider an exceptional raspberry and white-chocolate cheesecake "Southwestern"). Those wishing to try it without breaking the bank should either come at lunch or consider splitting appetizers as a light meal.

In Caesars Palace, 3570 Las Vegas Blvd. S. ℂ 702/731-7731. Main courses $12–$24 brunch and lunch, $23–$45 dinner. Mon–Fri 11am–3pm and 5–10:30pm; Sat–Sun 10:30am–3pm and 5–10:30pm.

The Palm 🏵🏵 STEAK/SEAFOOD   A branch of the venerable New York eatery, which has been branching ever further afield, this place attracts a star-studded clientele fond of the reliable and hearty, if not terribly exciting, bill of fare. (The famous may also be hoping to find their faces among the many caricatures that cover the walls.) This is plain but filling food—at manly prices. Red-meat lovers will be happy with the high-quality steaks found here, though those on a budget will shudder in horror. The tendency is to give the meat a good charring, so if you don't like yours blackened, start with it less well done and send it back for more, if necessary. All that money you've saved by not gambling will be well spent on one of the Palm's Buick-size lobsters. They're utterly succulent and outrageously priced, but given their size—they start at 3 pounds—they can easily be shared. Desserts are heavy and unspectacular.

In Caesars Palace Forum Shops, 3570 Las Vegas Blvd. S. ℂ 702/732-7256. www.thepalm.com. Reservations recommended. Main courses $10–$22 lunch, $20–$46 dinner. AE, DC, MC, V. Daily 11:30am–11pm.

Picasso 🏵🏵🏵 FRENCH   A Spanish chef who cooks French cuisine in an Italian-themed hotel in Vegas? Trust us, it works. This may well be the best restaurant in Vegas, and given the serious competition for such a title, that says a lot. Madrid-born chef Julian Serrano (whose Masa was considered the finest French restaurant in San Francisco) offers an extraordinary dining experience, along with the added thrill of having $30 million worth of Picassos gazing down over your shoulders while you eat.

Needless to say, Serrano's cooking is a work of art that can proudly stand next to the masterpieces. The menu changes nightly and always offers a choice between a four- or five-course fixed-price dinner or tasting menu. We were bowled over by roasted Maine lobster with a trio of corn—kernels, sauce, and a corn flan that was like slightly solid sunshine. Hudson Valley foie gras was crusted in truffles and went down most smoothly. A filet of roasted sea bass came with a light saffron sauce and dots of cauliflower purée. And finally,

---

Moments **A Dining Room, or Two, with a View**

Both the chic **Eiffel Tower** restaurant, in Paris Las Vegas, 3655 Las Vegas Blvd. S. (*©* **702/948-6937;** daily 11am–3pm and 5:30–10:45pm), located on the 11th floor of said Mid-Strip hotel, and the **Stratosphere's Top of the World,** in the Stratosphere Casino Hotel & Tower, 2000 Las Vegas Blvd. S. (*©* **702/ 380-7711;** daily 11am–3pm, Sun–Thurs 5:30–10:30pm, Fri–Sat 5:30–11pm), which is almost at the top of the North Strip's Stratosphere Tower, offer fantastic views. The latter revolves 360 degrees, while the former looks down on the Bellagio fountains. Both, however, match sky-high views with sky-high prices and, unfortunately, neither has food worth the price. Go for a special night out, or see if you can get away with just ordering appetizers and dessert (which are both superior to the entrees, anyway). You can also just have a drink at their respective bars, though each is set back far enough from the windows so that drinkers have less choice views than diners.

---

hope that they're serving the lamb rôti—it was an outstanding piece of lamb, perfectly done, tender, and crusted with truffles. Portions are dainty but so rich that you'll have plenty to eat without groaning and feeling heavy when you leave. Desserts are powerful yet prettily constructed.

In Bellagio, 3600 Las Vegas Blvd. S. *©* 877/234-6358. Reservations recommended. Prix-fixe 4-course dinner $113; 5-course degustation $123. AE, DC, DISC, MC, V. Wed–Mon 6–9:30pm.

The Range Steakhouse *✦* STEAK   This place is worth visiting, if only for the spectacular view of the Strip (few Strip restaurants take advantage of this view, oddly enough) from 40-foot-high wrap-around windows. The small menu features the usual steakhouse offerings—various cuts of beef and some chicken dishes, plus a few salads—but at a high-medium price. The quality, however, is better than we've found at the usual Vegas steakhouse suspects. We particularly liked the filet mignon on a Gorgonzola-onion croustade. All entrees come with family-style side dishes (they change nightly but can include such items as marinated mushrooms or horseradish mashed potatoes). Appetizers are also worth noting. The five-onion soup is thick, heavy, creamy, and served in a giant, hollowed-out onion. It's delicious, as was a smoked chicken quesadilla. Don't miss the bread, which comes with a sweet-and-savory apricot-and-basil butter.

In Harrah's, 3475 Las Vegas Blvd. S. (C) **702/369-5084**. Reservations strongly recommended. Main courses $20–$59. AE, DC, DISC, MC, V. Daily 5:30–10:30pm.

Spago *Overrated* AMERICAN/ASIAN/CALIFORNIA With Wolfgang Puck showing up in a different incarnation at every hotel in town these days (or so it seems), his original creation might get lost in the shuffle. Certainly, it's no longer the only foodie game in town—and you get the feeling it was so far ahead of the pack for so long that it has gotten a bit complacent. Which is not to say Spago is not worth the expense—it just means that others have caught up with and, in some cases, surpassed it.

Specialties include Puck's signature Chinois chicken salad and a superb mesquite-fried salmon served with a tangy toss of soba noodles and cashews in a coconut-sesame-chile paste vinaigrette nuanced with lime juice and Szechuan mustard. The main dining room menu changes seasonally, but the signature dish is a Chinese-style duck, moist but with a perfectly crispy skin. It's about as good as duck gets, served with a doughy steamed bun and Chinese vegetables. Lunch in the cafe brings nice enough pastas, salads, and quiches, but you do tend to wonder what the fuss is about.

In Caesars Palace, 3570 Las Vegas Blvd. S. (C) **702/369-6300**. www.wolfgang puck.com. Reservations recommended for the dining room, not accepted at the cafe. Dining room main courses $21–$45; cafe main courses $10–$25. AE, DC, DISC, MC, V. Dining room daily 5:30–10pm. Cafe Sun–Thurs 11am–11pm, Fri–Sat 11am–midnight.

EXPENSIVE

Bouchon ★★★ BISTRO Now here is where the whole celebrity-chef concept bursts into full glory. Thomas Keller made his name with his Napa Valley restaurant French Laundry, considered by many to be the best restaurant in the United States. (It's temporarily closed while Keller operates his new New York City restaurant, Per Se.) Bouchon is a version of his Napa Valley bistro. We had mixed expectations: On one hand, a certifiably genius chef. On the other hand, he's not going to be in the kitchen, which will be producing bistro (which is to say, not innovative) food and, what's more, is based on the rather lackluster Napa Bouchon.

Our negative expectations were confounded by the right, left, and center of the menu—we've tried nearly all of it and can report that, humble though these dishes sound, in nearly every case they are gold-standard versions of classics. Someone is certainly keeping a close eye on this kitchen, and that someone has learned their lessons well. Don't miss the bacon and poached-egg frisee salad, or the cleanly seared salmon over poached leaks, prepared to such rightness it doesn't need the accompanying sauce. Gnocchi is earthy and assertive, while beef bourguignon is exactly as you expect it to be, in the divine-perfection sense. Leg of lamb has all chewy bits excised before cooking, leaving it a garlic-permeated bit of tenderness. This is a superlative Vegas restaurant, and while it may be hard to reconcile the prices with the apparent simplicity of the food, recall that it takes serious skill to make even the most humble of dishes correctly, as your palate will reassure you.

In The Venetian, 3355 Las Vegas Blvd. S. ℂ 702/414-6200. www.bouchonbistro. com. Reservations strongly recommended. Main courses $10–$20 breakfast, $22–$45 dinner; Sat–Sun brunch $21–$25. AE, DC, DISC, MC, V. Daily 7–10:30am and 5–11pm; Sat–Sun brunch 8am–2pm. Oyster bar daily 3–11pm.

Canaletto ✾✾ ITALIAN Come here for solid, true Italian fare—and that means less sauce-intensive than the red-checked-tablecloth establishments of our American youths. Here, the emphasis is on the pasta, not the accompaniments. This place is all the more enjoyable for being perched on the faux St. Mark's Square; in theory, you can pretend you are sitting on the edge of the real thing, a fantasy we don't mind admitting we briefly indulged in. A risotto of porcini, sausage, and white truffle oil was full of strong flavors, while the wood-fired roast chicken was perfectly moist. A properly roasted chicken should be a much-celebrated thing, and that alone may be reason to come here.

In The Venetian Grand Canal Shoppes, 3377 Las Vegas Blvd. S. ℂ 702/733-0070. Reservations recommended for dinner. Main courses $14–$36. AE, DC, MC, V. Sun–Thurs 11:30am–11pm; Fri–Sat 11:30am–midnight.

Circo ✾✾ ITALIAN Yes, this is the less expensive offering from the same family who brings you Le Cirque, but going to one does not excuse you from going to the other.

Order the mista di Campo, a lovely little salad, both visually and in terms of taste; it's a creative construction of vegetables bound with cucumber and topped with a fab balsamic vinaigrette. Or start with the antipasto appetizer sampler of Tuscan sheep's milk cheese, marinated veggies, prosciutto, and Italian pastrami. Follow that with a perfect tagliatelle with rock shrimp—it comes loaded with various crustacean bits in a light sauce. Note that appetizer portions of pastas are plenty filling and cheaper than full-size servings. At dinner, opt for more elaborate dishes, such as breast of Muscovy duck with dried organic fruit in port-wine sauce.

In Bellagio, 3600 Las Vegas Blvd. S. © 702/693-8150. Reservations recommended. Main courses $14–$45. AE, DC, DISC, MC, V. Daily 5:30–10:30pm.

Pinot Brasserie 🦋🦋 BISTRO Pinot reliably delivers French and American favorites that are thoughtfully conceived and generally delicious. It's an excellent choice if you want a special meal that is neither stratospherically expensive nor too complex. And the space is highly attractive, with various props culled from French auctions and flea markets forming the archetypal, clubby bistro feel. (We particularly like the small room off the bar to the right—just perfect for a tête-à-tête.)

Salads are possibly fresher and more generous than other similar starters in town, and they can come paired with various toppings for crostini (toasted slices of French bread), such as herbed goat cheese. The signature dish, beloved by many, is a roasted chicken accompanied by heaping mounds of garlic fries, but if you wish to get a little more elaborate (and yet rather light), thin slices of smoked salmon with celery rémoulade could be a way to go. Desserts are lovely, and the ice cream is homemade—the chocolate alone should make you wish you'd never eaten at 31 Flavors because those were wasted calories compared to this. *Note:* It's easy to graze through this menu and have a less costly meal here than at most other high-end places, and the long operating hours mean you can also pop in for a nosh at times when other fine-dining options are closed.

In The Venetian, 3355 Las Vegas Blvd. S. © 702/414-8888. www.patinagroup.com. Reservations recommended for dinner. Main courses $10–$19 breakfast, $12–$25 lunch, $21–$36 dinner. AE, DISC, MC, V. Mon–Fri 8–10am, 11:30am–3pm, and 5:30–10pm; Sat-Sun 8am–3pm and 5:30–10:30pm.

MODERATE

See also the listing for **Spago** (p. 79), an expensive restaurant fronted by a more moderately priced cafe, and **Circo** (p. 80) and **Pinot Brasserie** (above), which are both in the expensive category but provide opportunities for moderately priced dining.

Isla 🦋🦋 MEXICAN Unless you absolutely do not consider Mexican food anything other than a specific form of Southern California burrito, you really should try this new establishment run by Richard Sandoval, who specializes in "modern Mexican cuisine." This means dishes both traditional and with potentially dangerous twists, but since the place starts with handmade tortillas and heads right to guacamole made on demand, it's all trustworthy, even if some of that guac contains lobster and passion fruit. Roast pork *pipian* with tamarind marinade is a lovely dish, as are the needlessly fried (though pleasantly crunchy) beef empanadas with dried cherries and chipotle tomato sauce, a satisfying mix of sweet and spicy. For the more timid, there is a nice assortment of particularly good tacos and burritos. Isla also has the most charming dessert menu in town, with Mexican themes both culinary and visual, like a desert-scape represented by a chocolate cactus stuck into a fudge hill, to complement the caramel cupcakes.

In TI at The Mirage, 3300 Las Vegas Blvd. S. 🕜 **866/286-3809** or 702/894-7223. Main courses $10–$25. AE, DC, DISC, MC, V. Wed and Fri–Sat 4pm–midnight; Sun–Tues and Thurs 4–11pm.

Mon Ami Gabi 🕜🕜 BISTRO   This charming bistro has it all: a delightful setting, better-than-average food, affordable prices. Sure, it goes overboard in trying to replicate a classic Parisian bistro, but the results are less cheesy than most Vegas attempts at atmosphere, and the patio seating on the Strip (no reservations taken there—first-come, first-served) actually makes you feel like you're in a real, not a prefab, city. You can be budget-conscious and order just the very fine onion soup, or you can eat like a real French person and order classic steak and *pommes frites* (the hanger steak is just a nice, juicy, and sweet cut of meat). There are plenty of cheaper options (which is why we listed this place in the "moderate" category, by the way), especially at lunch. Yes, they have snails, and we loved 'em. Desserts, by the way, are massive and should be shared (another way to save). The baseball-size profiteroles (three or four to an order) filled with fine vanilla ice cream and the football-size bananas-Foster crepe are particularly good. Ooh, la la!

In Paris Las Vegas, 3655 Las Vegas Blvd. S. 🕜 **702/944-GABI.** www.monamigabi.com. Reservations recommended. Main courses $18–$40. AE, DC, DISC, MC, V. Sun–Thurs 10:30–11pm; Fri–Sat 10:30pm–midnight.

Olives 🕜🕜 ITALIAN/MEDITERRANEAN   If there were an Olives cafe in our neighborhood, we would eat there regularly. A branch of Todd English's original Boston-based restaurant, Olives is a strong choice for a light lunch that need not be as expensive as you might think. Here's how to enjoy a moderately priced meal here: Don't fill up too much on the focaccia bread and olives they give you at the start (on the other hand, budget-obsessives, go ahead), and skip the small-size and thus costly salads, and instead go right to the flatbreads. Think pizza with an ultrathin crust (like a slightly limp cracker), topped with delicious combinations such as the highly recommended Moroccan spiced lamb, eggplant purée, and feta cheese; or the fig, prosciutto, and Gorgonzola. Split one between two people, along with that salad we just maligned, and you have an affordable and terrific lunch. Or try a pasta; we were steered toward the simple but marvelous spaghettini with roasted tomatoes, garlic, and Parmesan, and were glad. The food gets more complicated and costly at night, adding an array of meats and chickens, plus pastas such as butternut squash with brown butter and sage.

In Bellagio, 3600 Las Vegas Blvd. S. ℭ **702/693-7223.** www.toddenglish.com. Reservations recommended. Main courses $17–$25 lunch, flatbreads $15; $24–$52 dinner, flatbreads $17. AE, DC, DISC, MC, V. Daily 11am–10:30pm.

Payard Patisserie & Bistro ☆☆☆ BISTRO Breakfast here offers one of the few real remaining bargains in Vegas, given quality to price ratio. Surely it can't last, considering the state of things in modern day Vegas. But with some luck, this is what you have to look forward to; a continental breakfast like no other. Sixteen dollars gets you cereals, fruits, yogurt, lox and bagel, and, most significantly, all the breakfast pastries you can eat. Since the chef has his roots in Paris, these buttery bits of brioche and croissant perfection are as good as any you could consume by the Seine. One can easily spend that much on a breakfast buffet, or a lunch entrée, elsewhere in town, but there is no comparison for quality. Lunch is light and of the French variety, while evening brings dessert tastings of delicate, inspired flights of sugary whimsy. Both are of a particular high quality, and worth investigating, but it's breakfast that has already earned it a strong reputation, and justly so.

In Caesars Palace, 3570 Las Vegas Blvd. S. ℭ **702/731-7110.** Breakfast $16; lunch entrees $16–$26; evening desserts $15; prix fixe $45. AE, MC, V. Daily 6:30–11:30am, noon–7:30pm, and 9–11:30pm.

Sensi ☆☆ ECLECTIC It's usually a truism, as far as restaurants go, "jack of all trades, master of none." Sensi seems to be an exception, given that its menu is made up of Italian (fancy pizzas and pastas), wood-grilled American options (burgers, fish, chicken), and Asian-influenced dishes (and they mean "pan-Asian," thus tandoori and sushi both). And yet, it does it all credibly, if not very well indeed. You are probably best off here at lunchtime, sampling pizza al prosciutto or wok-fried shrimp, for more moderate prices than found at dinner. Best of all is the "Sensi 41," a healthy take on the

---

Value **Great Meal Deals**

We've already alluded to the rock-bottom budget meals and graveyard specials available at casino hotel restaurants— quality not assured and Pepto-Bismol not provided. Prices and deals can change without notice so your best bet is to keep your eyes open as you travel through town, as hotels tend to advertise their specials on their marquees.

---

bento box, featuring things like miso-glazed Chilean sea bass, some tender sashimi, piquant rice, and, disconcertingly, mozzarella salad. They finish it up with two small, cunning servings of fancy ice cream in wee cones. And do try that homemade ginger ale.

In Bellagio, 3600 Las Vegas Blvd. S. ⓒ **877/234-6358.** Main courses $14–$22 lunch, $22–$44 dinner. AE, DC, DISC, MC, V. Daily 11am–2:30pm and 5–10:30pm.

INEXPENSIVE

Canter's 🏵🏵 DELI   This is an offshoot of the venerable (1931!) Los Angeles establishment. That one is decidedly genuine old-school, while this one pretends it was built during the Jetsons-Googie age, but it wasn't. You know. Still, that perfect pastrami scent hits you as soon as you walk up, and if the portions aren't as large and the menu is only ⅕ the size of the one in Los Angeles, they still have some grand sandwiches (brisket with coleslaw and Russian dressing; we are fools for it). Not to mention black-and-white cookies. And it's open late, like a good deli should be.

In TI at The Mirage, 3300 Las Vegas Blvd. S. ⓒ **866/286-3809.** Everything under $17. AE, DC, DISC, MC, V. Daily 11am–midnight.

Cypress Street Marketplace 🏵🏵 *Kids* FOOD COURT   An interesting middle ground between the food court and the buffet, owing to an original arrangement wherein patrons get a card that gets swiped at whichever food booth is patronized, with the total added up at the end. Given the wide assortment—Vietnamese food, pot stickers, very fine burgers and pizza, salads, wraps, and pulled-pork sandwiches, there ought to be something for every single member of even the most finicky of families. With the real china and napkins, and the overall quality, we wish other hotel-casinos would put in a version of their own.

In Caesars Palace, 3570 Las Vegas Blvd. S. ⓒ **702/731-7110.** Most items under $15. AE, MC, V. Daily 11am–11pm.

3 North Strip

VERY EXPENSIVE

Alex ✿✿✿ NOUVEAU   Alex Strada (possibly familiar to you from his stint on the American *Iron Chef*) followed Steve Wynn from The Mirage, closing his Renoir venue to open this eponymous one instead. Strada comes from a cosmopolitan and international background; add to that some years working under Alain Ducasse and a general sense of food as pleasure and art, and you have one of the most special dining experiences in Vegas. The menu will change regularly—chef Alex is as exacting as a real chef should be, and so the readiness of seasonal ingredients will dictate any particular evening's selection. The result in a European restaurant would almost certainly earn a Michelin star. Diners have their choice of two set tasting menus or a three-course prix-fixe choice of appetizer, main, and dessert. Expect starters such as carpaccio of Santa Barbara prawn topped with Osetra caviar, or roasted scallop with basil purée, the whole topped by translucent fried zucchini flower. Porcini gnocchi dissolves in the mouth; a terrine of foie gras is paired with the chef's interpretation of Waldorf salad; a main course of squab and sautéed foie gras, rhubarb, and spiced pineapple is deep, rich, and bold. Even the palate cleansers are serious, such as apricot gelée topped with coconut granita ringed by passion fruit, or strawberry gelée with lemon-grass crème fraîche. You are in a master chef's hands; enjoy it.

In Wynn Las Vegas, 3131 Las Vegas Blvd. S. ⓒ **888/352-DINE [3463]** or 702/248-DINE [3463]. Reservations strongly recommended. Jacket recommended. 3-course prix-fixe menu $145; 7-course tasting menu $195. AE, DC, DISC, MC, V. Thurs–Mon 6–10pm.

Bartolotta Ristorante di Mare ✿✿✿ ITALIAN/SEAFOOD

James Beard Foundation Award–winning chef Paul Bartolotta trained in Italy under master chefs before opening up his highly acclaimed Spiaggia in Chicago. Now he's here, in this eponymous (and Best New Restaurant 2006 Beard finalist) kitchen, yet more proof that celebrity chefs are all very well and good, but it's not the same as having them on the premises. In this case, the result is as authentic Italian food as one can find outside of Italy. Determined to produce just that, Bartolotta went to his boss, Steve Wynn, and insisted that his fish not just be ultra-fresh, but be flown daily straight from the Mediterranean to his Vegas kitchen, saying, "I can't make authentic Italian food with American fish." Wynn's response? "Give the man his fish." And you will be introduced to the results after you sit down! You can choose your whole cooked fish right from that day's batch (you can get them big enough so one can be split among several people), which may include possibilities like Orata and purple snapper, each topped with a chunky "sauce" of sweet pachino tomatoes, arugula, garlic, and red onion. Pastas are perfect as well, especially the delicate sheep's milk ricotta handkerchief-style ravioli, made both sweet and savory with a veal Marsala wine-reduction glaze. Spaghetti allo scoglio comes with large chunks of lobster, langoustines are grilled to charred smoky rightness, seared scallops with porcini mushrooms in browned butter are what scallops should be—and all because this Italian staff learned their lessons well and they are passing that knowledge on to you. A jewel box of a place for cooking that is a treasure.

In Wynn Las Vegas, 3131 Las Vegas Blvd. S. ⓒ **888/352-DINE [3463]** or 702/352-DINE [3463]. Reservations recommended. Main courses $20–$58 dinner; family-style tasting $135 per person; Grand Seafood Feast served family style $155 per person. AE, DC, DISC, MC, V. Daily 5:30–10:30pm.

MODERATE

Cafe Heidelberg German Deli and Restaurant ⓡ GERMAN

A once-ponderous and dated German restaurant has been transformed into a German cafe well-packed (admittedly, with only six booths, that's not hard to do) with locals. Certainly, it's not a Vegas type of place, and since it's close enough to the Strip, it's a good place for refuge. The food is better than fine, though certainly not "lite" fare, by any means; you will be moaning and holding your stomach in sorrow if you don't share the huge portions. Recommended are the sausage sampler platter, so you can finally learn the difference between knockwurst and bratwurst, and the schnitzel sandwich of delicious breaded veal. Wash it down with a vast choice of imported beer. As you nosh, enjoy traditional (or, at times, not so) accordion music and note that the entire staff is German. This is also a full-service deli and German market, so it's a good place to pick up a picnic for sightseeing outside the city.

604 E. Sahara Ave. (at 6th St.). ⓒ **702/731-5310.** Reservations strongly recommended Fri–Sat nights. Main courses mostly under $13 lunch, $20–$26 dinner. AE, DC, DISC, MC, V. Mon–Tues 11am–3pm only; Wed–Sat lunch menu 11am–4pm, dinner 4–8pm; Sun 11am–8pm; the deli opens daily at 10am.

Fellini's ⓡ ITALIAN   A Vegas institution (in its original West Las Vegas location), much beloved by in-the-know locals, Fellini's is a classic Italian restaurant—you know, red gloopy sauce, garlicky cheesy bread—which isn't meant to be an insult at all. It might not

be ambitious, but it is reliable and more than satisfying. They do a strong version of pasta (rigatoni, in this case) Amatriciana, and they are generous with the pancetta, and while some Italian food purists would shudder at the gnocchi with tenderloin tips topped with Gorgonzola and shallot cream sauce, they are just missing out, that's all. The well-proportioned menu offers a variety of options from Osso Buco to basic pizza, and, given the prices, that makes it a good option for families with a similar range of tastes and needs.

In Stratosphere Hotel & Casino, 2000 Las Vegas Blvd S. © 702/383-4859. www.fellinislv.com. Main courses $11–$27. AE, DISC, MC, V. Mon–Thurs 5–11pm; Fri–Sat 5pm–midnight.

INEXPENSIVE

Capriotti's *Finds* SANDWICHES   It looks like a dump, but Capriotti's is one of the great deals in town, for quality and price. They roast their own beef and turkey on the premises and stuff them (or Italian cold cuts, or whatever) into sandwiches mislabeled "small," "medium," and "large"—the latter clocks in at 20 inches, easily feeding two for under $10 total. And deliciously so. The "Bobby" (turkey, dressing, and cranberry sauce, like Thanksgiving dinner in sandwich form) would be our favorite sandwich in the world had we not tried the "Slaw B Joe": roast beef, coleslaw, and Russian dressing. But other combos, such as the aforementioned Italian cold cuts, have their fans, too, and Capriotti's even has veggie varieties. There are outlets throughout the city, but this one is not only right off the Strip, but right by the freeway. We never leave town without a stop here, and you shouldn't, either.

322 W. Sahara Ave. (at Las Vegas Blvd. S.). © 702/474-0229. www.capriottis.com. Most sandwiches under $10. AE, MC, V. Mon–Fri 10am–5pm; Sat 11am–5pm.

Doña María Tamales MEXICAN   Decorated with Tijuana-style quiltwork and calendars, this is your quintessential Mexican diner, convenient to both the north end of the Strip and Downtown. They use lots of lard, lots of cheese, and lots of sauce. As a result, the food is really good—and really fattening. Yep, the folks who did those health reports showing how bad Mexican food can be for your heart probably did some research here. That just makes it all the better, in our opinion. Locals apparently agree; even at lunchtime the place is crowded. Meals are so large that it shouldn't be a problem getting full just ordering off the sides, which can make this even more of a budget option. Naturally, the specialty is the fantastic tamales, which come in red, green, cheese, or sweet. They also serve up excellent enchiladas, chiles rellenos, burritos, and fajitas. All dinners include rice, beans, tortillas, and soup or salad.

910 Las Vegas Blvd. S. (at Charleston Blvd.). ℂ **702/382-6538.** www.dona mariatamales.com. Main courses $8.20–$12 breakfast, $8.80–$12 lunch, $12–$15 dinner. AE, MC, V. Sun–Thurs 8am–10pm; Fri–Sat 8am–11pm.

Tiffany's at the White Cross Pharmacy ⋆⋆ *Value* DINER   You can go to any number of retro soda-fountain replicas (such as Johnny Rockets) and theme restaurants that pretend to be cheap diners, but why bother when the real thing is just past the end of the Strip? The decidedly unflashy soda fountain/lunch counter at the White Cross Pharmacy was Las Vegas's first 24-hour restaurant, and it has been going strong for 60 years. Plunk down at the counter and watch the cooks go nuts trying to keep up with the orders. The menu is basic comfort food: standard items such as meatloaf, steaks, and chops; fluffy cream pies; and classic breakfasts served anytime—try the biscuits and cream gravy at 3am. But the best bet is a ⅓-pound burger and "thick creamy shake," both the way they were meant to be and about as good as they get. At around $5, this is half what you would pay for a comparable meal at the Hard Rock Cafe. And as waitress Beverly says, "This is really real." Places like this are a vanishing species—it's worth the short walk from the Stratosphere. Note, however, that the neighborhood remains stubbornly rough in appearance, and that can be a turnoff.

1700 Las Vegas Blvd. S. (at East Oakley Blvd.). ℂ **702/383-0196.** Reservations not accepted. Most items under $7. No credit cards. Daily 24 hr.

4 East of the Strip

In this section, we cover restaurants close by the Convention Center, along with those farther south, on Paradise Road, Flamingo Road, and Tropicana Avenue.

VERY EXPENSIVE

Lawry's The Prime Rib ⋆⋆⋆ STEAK/SEAFOOD   If you love prime rib, come here. If you could take or leave prime rib, Lawry's will turn you into a believer. Yes, you can get prime rib all over town for under $10. But, to mix a food metaphor, that's a tuna fish sandwich when you can have caviar at Lawry's.

Eating at Lawry's is a ceremony, with all the parts played the same way for the past 60 years. Waitresses in brown-and-white English maid uniforms take your order—for side dishes, that is. The real decision, what cut of rib you are going to have, comes later. Actually,

Accommodations, Dining & Nightlife East of the Strip

ACCOMMODATIONS ■

Courtyard by Marriott **7**
Deserts Rose Suites **27**
Green Valley Ranch Resort **24**
Hard Rock Hotel & Casino **17**
Hyatt Place **19**
La Quinta **10**
Las Vegas Hilton **4**
Las Vegas Marriott Suites **5**
Residence Inn **6**
Ritz-Carlton, Lake
    Las Vegas **24**
The Westin Casuarina
    Las Vegas Hotel and Spa **14**

DINING ◆

Bougainvillea **15**
Carluccio's
    Tivoli Gardens **25**
Einstein Bros. Bagels **22**
Jason's Deli **9**
Lawry's The Prime Rib **12**
Lotus of Siam **3**
Memphis Championship
    Barbecue **24**
Pamplemousse **2**
Paymon's Mediterranean
    Café & Lounge **16**
Pink Taco **17**
Toto's **24**

NIGHTLIFE ●

The Buffalo **20**
Champagnes Cafe **8**
Club Paradise **18**
The Dispensary Lounge **23**
Double Down Saloon **21**
Drop Bar **24**
Ellis Isand Casino–Karaoke **13**
Gipsy **20**
Goodtimes Night Club **26**
Gordon Biersch
    Brewing Company **11**
Griffin **1**
Hogs & Heifers Saloon **1**
Whisky Bar **24**

Las Vegas Is for (Wine) Lovers

The Vegas restaurant boom of the late '90s continues unabated, which is also welcome news for those who worship the grape. If you're one of them, here's a sampling of places to eat *and* drink that we think you'll enjoy. They range from wine bars to haute cuisine, with a few in between:

The Wine Cellar & Tasting Room, in Rio All-Suite Hotel & Casino (3700 W. Flamingo Blvd.; ℂ 702/777-7962), offers more than 100 wines by the glass, ranging from under $10 to over $100. Its more than $10 million worth of inventory includes more than 6,500 labels. Though some may only be gazed upon, not purchased (like the 1890 bottle of Madeira once owned by Thomas Jefferson or the vertical of Chateau d'Yquem going back to 1898), you can indulge yourself with a flight of luxury champagnes. The nonsmoking tasting room is open Sunday through Thursday from 3 to 11pm, Friday and Saturday from 3pm until midnight.

If you agree with Oscar Wilde that "only people with no imagination can't find a good reason to drink champagne," then **Petrossian Bar,** in Bellagio (3600 Las Vegas Blvd. S.; ℂ 702/693-7111), is the place for you. If you're seeking crumpets with your chardonnay, you'll be glad to know that afternoon tea is served from 2 to 5pm; caviar (Petrossian, of course) is available from noon to midnight. To wash it down, you can select from any of 21 champagnes and sparkling wines (seven of them available by the glass) in addition to non-bubbly whites, reds, and ports. It's open 24 hours.

While you enjoy pizza, pasta, steak, and other expertly prepared traditional Italian dishes at **Valentino,** in The

that's the only part of the tradition that has changed. Lawry's has added fresh fish (halibut, salmon, or swordfish, depending on the evening) to its menu. Anyway, you tell the waitress what side dishes you might want (sublime creamed spinach, baked potato, and so on) for an extra price. Later, she returns with a spinning salad bowl (think of salad preparation as a Busby Berkeley musical number).

Venetian (3355 Las Vegas Blvd. S.; ℭ **702/414-3000**), you can select a wine from the 24,000 bottles on their full list. They also offer 40 different wines (which change regularly) by the glass or in 2-ounce pours. It's open daily from 11:30am to 11pm.

Rosemary's Restaurant, 8125 W. Sahara Ave. (btw. Buffalo Dr. and Cimarron Rd.; ℭ **702/869-2251**), is well off the Strip but equally well worth the trip. In addition to its impressive and well-balanced full-bottle list, Rosemary's offers 30 wines by the glass and three dozen by the half-bottle. For a full review, see p. 98.

Sure, you may want to visit just to see the "wine angels" rappel up and down the four-story glass wine tower at **Aureole,** in Mandalay Bay (3950 Las Vegas Blvd. S.; ℭ **877/632-7800;** www.aureolelv.com), to fetch your bottle, but the real reason we like this place is its innovative (patent-pending, even) Internet-based wine list. Customers use an "eWine Book" at their table to wirelessly access the restaurant's wine database. Better still, with a few taps of the stylus, you can check out which wine(s) the restaurant recommends to accompany various menu items before discussing your choices with the sommelier. Smoking is permitted in the bar and lounge only.

One of the most intriguing wine cellars is actually a wine loft, perched two-plus stories above the restaurant **Fleur de Lys** (in Mandalay Bay, 3950 Las Vegas Blvd. S.; ℭ **877/632-7800**), visible through floor-to-ceiling, candlelight-framed glass. With advance notice, diners can eat here, one of the most stunning, if chilly, tables in town. The "loft" is growing and promises to be most impressive.

The bowl, resting on crushed ice, spins as she pours Lawry's special dressing in a stream from high over her head. Tomatoes garnish. Applause follows.

Eventually, giant metal carving carts come to your table, bearing the meat. You name your cut (the regular Lawry's, the extra-large Diamond Jim Brady for serious carnivores, and the wimpy thin

English cut), and specify how you'd like it cooked. Flavorful, tender, perfectly cooked, lightly seasoned, this will be the best prime rib you will ever have. Okay, maybe that's going too far, but the rest is accurate, honest. It just has to be tasted to be believed. You can finish off with a rich dessert (English trifle is highly recommended), but it almost seems pointless.

4043 Howard Hughes Pkwy. (at Flamingo Rd., btw. Paradise Rd. and Koval Lane). *(* 702/893-2223. www.lawrysonline.com. Reservations recommended. Main courses $32–$49. AE, DC, DISC, MC, V. Sun–Thurs 5–10pm; Fri–Sat 5–11pm.

Pamplemousse *(* FRENCH   A little bit off the beaten path, Pamplemousse is a long-established Vegas restaurant that shouldn't be overlooked in the crush of new high-profile eateries. Evoking a cozy French-countryside inn (at least, on the interior), it's a catacomb of low-ceilinged rooms and intimate dining nooks with rough-hewn beams. It's all very charming and un-Vegasy. The restaurant's name, which means grapefruit, was suggested by the late singer Bobby Darin—one of the many celebrity pals of owner Georges La Forge.

Your waiter recites the menu, which changes nightly. Recent menu offerings have included out-of-this-world soups (French onion and cream of asparagus, to name a couple) and appetizers such as shrimp in cognac cream sauce and Maryland crab cakes with macadamia nut crust. Recommended entrees include a sterling veal with mushrooms and Dijon sauce, and an even better rack of lamb with pistachio nut crust and rosemary cream sauce (all sauces, by the way, are made with whatever the chef has on hand that evening in the kitchen). Leave room for the fabulous desserts, such as homemade ice cream in a hard chocolate shell.

400 E. Sahara Ave. (btw. Santa Paula and Santa Rita drives, just east of Paradise Rd.). *(* 702/733-2066. www.pamplemousserestaurant.com. Reservations required. Main courses $12–$21 lunch, $27–$58 dinner. AE, DC, DISC, MC, V. Lunch Mon–Sat 11:30am–2:30pm; dinner daily 5:30–10:30pm.

MODERATE

Carluccio's Tivoli Gardens *(* *Finds* ITALIAN   A bit of a drive, but well worth it for those seeking an authentic—read: older than 10 years—Vegas experience. This otherwise unimposing joint used to be owned by none other than the Rhinestone King Himself, Liberace. See, it was formerly Liberace's Tivoli's Gardens, and he designed the interior himself, so you know what that looks like (it was reopened a few years after his death, and they've kept the decor pretty much as is). Expect traditional Italian food (pasta, pasta, and scampi). This kind of history is more and more rare in this town with no memory, plus—no coincidence—it's right next door to the Liberace Museum, so go pay your giggling respects in the late afternoon and then stop in here for dinner.

1775 E. Tropicana Blvd. (at Spencer St.). © **702/795-3236**. Main courses $10–$18. AE, DC, DISC, MC, V. Tues–Sun 4:30–10pm. Closed Mon.

Memphis Championship Barbecue ⭐⭐ BARBECUE   Okay, we refuse, simply refuse, to get into the debate about Texas vs. Kansas City vs. Mississippi barbecue (and if you've got another state with the best dang barbecue, we really don't want to hear about it). But we can say that if you aren't physically in those places, you gotta take what you can get—and luckily for you, Memphis Championship Barbecue is hardly settling. Their vinegar-based sauce is sweet but has a kick. Food is cooked over mesquite applewood, and the meat falls off the bone just the way you want it to. And they have hot links, baked beans, and everything else you would want and hope for. Standouts include a pulled barbecue chicken sandwich, onion straws, and delicious mac and cheese. *Note this special:* A $60 feast includes a rack of baby back ribs, half pound of pork, half pound of beef brisket, half pound of hot links, a whole chicken, baked beans, coleslaw, rolls, creamed corn, and fries. It reportedly feeds four, though even if two of those four are teenage boys, we think you might have leftovers.

2250 E. Warm Springs Rd. (near 215 Fwy.). © **702/260-6909**. www.memphis-bbq.com. Entrees $10–$20; special barbecue dinner for 4 people $70. AE, MC, V. Sun–Thurs 11am–10pm; Fri–Sat 11am–10:30pm.

Pink Taco ⭐ MEXICAN   A mega-hip Mexican cantina, this folk-art-bedecked spot is a scene just waiting to happen, or rather, it's already happened. There are no surprises in terms of the food—you know the drill: tacos, burritos, quesadillas—but it's all tasty and filling, and some of it comes with some surprising accompaniments, such as tapenade, along with the usual guacamole and sour cream. This is hip Mexican as opposed to a mom-and-pop joint, and it's a good place to eat on this side of town.

In Hard Rock Hotel & Casino, 4455 Paradise Rd. © **702/693-5525**. www.pink taco.com. Reservations not accepted. Main courses $7.50–$15. AE, DC, DISC, MC, V. Sun–Thurs 11am–10pm; Fri–Sat 11am–midnight.

INEXPENSIVE

Bougainvillea ⭐⭐ *Value* COFFEE SHOP   Oh, how we love a Vegas coffee shop. You've got your all-day breakfasts, your graveyard-shift specials (build your own three-egg, three-ingredient omelet for around $5), your prime rib, and, of course, your full Chinese menu.

And it's all hearty and well-priced; we're talkin' New York steak and eggs for $5.99 all day long. You can get a full dinner entree or a nice light lunch also for around $5 (is that someone's lucky number?). And 24-hour specials, including a slab of meat, potato or rice, veggie, soup or salad, and a 12-ounce draft beer, is an astounding $9.99. Yep. That's the ticket.

In Terrible's Hotel, 4100 Paradise Rd. © **702/733-7000.** Main courses $5–$13. AE, MC, V. Daily 24 hr.

Einstein Bros. Bagels ⊛ BAGELS   You may not like digging into an enormous buffet first thing in the morning, and the continental breakfast in most hotels is a rip-off. A welcome alternative is a fresh-baked bagel, of which there are 15 varieties here—everything from onion to wild blueberry. Cream cheeses also come in many flavors, anything from sun-dried tomato to vegetable and jalapeño. Four special-blend coffees are available each day.

In the University Gardens Shopping Center, 4626 S. Maryland Pkwy. (btw. Harmon and Tropicana aves.). © **702/795-7800.** www.einsteinbros.com. All items under $6. MC, V. Mon–Fri 6am–5pm; Sat 6am–4pm; Sun 7am–3pm.

Jason's Deli ⊛ DELI   A chain popular with locals, there are four Jason's in the area, but this one is convenient to those staying east of the Strip. It's a busy, bustling deli where all items are advertised as free of artificial trans fat, plus a section of "slimwiches," so as multipurpose diner/delis go, this may be a fairly healthy option. They also do a brisk take-out business, again useful for those staying in nearby chain hotels without much in the way of room service. There is the usual deli fare—at least a dozen soups, sandwiches, wraps, and junior meals. The wraps tip you off that this is not a Brooklyn-style pastrami deli but fancy California-cuisine influenced froofy versions of sandwiches. A wild card is the New Orleans inspired muffalettas. The sandwiches are piled with meat, and the chicken potpie is huge. Naturally, the salad bar contains pudding and vanilla wafers—wouldn't want to carry "healthy" too far.

3910 S. Maryland Parkway. © **702/893-9799.** www.jasonsdeli.com. All items under $10. AE, DISC, MC, V. Daily 8am–9pm.

Lotus of Siam ⊛⊛⊛ *Finds* THAI   So we drag you out to a strip mall in the east end of Nowhere and you wonder why? Because here is what critic Jonathan Gold of *Gourmet* magazine called "no less than the best Thai restaurant in North America."

What makes this place so darn special? First of all, in addition to all the usual beloved Thai and Issan favorites and others, they have a separate menu featuring lesser-known dishes from northern Thailand—they don't routinely hand this one out (because most of the customers are there for the more pedestrian, if still excellent, $5.99 lunch buffet). Second, the owner drives at least twice a week back to Los Angeles (where his original venue, Renu Na Korn, is still operating under another family member) to pick up the freshest herbs and other ingredients needed for his dishes' authenticity. That's dedication that should be rewarded with superlatives.

You might be best off letting them know you are interested in northern food (with dried chiles and more pork, "it's not un-Cajun-like," says the owner) and letting them guide you through, though you must assure them that you aren't of faint heart or palate (some customers complain the heat isn't enough, even with "well-spiced" dishes, though others find even medium spice sufficient). Standouts include the Issan sausage, a grilled sour pork number, the *Nam Kao Tod* (that same sausage, ground up with lime, green onion, fresh chile, and ginger, served with crispy rice), *Nam Sod* (ground pork mixed with ginger, green onion, and lime juice, served with sticky rice), and *Sua Rong Hai* ("weeping tiger"), a dish of soft, sliced, grilled marinated beef. If you insist on more conventional Thai, that's okay, in that it's unlikely that you are going to have better *Tom Kah Kai* (note that this beloved soup can also be served northern-style, if asked, which is without the coconut milk). If in season, finish with mango with sticky rice, or if not, coconut ice cream with sticky rice, something you would find at many a street stall in Thailand.

In the Commercial Center, 953 E. Sahara Ave. ✆ **702/735-3033.** www.saipinchutima.com. Reservations strongly recommended for dinner, suggested you call at least a day in advance. Lunch buffet $9; other dishes $9–$20. AE, MC, V. Mon–Thurs 11:30am–2:30pm and 5:30–9:30pm; Fri–Sun 5:30–10pm.

Paymon's Mediterranean Café & Lounge ✮ MEDITERRANEAN

It's just so darn nice to find ethnic food in this town, and when it's served in a courtyard with some real, as opposed to ordered-up, character, full of pillows and fabrics and next to an honest-to-goodness hookah lounge, it's even nicer. It's not the best Middle Eastern food we've ever had, but getting away from the Strip makes it taste special. Kabobs take, the menu warns, 25 minutes, so order a *meze* plate to while away the time. The hummus is too reminiscent of its chickpea origins, but the baba ghanouj is properly smoky, and the falafel has the right crunch. Gyros may not be the most adventurous thing to order, but who cares about that when you've got a well-stuffed pocket of pita goopy with sweet yogurt sauce? *Fresenjan* is a dish of falling-apart chicken swimming in a tangy pomegranate sauce; ask to ensure that the ratio of sauce to chicken is greater than 10:1.

In the Tiffany Square strip mall, 4147 S. Maryland Pkwy. (at Flamingo Rd.). © 702/731-6030. www.paymons.com. Reservations not accepted. Main courses $10–$19 (most sandwiches under $8). AE, DISC, MC, V. Restaurant Mon–Thurs 11am–1am; Fri–Sat 11am–3am; Sun 11am–5pm. Lounge Mon–Thurs 5pm–1am; Fri–Sat 5pm–3am; closed Sun.

Toto's *Value* MEXICAN   A family-style Mexican restaurant favored by locals, with enormous portions and quick service, this is good value for your money. With all that food, you could probably split portions and still be satisfied. There are no surprises on the menu, though there are quite a few seafood dishes. The non-greasy chips come with fresh salsa, and the nachos are terrific. Chicken tamales got a thumbs-up, and non-meat eaters happily dug into the veggie burrito (although it's not especially healthful, all the ingredients were fresh, with huge slices of zucchini and roasted bell peppers). The operative word here is *huge;* the burritos are almost the size of your arm. The generous portions continue with dessert—a piece of flan was practically pie size. The Sunday margarita brunch is quite fun, and the drinks are large (naturally) and yummy.

2055 E. Tropicana Ave. (at Burnham Ave.). © 702/895-7923. Main courses $7–$15. AE, DISC, MC, V. Mon–Thurs 11am–10pm; Fri–Sat 11am–11pm; Sun 9:30am–10pm.

5 West Las Vegas

EXPENSIVE

Austins Steakhouse *Finds* STEAK/SEAFOOD   Now, understand that we don't send you out to nether regions such as Texas Station lightly. We do so here because Austins Steakhouse has gained a reputation for the best steak in town. Really. Even the snooty critics at the *Las Vegas Review-Journal* agree with the hoi polloi. And here's what has everyone, and us, raving: a 24-ounce rib-eye—yes, we know, just split it—aged and marinated, cooked over mesquite applewood, and then rubbed with peppercorns and pan-seared in garlic, butter, and cilantro. A massive chunk of meat with a smoky garlicky flavor like no other steak we can think of. For those not watching their cholesterol, there's shrimp sautéed in garlic butter sauce, dipped in cheese, and wrapped in bacon. The Maui onion soup is also a standout, as is just about anything on the dessert menu. Note that

Dining & Nightlife West of the Strip

NIGHTLIFE ●

Cheetah's **5**
Cherry **3**
Déjà Vu Showgirls **8**
ghostbar **12**
Little Darlings **5**
Playboy Club **12**
Rain **12**
Sand Dollar Blues
  Nightclub & Lounge **9**
Sapphire Gentleman's Club **7**
Spearmint Rhino **1**
Tommy Rocker's Mojave
  Beach Topless Bar **13**
VooDoo Lounge **11**

DINING ◆

Austins Steakhouse **2**
Cathay House **6**
Hash House A Go Go **4**
Rosemary's Restaurant **4**
Salt Lick **3**
Viva Mercado's **10**

a comparable meal on the Strip would cost $10 to $20 more per person—another reason to head out to the hinterlands.

In Texas Station, 2101 Texas Star Lane. © 702/631-1033. Reservations recommended. Main courses $15–$45. AE, DC, DISC, MC, V. Sun–Thurs 5–10pm; Fri–Sat 5–11pm.

Rosemary's Restaurant ★★★ (Finds) NOUVELLE AMERICAN
You don't have to eat at a name-brand temple of haute cuisine or celebrity chef showcase to have an outstanding meal in Vegas. Chefs Michael and Wendy Jordan cooked at some of the best places in New Orleans, came here to open Emeril's Seafood, then branched out on their own with two restaurants that showcase their clever twists on American cuisine. This is playful but hearty food; seared foie gras with peach coulis, candied walnuts, and vanilla-bean arugula is like a quilt, with distinct flavors that still all hang together nicely. Interesting sides include ultrarich bleu cheese slaw, slightly spicy crispy fried tortilla strips, and perfect cornmeal jalapeño hush puppies, to say nothing of "Grandma's pickled cucumbers." A recent visit found the crispy striped bass fighting it out with the pan-seared honey-glazed salmon for "best fish dish I've ever had." Desserts are similarly southern—lemon icebox pie!—and most pleasant.

There is a nice little wine list with a broad range. They also specialize in beer suggestions to pair with courses, including some fruity Belgium numbers. This is such a rare treat that if you drink, you must try some of their suggestions.

8125 W. Sahara. © 702/869-2251. www.rosemarysrestaurant.com. Reservations strongly recommended. Lunch $14–$17; dinner $27–$42. AE, DISC, MC, V. Mon–Fri 11:30am–2:30pm and 5:30–10:30pm; Sat–Sun 5:30–10:30pm.

MODERATE

Cathay House CHINESE   Las Vegas actually has a Chinatown—a very large strip mall (naturally) on Spring Mountain Road near Wynn. But ask locals who look like they know, and they will send you instead farther up Spring Mountain Road to the Cathay House, which is about a 7-minute drive from Treasure Island.

The standout at the Cathay House is a vegetable *bao* that includes Chinese glass noodles. Lightly browned and not overly doughy like many baos, it is slightly sweet and utterly delicious. The shrimp wrapped in rice noodles are big and plump, and anything fried is so good you should ignore your arteries for a while (we did!). Cathay House (which features quite a good view through the windows on one side) also has a full dinner menu, which includes the strawberry chicken invented by now-defunct local restaurant Chin's.

In Spring Valley, 5300 W. Spring Mountain Rd. (€ **702/876-3838.** www.cathay house.com. Reservations recommended. Main courses $6.75–$19. AE, DC, DISC, MC, V. Daily 10:30am–10pm.

Salt Lick 𝒢𝒢 BARBEQUE   An outpost of the much-beloved Austin barbeque spot, this looks both not at all like the Driftwood original and yet related in a double-first-cousin kind of way, with the same heavy pine wood tables and more importantly, the same heavenly smell. Many believe Salt Lick serves the platonic ideal of barbeque. That's not the case here. The meat is smoky, and the dry rub has its kick, but the results aren't as tender or as memorably flavorful. The sausage and ribs are better than the brisket, which is sublime back in Texas. Still, the all-you-can-eat plate is a good deal, and you can do take-out either on your way to a picnic in Red Rock Canyon or to munch back in your hotel after a long day of hiking.

In Red Rock Resort, 10972 W. Charleston. (€ **702/797-7535.** Main courses $9–$17. AE, MC, V. Sun–Thurs 11am–10pm; Fri–Sat 11am–11pm.

Viva Mercado's 𝒢𝒢 MEXICAN   Ask any local about Mexican food in Vegas, and almost certainly they will point to Viva Mercado's as the best in town. That recommendation, plus the restaurant's health-conscious attitude, makes this worth the roughly 10-minute drive from the Strip.

Given all those warnings about Mexican food and its heart-attack-inducing properties, the approach at Viva Mercado's is nothing to be sniffed at. No dish is prepared with or cooked in any kind of animal fat. Nope, the lard so dear to Mexican cooking is not found here. The oil used is an artery-friendly canola. This makes the place particularly appealing to vegetarians, who will also be pleased by the regular veggie specials. Everything is quite fresh, and they do particularly amazing things with seafood. Try the Maresco Vallarta, which is orange roughy, shrimp, and scallops cooked in a coconut tomato sauce, with capers and olives. They have all sorts of noteworthy shrimp dishes and 11 different salsas, ranked 1 to 10 for degree of spice (ask for advice).

6182 W. Flamingo Rd. (at Jones Blvd.). (€ **702/871-8826.** www.viva mercadoslv.com. Reservations accepted for large parties only. Main courses $8–$19. AE, DISC, MC, V. Sun–Thurs 11am–9:30pm; Fri–Sat 11am–10:30pm.

INEXPENSIVE
Hash House A Go Go 𝒢𝒢𝒢 DINER/AMERICAN   A hilarious twist on classic American cuisine ("Twisted farm food," they call it, and then they set it all in a sort of dairy barn on hallucinogens), with

such oversize, eccentric approaches to the business of eating that it really should be in a casino, rather than a several-mile drive down Sahara. Do take that drive, or risk missing out on pancakes the size of pizzas (we aren't kidding), waffles with strips of bacon baked right in them, rosemary chicken with brie sandwiches, grilled cheese with prosciutto, pork ribs on top of Caesar salads, and just about anything else a clearly fevered brain can think of, including the "O'Hare of the Dog That Bit You"—a 24-ounce Bud served in a paper bag with a side of bacon. Portions are enormous, to say the least, which makes sharing mandatory and prices even more reasonable, despite the small fee charged for sharing.

6800 W. Sahara Ave. ℂ 702/804-4646. www.hashhouseagogo.com. Main courses $9–$14 breakfast, $7–$16 lunch, $8–$25 dinner. Mon–Sat 7:30am–2:30pm and 5–10pm; Sun 7:30am–2:30pm.

6 Downtown

VERY EXPENSIVE

Hugo's Cellar ℛ INTERNATIONAL   Hugo's Cellar is indeed in a cellar, or at least below street level in the Four Queens hotel. No, they aren't ashamed of it—quite the opposite. This is their pride and joy, and it is highly regarded by the locals. This is Old School Vegas Classy Dining. Each female guest is given a red rose when she enters the restaurant—the first of a series of nice touches. The restaurant proper is dimly lit, lined with dark wood and brick. It's fairly intimate, but if you really want to be cozy, ask for one of the curtained booths against the wall.

The meal is full of ceremony, perfectly delivered by a well-trained and cordial waitstaff. Unfortunately, the main courses are not all that novel (various cuts of meat, seafood, and chicken prepared in different ways), but on a recent visit, not one of six diners was anything less than delighted. The filet of beef stuffed with crabmeat and wrapped with bacon is over the top for us, but others loved it, while the roast duckling rubbed with anise and flambéed at the table is a guilty pleasure, just the right effect for this Old School Vegas dining experience. The T-bone steak was tender enough to cut with a fork. Vegetables and excellent starchy sides are included, as is a finish of chocolate-dipped fruits with cream. While it's not worth going out of your way for the food (though here we admit that well-prepared old school is better than careless nouvelle any day), perhaps it is worth it for the entire package.

In the Four Queens, 202 Fremont St. ℂ 702/385-4011. www.hugoscellar.com. Reservations required. Main courses $36–$52. AE, DC, DISC, MC, V. Daily 5:30–11pm.

INEXPENSIVE

Ice House Lounge *☆* DINER   Don't let the dismal surroundings put you off; inside is a lively, popular modern-appearing club, with a menu full of, if not inspired, certainly reliable and well-priced, menu options. The late-night hours also make this a good choice for those located near Downtown. Lunch, in particular, is a bargain, as basketball-circumference-size plates are loaded with towering sandwiches or wide-reaching flatbread-style pizzas, mounds of coleslaw, or piles of crinkly fries. We like the plate of three miniburgers. None of it is thrillingly spiced or especially cleverly crafted, but it's all solidly good and, given the portions, eminently shareable.

650 S. Main St. (corner of Bonneville Ave.). *℗* **702/315-2570**. www.icehouse lounge.com. Most items under $15. AE, DISC, MC, V. Mon–Fri 10am–2am; Sat 11am–2am.

El Sombrero Cafe *☆☆* MEXICAN   This kind of hole-in-the-wall Mexican joint can be found all over California but not always so readily elsewhere. It's also the kind of family-run (since 1950) place increasingly forced out of Vegas by giant hotel conglomerates, making it even more worth your time (it's becoming harder and harder, particularly in Downtown, to find budget options that present you with food that is more than just mere fuel). Mexican food fans, in particular, should seek out this friendly place, though it's not in an attractive part of town. Portions are generous, better than average, and unexpectedly spicy. They also cater to special requests—changing the beef burrito to a chicken one (an option that comes highly recommended), for example, without batting an eyelash. The enchilada and taco combo also won raves.

807 S. Main St. (at Gass Ave.). *℗* **702/382-9234**. Lunch $8; dinner $13. MC, V. Mon–Thurs 11am–4pm; Fri–Sat 11am–8:30pm.

M&M Soul Food *☆☆* *(Finds)* SOUL FOOD   Though we've listed this in Downtown, it's really not too far from the Strip. At first glance, the neighborhood seems intimidating, but it's not actually threatening. Why come here? Because locals have voted this their favorite soul food place, and while the competition may not be all that high, the quality stands out regardless. It's, appropriately, a hole in the wall, with somewhat higher prices than one might expect, but the generous portions make up for it. Mini cornbread pancakes are served to every table. Smothered fried chicken is moist, slightly spicy, and topped with a robust gravy. The menu includes hot links, collard greens, and other typical options.

3923 W. Charleston. *℗* **702/453-7685**. $6–$17. AE, DISC, MC, V. Daily 7am–8pm.

7 Buffets & Sunday Brunches

Lavish, low-priced buffets are a Las Vegas tradition, designed to lure you to the gaming tables and make you feel that you got such a bargain for your meal that you can afford to drop more money. They're a gimmick, and we love them. Something about filling up on too much prime rib and shrimp just says "Vegas" to us. Of course, there is quite a range. Some are just perfunctory steam-table displays and salad bars heavy on the iceberg lettuce, while others are unbelievably opulent spreads, with caviar and free-flowing champagne. Some are quite beautifully presented as well. Some of the food is awful, some of it merely works as fuel, and some of it is memorable.

No trip to Vegas is complete without trying one or two buffets. Of the dozens, the most noteworthy are described here. Mind you, almost all buffets have some things in common. Unless otherwise noted, every one listed here has at least one carving station, a salad bar (quality differs), and hot main courses and side dishes. We will try to point out only when a buffet has something original or notable.

Note: Buffet meals are extremely popular, and reservations are usually not taken (we've indicated when they are accepted, and in all those cases, they are highly recommended). Arrive early (before opening) or late to avoid a long line, especially on weekends.

SOUTH STRIP
EXPENSIVE
Mandalay Bay's Bay Side Buffet ✦ BUFFET   This is a particularly pretty, not overly large buffet. Actual windows—floor-to-ceiling, no less—overlooking the beach part of the elaborate pool area make it less stuffy and eliminate that closed-in feeling that so many of the other buffets in town have. The buffet itself is adequately arranged but features nothing particularly special, though there are some nice cold salads, hearty meats, and a larger- and better-than-average dessert bar (they make their own desserts, and it shows).

In Mandalay Bay, 3950 Las Vegas Blvd. S. © 702/632-7777. Breakfast $17; lunch $21; dinner $28; Sun brunch $25; Shark Reef Brunch package $36. Reduced prices for children 11 and under. Children 3 and under eat free. AE, DC, DISC, MC, V. Mon–Fri 7am–2:30pm and 4:45–9:45pm; Sat–Sun 7am–10pm.

MGM Grand Buffet ✦ BUFFET   This rather average buffet does feature a fresh Belgian waffle station at breakfast. Dinner also has all-you-can-eat shrimp and an all-you-can-eat shrimp and prime-rib option. Also available: low-fat, sugar-free desserts! And at all meals, you get a full pot of coffee on your table.

In MGM Grand, 3799 Las Vegas Blvd. S. ℰ **702/891-7777.** Mon–Fri breakfast $13; Sat–Sun breakfast $12; lunch $15; Sun–Thurs dinner $25; Fri–Sat dinner $27; Sat–Sun brunch $20. Reduced prices for children 9 and under; free for children 3 and under. AE, DC, DISC, MC, V. Sun–Thurs 7am–2:30pm and 4–10pm; Fri–Sat 7am–2:30pm and 4–10:30pm.

MODERATE
Monte Carlo's Buffet ✿ BUFFET A "courtyard" under a painted sky, the Monte Carlo's buffet room has a Moroccan market theme, with murals of Arab scenes, Moorish archways, Oriental carpets, and walls hung with photographs of and artifacts from Morocco. Dinner includes a rotisserie (for chicken and pork loin, or London broil), a Chinese food station, a taco/fajita bar, a baked potato bar, numerous salads, and more than a dozen desserts, plus frozen yogurt and ice-cream machines. Lunches are similar. At breakfast, the expected fare is supplemented by an omelet station, and choices include crepes, blintzes, and corned beef hash. Fresh-baked New York–style bagels are a plus.

3770 Las Vegas Blvd. S. ℰ **702/730-7777.** Breakfast $12; lunch $14; dinner and Sun brunch $19 (all include tax). AE, DC, DISC, MC, V. Daily 7am–10pm.

MORE, The Buffet at Luxor ✿✿ BUFFET Located on the lower level, where the Luxor showroom used to be, this huge buffet looks like it was set in the middle of an archaeological dig, complete with wood braces holding up the ceiling, pot shards, papyrus, and servers dressed in khaki dig outfits. It's a unique and fun decor, but be sure to avoid tripping on the mummies and their sarcophagi sticking half up out of the ground. The food is better than at most cheap buffets. It features a Mexican station with some genuinely spicy food, a Chinese stir-fry station, and different Italian pastas. Desserts are disappointing, though there are plenty of low-fat and sugar-free options. Word has gotten out about this buffet, unfortunately, because the lines are always enormous.

In Luxor, 3900 Las Vegas Blvd. S. ℰ **702/262-4000.** Breakfast $12; lunch $14; dinner $20. AE, DC, DISC, MC, V. Daily 7am–10pm.

MID-STRIP
VERY EXPENSIVE
Bally's Sterling Sunday Brunch ✿✿ BUFFET Now, the admittedly high cost of this brunch seems antithetical to the original purpose of a buffet, which is a lot of food for minimal money. If you're a dedicated buffet fan, however, this is probably a better spree than one of the many new high-priced restaurants. It works out to less money in the long run, and you will get, for your purposes, more bang for your buck. It's a fancy deal—linen- and silver-bedecked tables, waiters to assist you, if you choose—and while the variety of food isn't as

massive as at regular buffets, the quality is much higher in terms of both content and execution. We're talking unlimited champagne, broiled lobster, caviar, sushi, and rotating dishes of the day (items such as monkfish with pomegranate essence, tenderloin wrapped in porcini mushroom mousse, and even ostrich). No French toast that's been sitting out for days here! Perfect for a wedding breakfast, business brunch, or just a big treat; stay a long time and eat as much as you can.

In Bally's, 3645 Las Vegas Blvd. S. ℂ 702/967-7999. Reservations recommended. Brunch $75. AE, DC, MC, V. Sun 9:30am–2:30pm.

EXPENSIVE

Bellagio's Buffet 🎭🎭 BUFFET   Pricier than its counterpart over at The Mirage, Bellagio's buffet gets comparably higher marks. The array of foods is fabulous, with one ethnic cuisine after another (Japanese, Chinese that includes unexpected buffet fare like dim sum, build-it-yourself Mexican items, and so on). There are elaborate pastas and semitraditional Italian-style pizza from a wood-fired oven. The cold fish appetizers at each end of the line are not to be missed—scallops, smoked salmon, crab claws, shrimp, oysters, and assorted condiments. Specialties include breast of duck and game hens. There is no carving station, but you can get the meat precarved. The salad bar is more ordinary, though prepared salads offer some fine surprises, such as eggplant tofu and an exceptional Chinese chicken salad. Desserts, unfortunately, look better than they actually are.

In Bellagio, 3600 Las Vegas Blvd. S. ℂ 877/234-6358. Mon–Fri breakfast $15; Sat–Sun brunch $23–$28; Mon–Thurs lunch $19; Fri lunch $18; Sun–Thurs dinner $27; Fri–Sat dinner $35. AE, DC, DISC, MC, V. Breakfast Mon–Fri 8–10:30am; lunch Mon–Thurs 11am–3pm, Fri 11am–3:30pm; dinner Mon–Thurs 4–10pm, Fri–Sat 4:30–11pm, Sun 4:30–10pm; brunch Sat–Sun 8am–4pm.

Paris Las Vegas's Le Village Buffet 🎭🎭🎭 BUFFET   One of the more ambitious buffets, with a price hike to match—still, you do get, even at the higher-priced dinner, a fine assortment of food, and more value for the dollar than you are likely to find anywhere else (unless it's another buffet).

Plus, the Paris buffet is the most pleasing room of the buffet bunch. It's a Disneyland-esque two-thirds replica of your classic French village clichés; it's either a charming respite from Vegas lights or sickening, depending on your tolerance level for eye candy. Buffet stations are grouped according to French regions, and though in theory entrees change daily, there do seem to be some constants, including most of the following dishes. In Brittany, you find things like made-to-order crepes, surprisingly good roasted duck with green peppercorn and peaches, and steamed mussels with butter and shallots. In Normandy, there's quiche and some dry bay scallops with honey cider. The carving station shows up in Burgundy but distinguishes itself by adding options of chateaubriand sauce and cherry sauce Escoffier. Lamb stew is a possibility for Alsace, while Provence has pasta to order and a solidly good braised beef. The salad station isn't strong on flavors, but the veggies are fresh, and there is even some domestic (darn it) cheese.

You can largely skip the dessert station in favor of heading back to Brittany for some made-to-order crepes, but you might want to try the Bananas Foster.

In Paris Las Vegas, 3655 Las Vegas Blvd. S. ② 702/946-7000. Breakfast $13; lunch $18; dinner $25; Sun brunch $25. AE, DC, DISC, MC, V. Sun–Thurs 7am–10pm; Fri–Sat 7am–11pm.

Wynn Las Vegas Buffet ✦✦✦ BUFFET   Now, we do get a bit giddy over a nice buffet, and this is a particularly nice one. But it's also a particularly expensive one. Let's think of it not as further proof of the overall increasing cost of Vegas (though it is that, we admit), but rather as an alternative to one of the more expensive eateries we rhapsodized about earlier. Instead of being limited to one $30 entree, plus cost of dessert and starters, you get, for just the one price, the ability to try all sorts of well-prepared options, like jerk chicken, beef rending, wood-fired pizza, honey-glazed pork, nice little salmon rolls, five kinds of ceviche, sweet Kansas City–style barbecue, and tandoori chicken among the stations, which include Mexican, Southern, seafood, and Italian. Best of all, desserts are superior to probably all the other buffets, in construction and in taste, giving the impression that a pastry chef is active on the premises. Don't miss the mini floating islands, the unusual tiramisu, the excellent chocolate mousse and ice creams, and even a plate full of madeleines.

In Wynn Las Vegas, 3131 Las Vegas Blvd. S. ② 702/770-3463. Breakfast $16; lunch $20; dinner $32–$36; Sat–Sun brunch $26–$32. AE, DC, DISC, MC, V. Breakfast Mon–Fri 8–10:30am; lunch Mon–Fri 11:30am–3:30pm; dinner Mon–Thurs 4–10pm; Fri–Sat 4:30–10:30pm, Sun 4:30–10pm; brunch Sat–Sun 8:30am–3:30pm.

MODERATE

Mirage's Cravings ✦ BUFFET   Newly remodeled so that it looks like a space-age cafeteria, this is both an ultramodern and a retro buffet, and as such it doesn't quite have any specific personality. You move through a line (you can jump ahead) past various stations—decent Chinese (fine pot stickers and barbecue pork), Japanese (tepid), quite good wood-oven pizza, solid barbecue, basic daily hot entrees with extra grease, decent Mexican (including sweet but dry slow-roasted pork), a dessert bar with strawberry soup (or was it sauce? Either way, we liked it), a sandwich stop with salads that is easy to miss (and a made-to-order salad spot that is always backed up), and cookies worth smuggling out in your purse—none of which are as vastly sized as one has come to expect from Vegas buffets over the years. On one hand, this helps reduce the amount of waste these places are prone to; on the other, it feels stingy, not good at these new inflated prices. Seniors may have trouble reading the small signs, and small children are likely to get fretful before they get through. Sure is nifty-looking, though.

In The Mirage, 3400 Las Vegas Blvd. S. ℂ **702/791-7111.** Breakfast $14; lunch $19; dinner $24; Sat–Sun brunch $23. Reduced prices for children ages 5–10; free for children 4 and under. AE, DC, DISC, MC, V. Mon–Fri 7am–10pm; Sat–Sun brunch 8am–3pm.

Rio's Carnival World Buffet 🌟🌟 BUFFET   This buffet has long been voted by locals as the best in town and just recently reopened after an extensive makeover. It's going to get mixed reactions. Quality-wise, it's probably as good as ever, and maybe even better. Decorwise, it's better still, since the overhaul was devoted mostly to improving the dining areas. The bad news? It can no longer pretend to be inexpensive—it's right at the top of the "moderate" category. Consider this an upscale food court, with "South American" cooked-to-order stir-fries, Mexican taco fixings and accompaniments, Chinese fare, a Japanese sushi bar and teppanyaki grill, a Brazilian mixed grill, Italian pasta and antipasto, and fish and chips. There's even a diner setup for hot dogs, burgers, fries, and milkshakes. (Make your own milkshakes—is there a happier concept anywhere?) All this is in addition to the usual offerings of most Las Vegas buffets. Best of all, it has a brand-new dessert station, featuring at least 70 kinds of pies, cakes, and pastries from an award-winning pastry chef, plus a large and decent selection of gelatos and sorbets.

In Rio All-Suite Hotel & Casino, 3700 W. Flamingo Rd. ℂ **702/252-7777.** Breakfast $15; lunch $17; dinner $24; Sat–Sun champagne brunch $24. Reduced prices for children 7 and under. Children 3 and under, free. AE, DC, MC, V. Mon–Fri 7am–10pm; Sat–Sun 7:30am–10pm.

INEXPENSIVE
Palms Fantasy Market Buffet 🌟🌟 *Finds* BUFFET   As a rule, you are better off fulfilling your buffet desires (unless they demand the cheapest of prices) at one of the newer hotels, and the Palms entry in the buffet sweepstakes bears this adage out. Not only does it look rather swell, but since the owners of the hotel are from a Middle Eastern background, that translates into some fresher concepts at the

stations—most notably, an emphasis on Middle Eastern fare such as gyros with warm pita bread, hummus, baba ghanouj, and kabobs of every variety. Plus there's a huge Chinese station, complete with dumplings; a Mongolian barbecue section (where they toss all your chosen ingredients into one stir-fry vat); some Jewish foods (knishes and kugel); an ambitious carving station with ribs and pastrami; and desserts that, as usual, aren't much of anything. And actually, this comes as close as any to classic buffet budget prices while still supplying food that can be described as better than "merely edible."

In Palms Resort & Casino, 4321 W. Flamingo Rd. © 702/942-7777. Breakfast $6; lunch $8; dinner $12; Sun brunch $12. AE, DC, DISC, MC, V. Mon–Sat 8–10am, 11am–3pm, and 4–9pm; Sun 8am–3pm and 4–9pm.

DOWNTOWN
INEXPENSIVE
Golden Nugget's Buffet ★★ BUFFET   This buffet, often voted number one in Las Vegas, has been completely redone in a new location overlooking a beautiful pool area. The buffet tables are also laden with an extensive salad bar (about 50 items), fresh fruit, and marvelous desserts, including the famous bread pudding made from the secret recipe of Zelma Wynn (Steve's mom). Every night, fresh seafood is featured. Most lavish is the all-day Sunday champagne brunch, which adds such dishes as made-to-order omelets and more breakfast meats than you can possibly ever eat.

In the Golden Nugget, 129 E. Fremont St. © 702/385-7111. Breakfast $10; lunch $11; dinner Mon–Thurs $18, Fri dinner $30, Sat–Sun dinner $21; Sat–Sun brunch $18; Children 3-12 half price, 2 and under free. AE, DC, DISC, MC, V. Mon–Fri 7am–10pm; Sat–Sun 8am–10pm.

Main Street Station's Garden Court ★★★ (Finds) BUFFET   Set in what is truly one of the prettiest buffet spaces in town, with very high ceilings and tall windows bringing in much-needed natural light, the Main Street Station Garden Court buffet is one of the best in town, let alone Downtown. Featuring nine live-action stations (meaning you can watch your food being prepared), including a wood-fired, brick-oven pizza (delicious); many fresh salsas at the Mexican station; a barbecue rotisserie; fresh sausage at the carving station; Chinese, Hawaiian, and Southern specialties (soul food and the like); and so many more we lost count. On Friday night, they have all this plus nearly infinite varieties of seafood, all the way up to lobster. We ate ourselves into a stupor and didn't regret it.

In Main Street Station, 200 N. Main St. © 702/387-1896. Breakfast $6; lunch $8; dinner $11–$16; Sat–Sun champagne brunch $10. Free for children 3 and under. AE, DC, DISC, MC, V. Daily 7–10:30am, 11am–3pm, and 4–10pm.

5

What to See & Do in Las Vegas

Need we tell you the primary activity in Las Vegas? Of course not. By now, you've certainly figured it out—if you were skeptical before you arrived, the slot machines waiting for you when you exited the plane into the airport erased any doubt.

But you won't lack for non-gambling activities in Vegas. The city isn't entirely happy when visitors aren't in the casinos, but it does acknowledge that not everyone (darn it) is going to gamble 24/7. A couple of the hotels have even conceded, for the time being, that some visitors may want a little culture along with their white tigers.

Your first order of business should be strolling the Strip, gaping at those impossible and impossibly large hotels, both during the day (when the hotels are less crowded) and at night (when the Strip is lit up in a garish display like nothing else in the country).

Don't forget to check out the **free hotel attractions,** such as Bellagio's water fountain ballet, The Mirage's volcano, the sexy sirens-battle-pirates epic at Treasure Island, and the Carnival in the sky show at the Rio.

You could also consider using a spa at a major hotel; they are too pricey (as high as $30 a day) to fill in for your daily gym visit, but spending a couple hours working out, sweating out Vegas toxins in the steam room, and generally pampering yourself will leave you feeling relaxed, refreshed, and ready to go all night again. Really treat yourself and get a massage or a facial.

There are also plenty of out-of-town sightseeing options, like **Hoover Dam** (a major tourist destination), **Red Rock Canyon,** and the **Grand Canyon.** We've listed the best of these side trips in chapter 8, "Side Trips from Las Vegas."

SUGGESTED ITINERARIES

The itineraries outlined here are for adults. If you're traveling with kids, incorporate some of the suggestions in "Especially for Kids," listed later in this chapter. The activities mentioned briefly here are described more fully later in this chapter and in chapters 7 and 8.

If You Have 1 Day

Spend most of the day **casino-hopping.** These are buildings like no other (thank goodness). Each grandiose interior tops the last. Be sure to see The Venetian, Bellagio, The Mirage (including the white tigers), TI, Paris Las Vegas, Caesars Palace (including the Forum Shops and the talking statues), New York–New York, MGM Grand, and the exteriors of Luxor and Excalibur. Then at night, take a drive (if you can) down **the Strip** ✦✦✦. As amazing as all this is during the day, you can't believe it at night. Aside from just the Strip itself, there are **Bellagio's water fountains** ✦✦✦, which "perform" to various musical numbers, the **siren-and-pirate battle at Treasure Island** (stupid and borderline vulgar now that it's turned into more of a showgirl piece than a stunt show), and the **volcano explosion** (no lava, just colored lights and smoke) next door, at The Mirage. Eat at a buffet (details in chapter 4), and have a drink at the top of the Stratosphere, goggling at the view from the tallest building west of the Mississippi.

If You Have 2 Days

Do more of the above since you may well have not covered it all. Then do something really Vegasy and visit the **Liberace Museum.** The **Dolphin Habitat at The Mirage** is also worth a look. At night, take in a show. We think *O, KÀ,* and *Mystère,* the productions from the avant-garde **Cirque du Soleil,** are the finest in Vegas, but there are plenty to choose from. Though buffets are still the most Vegas-appropriate food experience, genuine haute cuisine by celebrity chefs has invaded the town, and you should take advantage of it. **Joël Robuchon** and **L'Atelier de Joël Robuchon, Bartolotta, Bouchon,** and **Fleur de Lys** are our top choices, but you can't go wrong with **Aureole, Picasso,** or **Andre's,** plus there are branches of Olives, Circo, Pinot Brasserie, and Border Grill. You might also head Downtown to the classic Glitter Gulch and the **Fremont Street Experience** light show.

If You Have 3 Days

By now you've spent 2 days gawking. So take a break and drive out to **Red Rock Canyon.** The panoramic 13-mile Scenic Loop Drive is best seen early in the morning, when there's little traffic. If you're so inclined, spend some time hiking here. If you want to spend the whole day out, have lunch at nearby Red Rock Resort.

If You Have 4 Days

Plan a tour to **Hoover Dam.** Leave early in the morning, returning to Las Vegas after lunch via **Valley of Fire State Park,** stopping at the **Lost City Museum** in Overton en route (see chapter 8 for details). Alternatively, you can rest up by spending the day by the hotel pool or going to the hotel spa. At night, presumably refreshed and with toxins purged, eat some more and/or catch another show. If you aren't tired of magic, **Lance Burton** is a wonderful show for a reasonable price, or there is the arty weirdness of the **Blue Man Group** at The Venetian, or *Jubilee!* if your trip won't be complete without a topless revue. You can also feast at dinner since you certainly haven't tried all there is. Meet you at the Wynn Buffet?

1 The Top Attractions

See also the listings for theme parks and other fun stuff in "Especially for Kids," later in this chapter.

Note: At press time, there was serious talk of moving *Star Trek: The Experience* from its long time home at the Hilton (where it recently closed) to Neonopolis in downtown. If you call yourself a Trekker or a Trekkie, you can't miss this attraction, which includes a 4-D theater and motion simulator rides, if it does turn up again in town.

The Arts Factory *★★ (Finds* Believe it or not, Las Vegas has a burgeoning art scene (what some would consider soul-crushing is what others consider inspirational), and this complex, located in the Gateway District, is the place to find proof. It features a few galleries and a number of workspaces for local artists. Several of the spaces are closed to the public.

101–107 E. Charleston Blvd. ℂ **702/676-1111**. www.theartsfactory.com. Free admission. Hours vary by gallery.

The Atomic Testing Museum *★★★ (Finds* From 1951 until 1992, the Nevada Test Site was this country's primary location for testing nuclear weapons. Aboveground blasts in the early days were visible to the tourists and residents of Las Vegas, a mere 65 miles away. This well-executed museum, library, and gallery space offers visitors a fascinating glance at the test site from ancient days through modern times with memorabilia, displays, official documents,

Las Vegas Attractions

The Adventuredome **9**
The Arts Factory **6**
The Atomic
  Testing Museum **15**
Bellagio Gallery of Fine Art **13**
Bodies **18**
Eiffel Tower Tour **14**
Fremont Street Experience **5**
GameWorks **16**
Las Vegas Cyber Speedway/
  SPEED: The Ride **8**
Las Vegas Mini Gran Prix **4**
Las Vegas Motor Speedway **3**
Las Vegas Natural
  History Museum **1**
Liberace Museum **21**
Lied Discovery
  Children's Museum **2**
Madame Tussauds
  Las Vegas **11**
Marjorie Barrick Museum **20**
MGM Grand Lion Habitat **17**
Shark Reef at
  Mandalay Bay **19**
Siegfried & Roy's Secret Garden
  & Dolphin Habitat **12**
Springs Preserve **10**
Stratosphere Thrill Rides **7**
Titanic: The Exhibition **18**

0   0.5 mi
0   0.5 km

········· Monorail
▮ SAHARA Monorail
  station

videos, interactive displays, motion-simulator theaters (like sitting in a bunker watching a blast), and emotional testimony from the people who worked there. It respectfully treads that tricky line between honoring the work done at the site and understanding its terrible implications. Not to be missed, even if it's only because of the Albert Einstein action figure in the gift shop. Seriously.

755 E. Flamingo Rd. ⓒ 702/794-5151. www.atomictestingmuseum.org. Admission $10 adults; $7 seniors, military, students with ID and Nevada residents; free for children 5 and under. Mon–Sat 9am–5pm; Sun 1–5pm.

Bellagio Gallery of Fine Art 🅕   No one was more surprised than we were when then-Bellagio owner Steve Wynn opened up an art gallery—and people came to see the art. We were surprised again after Wynn's departure when not only did the gallery stay open, with traveling exhibits in place of Wynn's own collection, but that the popularity stayed high. Indeed, when the gallery hosted a show by Steve Martin (yes, that one), a longtime modern art collector, the show was reviewed in none other than *Time* magazine. In other words, this is serious, and for real.

Now, will there be as interesting a show up when you go? Beats us. Then there's that ticket price: Let us point out that the Louvre art collection—which is, needless to say, quite a bit larger and which does, one can safely say, have some notable works—costs around $11.

In Bellagio, 3600 Las Vegas Blvd. S. ⓒ 702/693-7871. www.bellagio.com/amenities/gallery-of-fine-art.aspx. Reservations suggested, but walk-ins taken every 15 min. Admission $17 adults; $14 seniors, Nevada residents; students with ID; children 12 and under free. Sun–Thurs 10am–6pm, Fri–Sat 10am–9pm. Last admission half hour prior to closing.

Bodies   A stunning and controversial exhibit featuring what can be perhaps best described as Real Live Dead Bodies. Utilizing a patented freeze dry-sort of operation, full bodies (in theory donated by their former inhabitants, though that's where the controversy comes in), artfully dissected body parts and stripped cadavers are on display not for sensationalism—though it is pretty sensational in nearly all senses of the word—but in order for visitors to fully appreciate the wonder and mechanics that go into this too, too transient flesh. When a body is positioned in an athletic pose you can see how the muscles work, and when a cross section of a lung afflicted with cancer is right in front of you, you may well be glad Vegas is increasingly a no-smoking town. It's educational and bizarre and not something you are likely to forget soon. Surprisingly not grotesque, but not for the ultra-squeamish.

In Luxor 3900 Las Vegas Blvd. S. © **702/946-7000.** Admission $31 adults, $29 seniors over 65, $23 children 4–14, free for children 3 and under. Daily 10am–10pm, last admission at 9pm.

Eiffel Tower Tour *Overrated* It's a view. From the top (more or less) of a half-size replica of the Pride of Paris. With an elevator operator giving you facts about the structure (a half-size replica, did we mention that?) during the few seconds it takes to ride to the top. If you like views, it might be worth the money.

In Paris Las Vegas, 3655 Las Vegas Blvd. S. © **702/946-7000.** Admission $10 adults, $7 seniors over 65 and children 6–12, free for children 5 and under. Daily 9:30am–12:30am, weather permitting.

Fremont Street Experience ★★ Poor Downtown. For years now, it's been overlooked in favor of the Strip. And no wonder; it's so . . . small . . . by comparison. Its once-dazzling collection of hotel marquee lights seems like candles next to the klieg-light voltage of the Strip. Even a $70-million revitalization project hasn't helped give it back its mojo. That's too bad; things are cheaper down here, and if you get tired of feeling not pretty or rich enough for the Strip, you are not alone. Come join us in admiring the project that closed off the heart of "Glitter Gulch" and turned it into a much more user-friendly pedestrian mall. The Fremont Street Experience is a 5-block open-air landscaped strip of outdoor snack shops, vendor carts, and colorful kiosks purveying food and merchandise. Overhead is a 90-foot-high steel-mesh "celestial vault;" at night, it is **Viva Vision,** a high-tech light-and-laser show (the canopy is equipped with more than 12.5 million lights) enhanced by a concert-hall-quality sound system that takes place four times nightly. But there's music between shows as well. Not only does the canopy provide shade, it cools the area through a misting system in summer and warms you with radiant heaters in winter. It's really cool, in that Vegas over-the-top way that we love so much. It still hasn't entirely given second life to a neighborhood that deserves such a revival, but it is still part of the good gawking that makes Vegas so, well, Vegas.

Fremont St. (btw. Main St. and Las Vegas Blvd.), Downtown. www.vegasexperience. com. Free admission. Shows nightly.

GameWorks ★★ *Kids* Though it shows a need for some maintenance here and there, this is the place for fun-loving families of teens to come because it has such a range of activities, from rock climbing to the most high-tech of virtual reality games (what would you expect when Steven Spielberg and DreamWorks get into the video

Free Vegas

Vegas used to be the land of freebies. Those days are a dim memory, but many hotels still offer free attractions designed to lure you into their casinos, where you might well then drop far more than the cost of a day ticket to Disney World. Do not give them the satisfaction. Meanwhile, here's a handy list of the best of the free bait, er, sights:

Bellagio Conservatory (in the Bellagio Hotel) ☆☆☆. A strange concept for today's money-grubbing Vegas: a greenhouse atrium, filled with seasonal living foliage in riotous colors and styles, changed every 6 weeks or so. From Easter to Chinese New Year, events are celebrated with carefully designed splashes of flowers, plants, and remarkable decorations. Open 24 hours.

Bellagio Fountains (outside the Bellagio Hotel) ☆☆☆. Giant spouts of water shoot up and down and sideways, and dance their little aquatic hearts out, in pieces carefully choreographed to tunes ranging from show to Chopin. Daily every half-hour starting early afternoon, then every 15 minutes 7pm to midnight. Closed when it's windy.

Forum Shops Fountain Shows (in the Forum Shops at Caesars) ☆. The first of the free shows, and easily the stupidest. We love it, in theory at least, as giant "marble" Greco-Roman statues come to creaky animatronic life and deliver a largely unintelligible speech, mostly exhorting the crowds to eat, drink, and get so merry they will think nothing of dropping a bundle on the slots. Daily every hour, starting at 10am.

Masquerade Show in the Sky (in the Rio) ☆☆. Think those Skyway buckets from Disneyland turned into carnival-themed floats, some featuring rather adult skits (like the one on the giant bed), and you've got the basic idea of this overhead parade. Mardi Gras-by-way-of-Rio costumed extras toss beads to the cheering crowd, which probably isn't noticing how creepy-cool the floating floats really are. Daily 3, 4, 5, 6:30, 7:30, 8:30, and 9:30pm.

Mirage Volcano (outside The Mirage). The first curbside free attraction, and one of the reasons Wynn made it so you can't see his new mountain and lake show from the street (see below)—because that doesn't bring guests *into* the property—this may finally be more thrilling than disappointment after an expensive makeover has amped up the effects. Still, don't expect much in the way of lava. Every 15 minutes after dark until midnight.

Sirens of TI (outside Treasure Island at The Mirage) ⓕ. We gave it the star because it has such high production values, but we did so grudgingly. See, this used to be a fun, hokey stunt show, where pirates attacked a British sailing vessel. Now the pirates are lured by singing and dancing lingerie-clad lovelies more suited to the Victoria's Secret catalogue than Homer. Stuff happens, but no one really cares; either you like the nekkid chicks or you are so horrified by the whole spectacle because it's so appallingly bad that plot twists don't matter much. Parents, be warned. Daily at 5:30, 7, 8:30, and 10pm, weather permitting.

Wynn Conservatory (in the Wynn Las Vegas) ⓕ. Yes, remarkably like the one at Bellagio, only we have to admit this one is better placed, situated just inside the door, and laid out so that one can stroll through it on one's way to other parts of the hotel, as opposed to the tucked-in-a-corner Bellagio version. The floral displays will change regularly. Open 24 hours.

Wynn Lake of Dreams (in the Wynn Las Vegas) ⓕ. The 150-foot-tall mountain, complete with mature trees saved from the old Desert Inn golf course, plus several waterfalls, cannot be seen in its entirety from anywhere other than hotel rooms facing west. The show itself can be watched only if you are dining in the Daniel Boulud Brasserie or SW Steakhouse, the Parasol or Chanel bars, or a small viewing platform set above those venues on the casino level. Should you bother? Maybe. Basically, twice an hour, the lake lights up with pretty colors, cued to tunes ranging from classical to Louis Armstrong for "interludes." At the top of the hour are bigger extravaganzas of weird, hologram erotic-psychedelic images projected on the wall waterfall, while shapes and puppets pop out for even more wacky action, with some rather adult imagery at times. Not worth the overpriced drink unless you can nurse it all night. Shows begin at 7pm, with a new one starting every 20 minutes through midnight.

game arcade business?). Hunt dinosaurs in the *Jurassic Park* game, take swings in a virtual-reality batting cage, or just play classics ranging from pool to Pac-Man. There is something for everyone, pretty much, though none of it comes cheap. Games are priced on a point system: $5 gets you $7 worth play points, $10 gets you $16 in game play, $20 gets you $36, $25 gets you $50. Thursday nights from 9pm until the midnight closing, you can purchase a card to play for the final 3 hours for $30. Purchased points go on a debit card that you then insert into the various machines to activate them. It's geared for people college-age and up, children should probably be at least 10 years old, unless part of their fun is playing with their folks.

In the Showcase Mall, 3785 Las Vegas Blvd. S. ✆ **702/432-4263.** www.gameworks. com. Sun–Thurs 10am–midnight; Fri–Sat 10am–1am. Hours may vary.

Las Vegas Cyber Speedway/SPEED: The Ride ★★ Auto racing is the fastest-growing spectator sport in America, so this is a popular stop. The first part of this attraction is an 8-minute virtual-reality ride, Cyber Speedway, featuring a three-quarter-size replica of a NASCAR race car. Hop aboard for an animated, simulated ride—either at the Las Vegas Motor Speedway or a race around the streets of Las Vegas (starting with the Strip, with all the hotels flashing by, and then going through the Forum Shops—whoops! there goes Versace!—and so forth). Press the gas, and you lean back and feel the rush of speed; hit a bump, and you go flying. Should your car get in a crash, off you go to a pit stop. At the end, a computer-generated report tells you your average speed, how many laps you made, how you did racing against the others next to you, and so forth. It's a pretty remarkable experience.

SPEED: The Ride is a roller coaster that blasts riders out through a hole in the wall by the NASCAR Cafe, then through a loop, under the sidewalk, through the hotel's marquee, and finally straight up a 250-foot tower. At the peak, you feel a moment of weightlessness, and then you do the whole thing backward! Not for the faint of heart.

In Sahara Hotel & Casino, 2535 Las Vegas Blvd. S. ✆ **702/737-2111.** $20 for all-day pass on both rides. Stock-car simulator only $10 (you must be at least 48 in. tall to ride), Speed: The Ride (roller coaster) $10 for single ride. Sun–Thurs 10am–9pm; Fri–Sat 10am–11pm (closing hours may vary).

Tips **Insider Info**

A good place to view the Sky Parade light show is from the balcony at Fitzgeralds Casino/Hotel.

Las Vegas Mini Gran Prix ✶✶✶ *Kids*   Here's an absolute gem of a family fun center, featuring a good-size and well-stocked arcade (both current video and classic arcade games), a mini-roller coaster, a giant slide, and, best of all, four go-cart tracks. The latter features not just basic whizzing around a circle, but a track where drivers can time themselves through a twisting course that, in your head, takes on whatever race fantasy you have—Formula One or chasin' after bad guys in the General Lee, whatever. The facility is well-maintained by the family owners/operators, and it features a genuinely good snack stand, including pizzas bigger and better than what you will find in your hotel, which just adds to the pleasures of this as an outing. It's also affordable, assuming that you have your own car, because otherwise it's a costly cab ride from the Strip.

1401 N. Rainbow Rd., just off U.S. 95 N. ✆ **702/259-7000.** www.lvmgp.com. Ride tickets $6.50 each, $6 each for 5 or more; tickets good on all ride at any time. Sun–Thurs 10am–10pm; Fri–Sat 10am–11pm.

Las Vegas Motor Speedway ✶✶   This 176,000-seat facility was the first new super-speedway to be built in the Southwest in over 2 decades. A $200-million state-of-the-art motor-sports entertainment complex, it includes a 1½-mile super-speedway, a 2½-mile FIA-approved road course, paved and dirt short-track ovals, and a 4,000-foot drag strip. Also on the property are facilities for Go-Kart, Legends Car, Sand Drag, Motocross competition, driving schools and attractions, and more. The place is so popular, condos are being constructed overlooking the track for those who apparently don't want to sleep on race days. Some major hotels have their own shuttles to the speedway during big events so check with your hotel's front desk or concierge.

7000 Las Vegas Blvd. N., directly across from Nellis Air Force Base (take I-15 north to exit 54). ✆ **800/644-4444** or 702/644-4443. www.lvms.com. Tickets $10–$75 (higher prices for major events). Race days vary.

Liberace Museum ✶✶✶ *Moments*   Culture, schmulture. You can keep your Louvres and Vaticans and Smithsonians; *this* is a museum. Housed, like everything else in Vegas, in a strip mall, this is a shrine to the glory and excess that was the art project known as Liberace. You've got your costumes (bejeweled), your many cars (bejeweled), your many pianos (bejeweled), and many jewels (also bejeweled). It's a testament to what can be bought with lots of money and no taste.

This is a one-of-a-kind place. Unless you have a severely underdeveloped appreciation for camp or take your museum-going very

When Temptation Strikes

You are not a gambler. You are not interested in wagering or betting of any sort. We can respect that. We can also respect the effects the bells and whistles of the ubiquitous slot machines (they'll greet you at the airport, for heaven's sake!) and the cries of victory from the casino floor may have on even the most rabid non-gamblers. After all, we watched just such a person transform before our very eyes one summer when she discovered craps on her first trip to Vegas. By the end of her vacation, she was tossing the dice with the best of them.

So, should the siren song of the casinos lure you to take part in the primary sin of Sin City, we offer the following advice to help you avoid losing your halo, wings, and—most important—your wallet:

1. **Go back to school.** Many of the casino hotels offer free gambling lessons (ask a dealer to find out if lessons are offered in a particular casino) to those interested in the major table games. If you're merely curious instead of highly interested, these will more than satisfy your casino cravings. Note that most lessons are given on weekdays, so if you're in town for the weekend, you'll be out of luck.

2. **Daylight is your friend.** Unless you decide to try your luck at the slot machines, stick to playing during mornings and afternoons, when table limits (the minimum bet you must make) will be lower. The excitement level may not be as high, but neither will the risk. The same advice holds for weekdays (lower) vs. weekends (higher).

3. **Find a friendly table.** Gambling is supposed to be fun. If you're not having any (and not just because you're losing—that's just plain old probability in action) then you're in the wrong place. If a dealer is being surly, a casino is too smoky or too crowded, or the players at your table rub you the wrong way, go someplace else.

4. **Gamble by proxy.** If your personal risk quotient is zero, there is perhaps no bigger thrill in Vegas than to watch others gamble their own fortunes. Watching the games on the floor costs nothing and is a lot more entertaining than you might think.

seriously, you shouldn't miss it. And you probably won't, given a renovation that added an entrance shaped like a giant rhinestone topped with a giant pink piano. The museum is 2½ miles east of the Strip, on your right.

1775 E. Tropicana Ave. (at Spencer St.). ⓒ 702/798-5595. www.liberace.org. Admission $15 adults, $10 seniors over 64 and student with ID, free for children 10 and under. Tues–Sat 10am–5pm; Sun noon–4pm. Closed Mondays, Thanksgiving, Dec 25, and Jan 1.

Madame Tussauds Las Vegas 𝕲 ⓚⓘ⓭⓼

Madame Tussauds waxworks exhibition has been the top London attraction for nearly 2 centuries, so even if you aren't a fan of wax museums, this, its sole branch west of the Mississippi, may be worth a stop—if you can stomach the price. We, frankly, cannot. Figures here are state-of-the-art, painstakingly constructed to perfectly match the original person. (Truth be told, though some are nearly identical to their living counterparts—Brad Pitt gave us a start—others look about as much like the celebrity in question as a department store mannequin.) They have recently upped the interaction quotient; figures are not only freestanding (go ahead, give 'em a poke and see if they squeal) but you can put on a wedding dress and get married to "George Clooney" (oh, like you don't want to). You can fondle a certain part of J. Lo's anatomy (oh, like you don't want to). There's a bunch more, plus a sort of glorified haunted house where living folks might jump out and scare you. Consequently, it's all quite a bit more entertaining than it used to be, but the price still makes one pause. *Tip:* Book online for a 10% discount.

In The Venetian, 3355 Las Vegas Blvd. S. ⓒ 702/862-7800. www.madametussauds. com/lasvegas. Admission $25 adults, $18 seniors, and students, $15 children 7–12, free for children 6 and under. Daily 10am–10pm, but hours vary seasonally, and museum may close early for private events.

Marjorie Barrick Museum 𝕲

Formerly known as the Natural History Museum (as opposed to the Las Vegas Natural History Museum, which still exists—and now you can see why they changed the name), this is a cool place to beat the heat and noise of Vegas while examining some attractive, if not overly imaginative, displays on Native American craftwork and Las Vegas history. Crafts include 19th-century Mexican religious folk art, a variety of colorful dance masks from Mexico, and Native American pottery. The first part of the hall is often the highlight, with impressive traveling art exhibits. Children won't find much that's entertaining, other than some glass cases containing examples of local, usually poisonous, reptiles (who,

if you are lucky—or unlucky, depending on your view—will be dining on mice when you drop by).

On the UNLV campus, 4505 Maryland Pkwy. ⓒ **702/895-3381.** http://hrcweb.
nevada.edu/museum. Free admission. Mon–Fri 8am–4:45pm; Sat 10am–2pm.
Closed on state and federal holidays.

MGM Grand Lion Habitat ⓕⓕ *Kids*   Hit this attraction at the
right time and it's one of the best freebies in town. It's a large, multilevel glass enclosure, in which various lions frolic during various
times of day. In addition to regular viewing spots, you can walk
through a glass tunnel and get a worm's-eye view of the underside of
a lion. Multiple lions share show duties (about 6 hr. on and then 2
days off at a ranch for some free-range activity, so they're never
cooped up here for long). So you could see any combo from one
giant male to a pack of five females who have grown from cub to
near adult size during their MGM time.

In MGM Grand, 3799 Las Vegas Blvd. S. ⓒ **702/891-7777.** Free admission. Daily
11am–10pm.

Shark Reef at Mandalay Bay *(Overrated*   It's just a big aquarium,
and mind you, we love big aquariums, so our only beef (or is that
fish?) with his exhibit is the price. (Though standing in the all-glass
tunnel, surrounded by sharks and finny friends, is kinda cool.) Note
also that it is waaay off in a remote part of Mandalay Bay, which
might be a hassle for those with mobility problems.

In Mandalay Bay, 3950 Las Vegas Blvd. S. ⓒ **702/632-4555.** www.mandalay
bay.com. Admission $16 adults, $11 children 5–12, free for children 4 and under.
Daily 10am–11pm. Last admission at 10pm.

Siegfried & Roy's Secret Garden & Dolphin Habitat *Kids*
The **Secret Garden** ⓕⓕ is an ample (though not zoo-size) display of
several of S&R's feline friends, plus an elephant or two. It's surprisingly charming, full of foliage and close-up views of some very large
cats. Zoo purists shouldn't fret; these are just the daytime digs for
these animals, who spend their nights in great, and often entirely
unfettered, luxury, over at their owners' home. It's a little weird of a
vibe, given the abrupt end to the animals'—to say nothing of their
owners'—performing careers, but it's still a pleasant diversion.

The **Dolphin Habitat** ⓕⓕⓕ is even more satisfying than the
Secret Garden—maybe the most fun thing to do in all of Vegas. It
was designed to provide a healthy and nurturing environment and to
educate the public about marine mammals and their role in the
ecosystem. Specialists worldwide were consulted in creating the

habitat, which was designed to serve as a model of a quality, secured environment. It must be working because the adult dolphins here are breeding regularly. The Mirage displays only dolphins already in captivity—no dolphins are taken from the wild. You can watch the dolphins frolic both above and below ground through viewing windows, in three different pools. (There is nothing quite like the kick you get from seeing a baby dolphin play.) The knowledgeable staff, who surely have the best jobs in Vegas, will answer questions and frequently play with the dolphins to help stimulate them. If you are lucky, you can toss a ball to a dolphin, who will knock it back to you with its snout, and if you do anything cooler than that during your trip, we'd like to hear about it. There is also a video of a resident dolphin (Duchess) giving birth (to Squirt) underwater. You can stay as long as you like, which might just be hours.

In The Mirage, 3400 Las Vegas Blvd. S. © **702/791-7111.** www.mirage.com. Admission $15 adults, $10 children 4–10, free for children 3 and under if accompanied by an adult. Memorial Day to Labor Day daily 10am–7pm; Labor Day to Memorial Day Mon–Fri 11am–5:30pm, Sat–Sun 10am–5:30pm. Hours subject to change.

Springs Preserve ✮✮✮   By now, perhaps you've learned that "Las Vegas" is Spanish for "the meadows." This facility is set on the 180-acre site of the original springs that fed Las Vegas until it dried in the 1960s. (Told you that Hoover Dam comes in handy.) These days, Las Vegas is an environmental nightmare, along with much of the rest of this planet, and this remarkable recreational attraction is here to educate us about the possibilities to reverse some of the damage.

Set amidst nature and hiking trails, plus man-made wetlands, which is an interesting concept, the focal point is a large interpretive center that gives the history of Las Vegas from a land- and water-use perspective. The displays are creative and interactive, including a room with a reproduction flash flood that uses 5,000 gallons of water and one with a simulation of the experience of working on Hoover Dam. The other buildings are all done according to standards that have the least environmental impact, using modern construction versions of adobe and other green concepts. There are only 30 such structures in the world and seven of them are here. Each building tackles an aspect of desert living and the environment, including one that instructs kids on the glories of recycling, complete with a compost tunnel to crawl through! The outdoor kids play area is made from recycled materials and has big animals to climb on, in case they've grown tired about learning responsible stuff. The cafe menu is designed by Wolfgang Puck with further green emphasis.

Finally, this will be the eventual location of the Nevada state historical museum. Given the care, knowledge, and urgency of the issues addressed, this is an extraordinary facility for any town but particularly for this one.

3333 S. Valley View Blvd. © **702/822-8344.** www.springspreserve.com. $19 adults, $17 seniors and students with ID, $11 children 5–17. Admission to trails is free. Daily 10am–10pm summer; 10am–6pm winter.

Stratosphere Thrill Rides ★★ (Kids)

You won't get this kind of a thrill-ride experience anywhere else. You also will never, ever see us on any of it. Atop the 1,149-foot Stratosphere Tower are three stomach-churning thrill rides: **Big Shot** ★★, a breathtaking free-fall ride that thrusts you 160 feet in the air along a 228-foot spire at the top of the tower, then plummets back down again. Sitting in an open car, you seem to be dangling in space over Las Vegas. We have one relative, a thrill-ride enthusiast, who said he never felt more scared than when he rode the Big Shot. After surviving, he promptly put his kids on it; they loved it. And then there is the **X-Scream,** a giant teeter-totter that plunges one end over the edge of the Strat—you know, so you feel like you are plunging to the Strip, 1,149 feet below. There are so many languages we can say "no" in, and when we aren't using them on that ride, we will be saving them for the aptly named **Insanity: the Ride,** a spinning whirligig of a contraption that straps you into a seat and twirls you around 1,000 feet or so above terra firma in a whirligig contraption. *Nein, nyet, non!* But don't let our scaredy-cat attitude stop you. *Note:* The rides are shut down in inclement weather and high winds.

Atop Stratosphere Las Vegas, 2000 Las Vegas Blvd. S. © **702/380-7777.** www.stratospherehotel.com. Admission: Big Shot $10; X-Scream $10; Insanity $10; plus fee to ascend Tower: $12 for adults; $8 for locals, seniors, hotel guests, and children 4–12; free for children 3 and under and those dining in the buffet room or Top of the World. Multiride and all-day packages also available for varying costs. Sun–Thurs 10am–1am; Fri–Sat 10am–2am. Hours vary seasonally. Minimum height requirement for Big Shot is 48 inches, minimum height requirement for X-Scream and Insanity are 52 inches.

Titanic: The Exhibition ★

While this is obviously a can't-miss for buffs, it might still be of some interest for those with only marginal feelings about the massive 1912 disaster. (It is interesting to muse about what turns historical trivia into romantic significance.) It features displays explaining the ship's ill-fated maiden voyage; relics salvaged from the sunken liner; and even recreations of sample cabins from first, second, and third class, including atmospheric conditions, giving you a sense of how it felt to travel aboard what was an incredible vessel. There is even a large chunk of real ice standing in for the culprit berg. It's tastefully done, except for the proposed adjoining bar wherein patrons will be lifted into the establishments via lifeboat. Let's hope that one doesn't come to pass.

In the Luxor, 3900 Las Vegas Blvd. S. No prices or hours available at press time.

2 Getting Married

Getting married is one of the most popular things to do in Las Vegas. Why? It's very easy to get married here. Too easy. See that total stranger standing next to you? Grab him or her, and head down to the **Clark Country Marriage License Bureau,** 201 Clark Ave. (© **702/761-0600;** open daily 8am–midnight, including holidays), to get your license. Find a wedding chapel (not hard, as there are about 50 of them in town; they line the north end of the Strip, and most hotels have them), and tie the knot. Just like that. No blood test, no waiting period—heck, not even an awkward dating period. Ah, c'mon. If we've learned anything from the impetuous actions of Britney Spears and Nicky Hilton, it's that annulments are almost as easy as weddings!

But even if you have actually known your intended for some time, Las Vegas is a great place to get married. The ease is the primary attraction, but there are a number of other appealing reasons. You can have any kind of wedding you want, from a big, traditional production number to a small, intimate affair; from a spur-of-the-moment "just-the-happy-couple-in-blue-jeans" kind of thing to an Elvis-in-a-pink-Cadillac-at-a-drive-through-window kind of thing. (Oh, yes. More on that later.) The wedding chapels take care of everything; usually they'll even provide a limo to take you to the license bureau and back. Most offer all the accessories, from rings to flowers to a videotaped memory of the event.

We personally know several very happy couples who opted for the Vegas route. Motivations differed, with the ease factor heading the list (though the Vegasness of the whole thing came in a close second), but one and all reported having great fun. Really, is there a more romantic way to start off your life together than in gales of laughter?

In any event, the more than 100,000 couples who yearly take advantage of all this can't be wrong. If you want to follow in the footsteps of Elvis and Priscilla (at the original Aladdin hotel), Michael Jordan, Joan Collins, Bruce Willis and Demi Moore, and, of course, Dennis Rodman and Carmen Electra, you'll want to peruse the following list of the most notable wedding chapels on or near the Strip. There are many more in town, and almost all the major hotels offer chapels as well; though the latter are cleaner and less tacky than some of the Strip chapels, they do tend to be without any personality at all. (Two exceptions might be the chapel at the Excalibur Hotel, where you can dress in medieval costumes, and the lovely chapel at the Bellagio, which has personal wedding coordinators and a high level of customer service, holding only 8–10 weddings a day—seems like a lot, but it's nothing compared to the volume on the Strip.)

With regard to decor, there isn't a radical difference between the major places (hence, no star ratings here), though some are decidedly spiffier and less sad than others. Attitude certainly makes a difference with several and varies radically, depending on who's working at any given time. Given how important your wedding is—or should be— we encourage you to give yourself time to comparison-shop, and spurn anyone who doesn't seem eager enough for your business.

You can also call **Las Vegas Weddings and Rooms** (℃ **800/488-MATE [6283];** www.lasvegasweddings.com), which offers one-stop shopping for wedding services. They'll find a chapel or an outdoor garden that suits your taste (not to mention such only-in-Vegas venues as the former mansions of Elvis Presley and Liberace); book you into a hotel for the honeymoon; arrange the ceremony; and provide flowers, a photographer (or videographer), wedding cake, limo, car rental, music, champagne, balloons, and garter for the bride. Basically, they can arrange anything you like.

Weddings can be very cheap in Vegas: A license is about $55, and a basic service not much more. Even a full-blown shebang package— photos, music, some flowers, video, cake, and other doodads—will run only about $500 total. We haven't quoted any prices here, since the ultimate cost depends entirely on how much you want to spend. Go cheap, and the whole thing will put you back maybe $100, including the license (maybe even somewhat less); go elaborate, and the price is still reasonable by today's wedding price standards. Be sure to remember that there are often hidden charges, such as expected gratuities for the minister (about $25 would do; no real need to tip anyone else), and so forth. If you're penny-pinching, you'll want to keep those in mind.

Be aware that Valentine's Day is a very popular day to get married in Vegas. Some of the chapels perform as many as 80 services on February 14.

But remember, you also don't have to plan ahead. Just show up, get your paperwork, close your eyes, and pick a chapel. And above all, have fun. Good luck and best wishes to you both.

Chapel of the Bells   Sporting perhaps the largest and gaudiest sign on the Strip, this chapel also shares a parking lot with the bright pink Fun City Motel. We won't make any jokes. Kitschy on the outside, but nice kitsch on the inside. The chapel has wood paneling, sage carpeting, and gilt trim up by the pulpit. Electric candles light the walls. It seats only about 25. They prefer advance booking but can do same-day ceremonies if called to.

2233 Las Vegas Blvd. S. (at Sahara Ave.). ℂ 800/233-2391 or 702/735-6803. www.chapelofthebellslasvegas.com. Mon–Thurs 9am–10pm; Fri–Sat 9am–1am. Open as late as needed on holidays.

Cupid's Wedding Chapel   "The little chapel with the big heart." Well, it just might be. The manager explains that, unlike other chapels on the Strip, this one schedules weddings an hour apart to provide time for the full production number. The folks at Cupid's pride themselves on offering "a traditional church wedding at a chapel price." The chapel is pleasantly low-frills and down-to-earth, with white walls and pews, and modern stained glass with doves and roses. (Kitsch-phobes will be pleased to know the cupids are only in the lobby.) It seats 60 to 70. They have two reception rooms, one rather banquet-hall in style, the other more '50s diner in feel. And a video of your wedding can be archived and posted online within an hour.

827 Las Vegas Blvd. S. (btw. Gass and Hoover aves.). ℂ 800/543-2933 or 702/598-4444. www.cupidswedding.com. Weddings by appointment only, hours vary.

Graceland Wedding Chapel   Housed in a landmark building that's one of the oldest wedding chapels in Vegas, the Graceland bills itself as "the proverbial mom-and-pop outfit. We offer friendly, courteous service, and are willing to go that extra step." No, there's no Elvis connection (one of the owners was friends with Elvis and asked his permission to use the name). This is a tiny New England church building with a small bridge and white picket fence out front. Inside is a 33-seat chapel; the walls are burgundy and white, with a large, modern stained-glass window of doves and roses behind the pulpit. The pews are dark blond wood. It's not the nicest of the chapels, but Catherine Oxenberg and Casper Van Dien got married here. Jon Bon Jovi and Lorenzo Lamas did also, though not to each other.

Note: If the King is important to you, you should know that there is an Elvis impersonator on-site who will do your ceremony—for the

Tips   Photo Ops

In a town full of nothing but Artificial Wonders of the World, camera shutters will be kept busy clicking. For those looking for Christmas card possibilities, gather your brood around the famous vintage **"Welcome to Las Vegas"** sign on the outskirts of town (or call up Jesse Garon, an Elvis impersonator, at ℂ **702/588-8188**—and see if you can pay him to pose in his pink Caddie along with you).

From there, you can choose among posing with the replica of Michelangelo's David or the talking animatronic statues at **The Forum Shops at Caesars Palace** or the non-talking lions at the **MGM Grand Lion Habitat** (glass safely between you and Kitty, of course—you'll need a polarizing filter on your camera to capture them properly). More kitty critters can be found at The Mirage behind bars at **Siegfried & Roy's Secret Garden.** Ask nicely, and maybe a trainer at the **Dolphin Habitat** will get a finny friend to leap behind you at just the right moment.

If beasties aren't your thing, you can stand with a glad-iator back at **Caesars** or with one of the roaming Italian Renaissance–dressed figures (Casanova, perhaps) at **The Venetian.** Confuse the folks at home and pose by the **Statue of Liberty** outside New York–New York (while the tugboats shoot water into the air), or really confuse them with shots of you amid the gorgeously arranged seasonal flora in **The Conservatory** at Bellagio.

right price. Weddings available for viewing online 45 minutes after the ceremony.

619 Las Vegas Blvd. S. (at E. Bonneville Ave.). ℂ **800/824-5732** or 702/382-0091. www.gracelandchapel.com. Sun–Thurs 9am–9pm; Fri–Sat 9am–midnight.

Little Chapel of the Flowers   This chapel's claim to fame is that Dennis Rodman and Carmen Electra exchanged their deathless vows here. Don't hold it against the place; this is the slickest operation on the Strip, a big complex that offers your best shot at a traditional wed-ding. The Heritage Chapel fits 65 and has a cutesy church feel, with wood pews and a ghastly brass chandelier. The Victorian Chapel, which holds only 30, has white walls and dark-wood pews and doesn't look very Victorian at all—but as the plainest, it's also the nicest. The smallest is the Magnolia Chapel, full of artificial flowers and a free-standing archway. If you want an outdoor vow exchange, you might choose the gazebo by a running stream and waterfall that nearly drowns out Strip noise. The Heritage Chapel holds 70 and adds rose-colored drapes and electric candle chandeliers. There's also a medium-size reception room and live organ music upon request. It's a pretty, friendly place that seems to keep an eye on its bustling business. It does not allow rice or confetti throwing.

1717 Las Vegas Blvd. S. (at E. Oakey Blvd.). ℂ 800/843-2410 or 702/735-4331. www.littlechapel.com. Mon–Thurs 8am–8pm; Fri–Sat 8am–9pm; Sun noon–6pm (sometimes).

Little White Wedding Chapel   This is arguably the most famous of the chapels on the Strip, maybe because blue-jean-clad Brit strolled down this aisle with What's His Name, maybe because it has the big sign saying Michael Jordan and Joan Collins were married there (again, not to each other), maybe because it was the first to do the drive-up window. It is indeed little and white. There is a factory-line atmosphere, however, as the place processes wedding after wedding after wedding, 24 hours a day. Move 'em in, and move 'em out. (No wonder they put in that drive-up window!) The staff are brusque, hasty, and can have a bit of an attitude (though we know one couple who got married here and had no complaints). Little White Chapel does offer full wedding ceremonies, complete with candlelight service and traditional music. There are two chapels, the larger of which—decorated with tulle and white fake flowers—is the nicest. There is also a gazebo for outdoor services, but since it's right on the Strip, it's not as nice as it sounds. If you want something special, there are probably better choices, but for a true Vegas wedding experience, this is Kitsch Wedding Central.

1301 Las Vegas Blvd. S. (btw. E. Oakey and Charleston boulevards). ℂ 800/545-8111 or 702/382-5943. www.alittlewhitechapel.com. Daily 24 hr.

Wee Kirk O' the Heather   This is the oldest wedding chapel in Las Vegas (it's been here since 1940) and the one at the very end of the Strip, right before Downtown (and thus really close to the license bureau). It would be declared a historic landmark except that some renovations in the past moved just enough interior walls to alter it sufficiently to keep it from being official. A recent renovation has gussied it up nicely.

231 Las Vegas Blvd. S. (btw. Bridger and Carson aves.). ℂ 800/843-5266 or 702/382-9830. www.weekirk.com. Daily 10am–midnight.

3 Especially for Kids

Like much of the rest of the world, you may be under the impression that Las Vegas has evolved from an adults-only fantasyland into a vacation destination suitable for the entire family. The only explanation for this myth is that Las Vegas was referred to as "Disneyland for adults" by so many and for so long that the town became momentarily confused and decided it actually *was* Disneyland. Some of the gargantuan hotels then spent small fortunes on redecorating in an attempt to lure families with vast quantities of junk food and a lot of hype. They now vehemently deny that any such notion ever crossed their collective minds, and, no, they don't know how that roller coaster got into the parking lot.

To put things simply, Las Vegas makes money—lots and lots of money—by promoting gambling, drinking, and sex. These are all fine pursuits if you happen to be an adult, but if you haven't reached the magical age of 21, you really don't count in this town. In any case, the casinos and even the Strip itself are simply too stimulating, noisy, and smoky for young kids.

Older progeny may have a tolerance for crowds and the incessant pinging of the slot machines, but they will be thoroughly annoyed with you when casino security chastises them if they so much as stop to tie their shoelaces anywhere near the gaming tables. Since you can't get from your hotel room to the parking lot without ambling through a casino, you can't reasonably expect a teenager to be in a good mood once you stagger outside. And those amusement parks and video halls that haven't yet been purged are expensive places to park your kids for an afternoon or evening, assuming that they are old enough to be left unsupervised. And it can be tough just going about your business on the Strip, what with the two-story-tall, thong-clad showgirl rear ends advertising *Jubilee!* and *Folies Bergere* on the sides of Bally's and the Tropicana, respectively, to say nothing of the bare-breasted giantess on the prow of the pirate boat at the Strip entrance to TI. Or the guys handing out flyers for "escort" services and porn phone lines. Really, if you don't want to engage in any biology discussions with your progeny, you might want to keep them at home.

Nevertheless, you may have a perfectly legitimate reason for bringing your children to Las Vegas (like Grandma was busy, or you were just stopping off on your way from somewhere else), so here are some places to take the children both on and off the Strip.

Circus Circus (p. 58) has ongoing circus acts throughout the day, a vast video-game and pinball arcade, and dozens of carnival games on its mezzanine level. Behind the hotel is **The Adventuredome,** detailed below.

Excalibur (p. 39) also offers video and carnival games, plus thrill cinemas and free shows (jugglers, puppets, and so on).

At **Caesars Palace** (p. 44), animated talking statues in the **Forum Shops** are a kick, while kids should also be wowed by clamoring around inside the giant moving Trojan horse outside FAO Schwarz, exploring the shops, and marveling at the fountain show.

Star Trek: The Experience, if it has reopened somewhere by the time you read this (p. 110), will appeal to some families, but it may be a bit much for younger children.

The **battle** in front of **Treasure Island** (p. 47) is no longer G-rated, thanks to the addition of nekkid girls, so stick with the erupting volcano and **Siegfried & Roy's Secret Garden** and **Dolphin Habitat** at **The Mirage** (p. 44) and **Shark Reef at Mandalay Bay** (p. 120). Kids into gross out might find Bodies at the Luxor of icky interest; you don't need to tell them it's also educational. Or let them zoom zoom zoom at **Las Vegas Cyber Speedway** (p. 116) at the **Sahara.**

Children 10 and up will love the many options for play (from high-tech to low-tech, from video wonders to actual physical activity) offered at **GameWorks** (p. 113), as will their parents.

Appropriate shows for kids include *Tournament of Kings* at Excalibur, *Lance Burton* at the Monte Carlo, and Cirque du Soleil's *Mystère* at Treasure Island. As a general rule, early shows are less racy than late-night shows. All these productions are reviewed in detail in chapter 7.

Lake Mead has great recreational facilities for family vacations. Finally, organized tours (see "Organized Tours," below) to the Grand Canyon and other interesting sights in southern Nevada and neighboring states can be fun family activities. Check with your hotel's sightseeing desk. Kids would also be entertained by the personalized tours offered by **Creative Adventures** (© **702/893-2051;** www. pcap.com/creativeadventures); see p. 133.

Specifically kid-pleasing attractions are described below.

The Adventuredome ⋆ *Kids*   This isn't a half-bad place to spend a hot afternoon, especially since Circus Circus, the casino hotel that built this somewhat worn indoor amusement park, is still more child-friendly than not. The glass dome that towers overhead lets in natural light, a solace to those of us who look peaked under the glow of the artificial kind. A double-loop roller coaster careens around the simulated Grand Canyon, and there's the requisite water flume and a modest number of other rides for kids of all ages. Video games and an arcade are separate from the attractions, cutting down just a tad on the noise level. Our only caveat is not to leave kids here alone; they could easily get lost.

2880 Las Vegas Blvd. S. (behind Circus Circus). (C) 702/794-3939. www.adventure dome.com. Free admission; pay per ride $4–$7; daily pass $25 adults, $15 children 33–47 in. tall. AE, DC, DISC, MC, V. Park hours vary seasonally but are usually Mon–Thurs 10am–6pm; Fri–Sat 10am–midnight; Sun 10am–9pm.

Las Vegas Natural History Museum *Kids*

Conveniently located across the street from the Lied Discovery Children's Museum (described below), this humble temple of taxidermy harkens back to elementary school field trips around 1965, when stuffed elk and brown bears forever protecting their kill were as close as most of us got to exotic animals. Worn around the edges but very sweet and relaxed, the museum is enlivened by a hands-on activity room and two life-size dinosaurs that roar at one another intermittently. A small boy was observed leaping toward his dad upon watching this display, so you might want to warn any sensitive little ones that the big tyrannosaurs aren't going anywhere. Surprisingly, the gift shop here is particularly well-stocked with neat items you won't too terribly mind buying for the kids.

900 Las Vegas Blvd. N. (at Washington Ave.). (C) 702/384-3466. www.lvnhm.org. Admission $8 adults; $7 seniors, students, and military; $4 children 3–11; free for children under 3. Daily 9am–4pm.

Lied Discovery Children's Museum *Finds Kids*

A hands-on science museum designed for curious kids, the bright, airy, two-story Lied makes an ideal outing for toddlers and young children. Lots of interactive exhibits to examine; they change periodically, but past exhibits have included a miniature grocery store, a tube for encasing oneself inside a soap bubble, a radio station, and music and drawing areas. Clever, thought-inducing exhibits are everywhere. Learn how it feels to have a disability by playing basketball from a wheelchair. Feed a wooden "sandwich" to a cutout of a snake and to a human cutout, and see how much nutrition each receives. See how much sunscreen the giant stuffed mascot needs to keep from burning. On Saturday afternoons from 1 to 3pm, free drop-in art classes are offered, giving adults a bit of time to ramble around the gift store or read the fine print on the exhibit placards. The Lied also shares space

(Kids) Hotel Arcades

Virtually every hotel has some kind of video arcade—all the better to prep the under-21s for their upcoming gambling days, we say, because we are cynical (and also probably right). These vary considerably in size and quality. The top dog in town is the **Coney Island Emporium** (© 702/740-6969) at New York–New York, where video machines are joined by carny style, and kids can redeem tickets earned from wins for various cheap trinkets and stuffed animals. The **Fantasy Faire** at Excalibur (© 702/597-7777) has motion-simulator rides next to their arcades. And the Sahara's **Pit Pass Arcade** (© 702/737-2111) has additional racing-themed games, as the arcade is part of the NASCAR Cafe.

Note: Several arcades restrict the times those under 18 can play while unaccompanied by an adult. Call or stop in to check on policies if you plan to leave your kids in the arcade for a while.

with a city library branch, so after the kids run around, you can calm them back down with a story or two.

833 Las Vegas Blvd. N. (½ block south of Washington, across the street from Cashman Field). © 702/382-3445. www.ldcm.org. Admission $7 adults; $6 seniors, military, and children 1–17; free for under 1 year. Tues–Sun 10am–5pm. Closed Easter, Thanksgiving, Dec 24, Dec 25, and Jan 1.

4 Organized Tours

Just about every hotel in town has a sightseeing desk offering a seemingly infinite number of tours in and around Las Vegas. You're sure to find a tour company that will take you where you want to go.

Gray Line Tours (© 800/634-6579; www.grayline.com) offers a rather comprehensive roster, including:

- A pair of 5- to 6-hour **city tours** (1 day, 1 night), with various itineraries, including visits to Ethel M Chocolates, the Liberace Museum, and the Fremont Street Experience
- Half-day excursions to **Hoover Dam** and **Red Rock Canyon** (see chapter 8 for details)
- A half-day tour to **Lake Mead** and **Hoover Dam**
- Several full-day **Grand Canyon** excursions

Going Vegas

If you're looking for a quintessential Las Vegas experience, try these suggestions from James P. Reza, Geoff Carter, and the editors of *Las Vegas Weekly:*

- **Peppermill's Fireside Lounge** (p. 169). This lounge is so evocative of the Me Decade, it's impossible not to love it. Dark, cozy, sexy, and somewhat kitschy, it's a great place for romantic encounters. Try to sit by the year-round fire pit, if you can stand the heat.

- **GameWorks** (p. 113). This multilevel entertainment center gives visitors a chance to wreak digitized havoc on the latest video-game creations. A few brave souls try the 75-foot climbing wall; most just hang in the lounge and shoot pool.

- **Cheetah's** (p. 177). How could you possibly visit Sin City and not sample the ubiquitous lap dance? Couples are welcome at Cheetah's, the site of Paul Verhoven's laughably overdone film *Showgirls.* More quality, less silicone, and a VIP lounge that has hosted lap dances for the likes of Sting and Drew Barrymore.

- **The Forum Shops at Caesars Palace** (p. 143). The most unique shopping experience in the world. Take Rodeo Drive, marry it to Rome, douse the whole thing in Spielberg, and you're still nowhere near this elegant retail space.

- **Hard Rock Hotel & Casino** (p. 50). Everything about this hotel/casino—the bars, The Joint showroom, Mr. Lucky's 24/7—manages to evoke classic Vegas, a city that was built for young hipsters, not fanny-pack-wielding families.

- **Red Rock Canyon** (p. 192). Providing needed respite from the neon jungle, Red Rock is as beautiful as the desert gets. This haven for hikers and rock climbers gets a bit overrun at times, but it is still worth the trip. *Note:* Don't feed the wild burros. Unlike the entertainers at Cheetah's, they bite.

GRAND CANYON TOURS

Generally, tourists visiting Las Vegas don't drive 300 miles to Arizona to see the Grand Canyon, but plenty of sightseeing tours are available for those who are interested. See chapter 8 for details.

UNIQUE DESERT TOURS BY CREATIVE ADVENTURES ★★★

A totally different type of tour is offered by Char Cruze of **Creative Adventures** (© 702/893-2051; www.creativeadventuresltd.net). Char, a charming fourth-generation Las Vegan (she was at the opening of the Flamingo), spent her childhood riding horseback through the mesquite and cottonwoods of the Mojave Desert, discovering magical places you'd never find on your own or on a commercial tour. A lecturer and storyteller as well as a tour guide, Char has extensively studied southern Nevada's geology and desert wildlife, its regional history, and its Native American cultures. Her personalized tours, enhanced by fascinating stories about everything from miners to mobsters, visit haunted mines, sacred Paiute grounds, ghost towns, canyons, and ancient petroglyphs. She also has many things to entertain and educate children, and she carries a tote bag full of visual aids, like a board covered in labeled rocks to better illustrate a lecture on local geology. Char has certain structured tours, but she loves to do individual tours tailored to the group. This is absolutely worth the money—you are definitely going to get something different than you would on a conventional tour, while Char herself is most accommodating, thoughtful, knowledgeable, and prompt. Char rents transport according to the size of the group and can handle clients with disabilities.

Each tour is customized based on your interests so pricing varies dramatically. Figure at least $150 for the basics (which are much more than basic), with costs going up from there. It's a good idea to make arrangements with Char prior to leaving home.

5 Fore! Great Desert Golf

In addition to the listings below, there are dozens of local courses, including some very challenging ones that have hosted PGA tournaments. *Note:* Greens fees vary radically depending on time of day and year. Because of the heat, you will want to take advantage of the cart which in most cases is included in the greens fee.

If you're a serious golfer, you may want to contact **American Golf** (© 800/468-7918), a nationwide reservations service that's based in Arizona. They can help you arrange golf packages and book hard-to-get tee times.

Note also that the **Rio All-Suite Hotel & Casino** has a golf course; see p. 58.

Angel Park Golf Club ✶✶   This 36-hole par-70/71 public course is a local favorite. Arnold Palmer originally designed the Mountain and Palm courses (the Palm Course was redesigned several years later by Bob Cupp). Players call this a great escape from the casinos, claiming that no matter how many times they play it, they never get tired of it. The Palm Course has gently rolling fairways that offer golfers of all abilities a challenging yet forgiving layout. The Mountain Course has rolling natural terrain and gorgeous panoramic views. In addition to these two challenging 18-hole courses, Angel Park offers a night-lit Cloud 9 Course (12 holes for daylight play, 9 at night), where each hole is patterned after a famous par-3. You can reserve tee times up to 60 days in advance with a credit card guarantee.

Yardage: Palm Course 6,525 championship and 5,438 resort; Mountain Course 6,722 championship and 5,718 resort.

Facilities: Pro shop, night-lit driving range, 18-hole putting course, restaurant, snack bar, cocktail bar, and beverage cart.

100 S. Rampart Blvd. (btw. Summerlin Pkwy. and Alta St.; 20 min. northwest of the Strip). © 888/629-3929 or 702/254-0566. www.angelpark.com. Greens fees for 18 hole courses, which include cart rental practice balls and tax $75–$155, short course fees $25, excluding optional cart rental. Discounted twilight rates available for 18 hole course.

Bali Hai Golf Club ✶✶✶   One of the newest and most exclusive golf addresses belongs to this multimillion-dollar course built in 2000 on the strip just south of Mandalay Bay. Done in a wild South Seas theme, the par-72 course features over 7 acres of water features, including an island green, palm trees, and tropical foliage. Not impressed yet? How about the fact that all of their golf carts are equipped with global positioning systems (GPSs)? Or that celeb chef Wolfgang Puck chose to open his newest Vegas eatery here (now run by someone else)? Okay, if that doesn't convince you of the upscale nature of the joint, check out the greens fees. Even at those prices, tee times are often booked 6 months in advance.

Yardage: 7,002 championship.

Facilities: Pro shop, putting green, gourmet restaurant, grill, and lounge.

5150 Las Vegas Blvd. S. © 888/427-6678. www.balihaigolfclub.com. Greens fees, which include cart, range balls, and taxes $99–$395.

Black Mountain Golf & Country Club ✶✶   Two new greens have recently been added to this 18-hole, par-72 semiprivate course, which requires reservations 4 days in advance. It's considered a great old course, with lots of wildlife, including roadrunners. Unpredictable winds, however, may blow during your game.

Yardage: 6,550 championship, 6,223 regular, and 5,518 ladies'.

Facilities: Pro shop, putting green, driving range, restaurant, snack bar, and cocktail lounge.

500 Greenway Rd., Henderson. © 866/596-4833. www.golfblackmountain.com. Greens fees, which include cart rental, $75–$120; call for twilight rates.

Craig Ranch Golf Club *Value*   This is a flat 18-hole, par-70 public course with many trees and bunkers; both narrow and open fairways feature Bermuda turf. The greens fees are a bargain, and you can reserve tee times 7 days in advance.

Yardage: 6,001 regular and 5,221 ladies'.

Facilities: Driving range, pro shop, PGA teaching pro, putting green, and snack bar.

628 W. Craig Rd. (btw. Losee Rd. and Martin Luther King Blvd.). © 702/642-9700. Greens fees $19 walking, $30 in golf cart.

Desert Rose Golf Course *Value*   This is an 18-hole, par-71 public course built in 1963 and designed by Dick Wilson/Joe Lee. Narrow fairways feature Bermuda turf. You can reserve tee times up to 7 days in advance.

Yardage: 6,511 championship, 6,135 regular, and 5,458 ladies'.

Facilities: Driving range, putting and chipping greens, PGA teaching pro, pro shop, restaurant, and cocktail lounge.

5483 Clubhouse Dr. (3 blocks west of Nellis Blvd., off Sahara Ave.). © 800/470-4622 or 702/566-7618. Greens fees, including cart rental $60–$80.

Las Vegas National Golf Club   This is an 18-hole (about eight with water on them), par-72 public course, and a classic layout (not the desert layout you'd expect). If you play from the back tees, it can really be a challenge. The 1996 Las Vegas Invitational, won by Tiger Woods, was held here. Discounted tee times are often available. Reservations are taken up to 60 days in advance; a $5 to $7 fee applies.

Yardage: 6,815 championship, 6,418 regular, and 5,741 ladies'.

Facilities: Pro shop, golf school, driving range, restaurant, and cocktail lounge.

1911 Desert Inn Rd. (btw. Maryland Pkwy. and Eastern Ave.). © 702/734-1796. www.lasvegasnational.com. Greens fees $60–$179, some including cart rental.

6 Staying Active

For our tastes, it's way too hot (or, alternatively, too cold) to do much outside—that's why they invented indoor climate control. But if you are more active than we, first of all, we are impressed, and second, here are some ways to get physical in and around Vegas.

BOWLING   Lucky Strike at the Rio, 3700 W. Flamingo Blvd. (© 702/777-7777). It has only 10 lanes, but you don't come to this clublike spot to bowl. You come to eat items like fried mac 'n' cheese and other salty, tasty snacks. This then makes you thirsty for various goofy drinks, such as cotton candy–flavored martinis (the glass is lined with the vibrant spun sugar, and when the drink is poured into it, a curious colored effect appears) or the Mambo for Two, from which dry ice dramatically froths out. You then lounge on some couches and think "Bowling? Eh." Open daily from 2pm to 2am; no one under 21 admitted after 9pm.

Gold Coast Hotel, 4000 W. Flamingo Rd. (at Valley View; © 702/367-7111), has a 72-lane bowling center open 24 hours a day.

The **Orleans,** 4500 W. Tropicana Ave. (© 702/365-7111), has 70 lanes, a pro shop, lockers, meeting rooms, and more. Open 24 hours.

Out on the east side of town, you'll find 56 lanes at **Sam's Town,** 5111 Boulder Hwy. (© 702/456-7777), plus a snack shop, cocktail lounge, video arcade, day-care center, pro shop, and more. Open daily 24 hours.

In 2005, **Sunset Station,** 1301 W. Sunset Rd. in Henderson (© 702/547-7777), added a high-tech 72-lane facility called Strike Zone. It's got all the latest automated scoring gizmos, giant video screens, a full bar, a snack shop, a pro shop, a video arcade, and more.

Up north at **Santa Fe Station,** 4949 N. Rancho Rd. (© 702/658-4900), you'll find a newly remodeled (as of 2005) 60-lane alley with the most modern scoring equipment, all new furnishings, a fun and funky bar, a small cafe, and much more.

Just down the road is sister hotel **Texas Station,** 2101 Texas Star Lane (© 702/631-8128), with a 60-lane alley, video arcade, billiards, snack bar and lounge, and more. They are open 24 hours.

Suncoast, 9090 Alta Dr., in Summerlin (© 702/636-7111), offers one of the newer facilities in town, with 64 lanes divided by a unique center aisle. The high-tech center with touch-screen scoring has become a regular stop on the Pro Bowlers tours. Open daily 24 hours.

HORSEBACK RIDING   Cowboy Trail Rides ⚜ (© 702/387-2457; www.cowboytrailrides.com) offers a variety of rides on trails in Red Rock Canyon and on Mt. Charleston (at the 12-mile marker), ranging in price from $69 to $389. The high end is for a

Tips Desert Hiking Advice

Except in summer, when temperatures can reach 120°F (49°C) in the shade, the Las Vegas area is great for hiking. The best hiking season is November to March. Great locales include the incredibly scenic Red Rock Canyon and Valley of Fire State Park (see chapter 8 for details on both).

Hiking in the desert is exceptionally rewarding, but it can be dangerous. Here are some safety tips:

1. Don't hike alone.
2. Carry plenty of water and drink it often. Don't assume that spring water is safe to drink. A gallon of water per person per day is recommended for hikers.
3. Be alert for signs of heat exhaustion (headache; nausea; dizziness; fatigue; and cool, damp, pale, or red skin).
4. Gauge your fitness accurately. Desert hiking may involve rough or steep terrain. Don't take on more than you can handle.
5. Check weather forecasts before starting out. Thunderstorms can turn into raging flash floods, which are extremely hazardous to hikers.
6. Dress properly. Wear sturdy walking shoes for rock scrambling, long pants (to protect yourself from rocks and cactuses), a hat, sunscreen, and sunglasses.
7. Carry a small first-aid kit.
8. Be careful when climbing on sandstone, which can be surprisingly soft and crumbly.
9. Don't feed or play with animals, such as the wild burros in Red Rock Canyon. (It's actually illegal to approach them.)
10. Be alert for snakes and insects. Though they're rarely encountered, you'll want to look into a crevice before putting your hand into it.
11. Visit park or other information offices before you start out and acquaint yourself with rules and regulations and any possible hazards. It's also a good idea to tell the staff where you're going, when you'll return, how many are in your party, and so on. Some park offices offer hiker registration programs.
12. Follow the hiker's rule of thumb: Take only photographs and leave only footprints.

Red Rock Canyon ride beginning at sundown and going high up in the mountains. It's about 5 hours, and is for the more experienced, high stamina rider. We prefer the 2 hour sunset ride through Red Rock with the canyon providing a glorious backdrop for the end of the day. Riders then return to camp for a barbecue dinner (including a 16-oz. T-bone steak), joined by the cowboys for singalongs and marshmallow roasting.

Riding stables at **Bonnie Springs Ranch** (© 702/875-4191; www.bonniesprings.com/ranch.html) also offer guided trail rides daily. Rates are $45 per person for a 1-hour ride and go up to $150 for a 4-hour adventure with breakfast. Prices do vary on the season, and inclement weather makes rides impractical, so be sure to call ahead.

ROCK CLIMBING   Red Rock Canyon ✦✦✦, just 19 miles west of Las Vegas, is one of the world's most popular rock-climbing areas. In addition to awe-inspiring natural beauty, it offers everything from boulders to big walls. If you'd like to join the bighorn sheep, Red Rock has more than 1,000 routes to inaugurate beginners and challenge accomplished climbers. Experienced climbers can contact the **visitor center** (© 702/515-5350; www.nv.blm.gov/redrockcanyon) for information.

TENNIS   Tennis buffs should choose one of the many hotels in town that have tennis courts.

Bally's ✦✦ (© 702/739-4111) has eight night-lit hard courts. Fees per hour start at $10 for guests and $15 for non-guests. Facilities include a pro shop. Hours vary seasonally. Reservations are advised.

The Flamingo Las Vegas ✦✦ (© 702/733-3444) has four outdoor hard courts (all lit for night play) and a pro shop. It's open to the public daily from 7am to 7pm. Rates are $12 per hour for guests, $20 for non-guests. Lessons are available. Reservations are required.

6

Shopping

Where you rank shopping in Vegas will depend on your own personal philosophy toward shopping. If shopping is its own excuse for being, then you ought to find this a sublime experience. In addition to four major malls, plus three outlet centers, every hotel has its own shopping arcade, including three (The Forum Shops at Caesars, the Grand Canal Shoppes at The Venetian and Miracle Mile at Planet Hollywood) that are possibly things of great beauty and certainly joys forever, provided that you don't want much in the way of quaint, original stores.

Because, dropping the Keats references for the moment, while Vegas has at least one representative of every major name-brand store you can think of (don't just start and stop with Gap and Victoria's Secret; go to Sur La Table and Tiffany & Co.), what it does not have is much of anything that would distinguish shopping here from shopping in, say, Miami, or even Duluth. Sure, everything you could want, from Chanel to Cost Plus, is somewhere within a 5-mile radius, so if all you want to do is drop some change, or kill some time in between conferences or while other members of your family are whooping it up in a casino, you're in luck. But there is probably nothing here you can't get at home, with perhaps the exception of the high-end stores found in some of the hotel arcades.

You might consider driving **Maryland Parkway,** which runs parallel to the Strip on the east and has just about everything: Target, Toys "R" Us, major department stores, drugstores, some alternative-culture stores (tattoo parlors and hip clothing stores), and so forth. It goes on for blocks.

1 The Malls

You aren't going to find any surprises in any of the following malls—name brands and chain stores rule the day—but some are better in terms of ambience and location.

The Boulevard ⋒   This is the second-largest mall in Las Vegas—Fashion Show on the Strip has it beat. Its 150-plus stores and restaurants are arranged in arcade fashion on a single floor—read: strictly formula mall layout—occupying 1.2 million square feet. Geared to the average consumer, it has anchors like Sears, JCPenney, Macy's, Dillard's, and Marshalls. There's free valet parking. Open Monday through Saturday from 10am to 9pm and Sunday from 11am to 6pm. 3528 S. Maryland Pkwy. (btw. Twain Ave. and Desert Inn Rd.). ℂ **702/732-8949**. www.blvdmall.com.

Fashion Show 𝒜𝒜   This luxurious and centrally located mall, the city's largest, is bigger than ever, thanks to a $300-million expansion that added the city's first Nordstrom and a Bloomingdale's, in addition to Neiman Marcus, Saks Fifth Avenue, and Macy's. It also added a weird spaceship-shaped doohickey on top, and a block-long LED screen, neither of which adds to our shopping experience, but even a mall in Vegas has to have a visual and electronic gimmick, apparently. It's well-located for visitors since it's the only real mall on the Strip, and it's a nicely posh-feeling one. Valet parking is available, and you can even arrange to have your car hand-washed while you shop. Open Monday through Friday from 10am to 9pm, Saturday from 10am to 8pm, and Sunday from 11am until 6pm. 3200 Las Vegas Blvd. S. (at the corner of Spring Mountain Rd.). ℂ **702/784-7000**. www.thefashion show.com.

Galleria at Sunset 𝒜   This is the farthest-away mall of the bunch (9 miles southeast of Downtown Las Vegas, in Henderson) but the most aesthetically pleasing, a 1-million-square-foot Southwestern-themed shopping center, with topiary animals adding a sweet touch to the food court. Anchored by Dillard's, JCPenney, Mervyn's, and Robinsons-May, the Galleria's 140 emporia include branches of Gap/Gap Kids/Baby Gap, Limited Too, Ann Taylor, bebe, Caché, Lane Bryant, Victoria's Secret, The Body Shop, B. Dalton, and Sam Goody. Open Monday through Saturday from 10am to 9pm and Sunday from 11am to 7pm. In nearby Henderson, 1300 W. Sunset Rd. (at Stephanie St., just off I-515). ℂ **702/434-0202**. www.galleriaatsunset.com.

Meadows Mall 𝒜   Another immense mall, this one has more than 144 shops, services, and eateries, anchored by four department stores: Macy's, Dillard's, Sears, and JCPenney. Fountains and trees enhance Meadows Mall's ultramodern, high-ceilinged interior, and there are a few comfortable conversation/seating areas for resting your feet a moment. Meadows Mall is open Monday through Saturday from 10am to 9pm and Sunday from 10am to 6pm. 4300 Meadows Lane (at the intersection of Valley View and U.S. 95). ℂ **702/878-3331**. www. meadowsmall.com.

2 Outlet Centers

To reach the Las Vegas Outlet Center, you can drive or take the double-decker Deuce bus from anywhere on the Strip or Downtown Las Vegas all the way to the shopping center.

Fashion Outlets Las Vegas ⊀⊀⊀ Dedicated bargain hunters may want to make the roughly 40-minute drive along I-15 (there's also a $15 shuttle from New York–New York or MGM Grand, though note that MGM just sold the hotels next to the outlet and this shuttle service may disappear) to this big outlet complex, right on the border of California and Nevada. On your left is a large factory outlet with some designer names prominent enough to make that drive well worthwhile—Kenneth Cole, Gap, Banana Republic, Old Navy, even a rare Williams-Sonoma, among several others. Why so far out of town? Our guess is because all these designers have full-price boutiques in various hotels, and they don't want you ignoring those in favor of discounted items. Open daily from 10am to 8pm. 32100 Las Vegas Blvd. S. ☎ **888/424-6898.** www.fashionoutletlasvegas.com.

Las Vegas Outlet Center Formerly Belz Outlet Center, this massive complex houses more than 150 air-conditioned outlets, including a few dozen clothing stores and shoe stores. It offers a range of merchandise, but even given our understanding of the hit-and-miss nature of outlets, we've never bought a thing here and feel nothing but apathy for the center. Among other stores (which you will perhaps find less disappointing than we have), you'll find Liz Claiborne, Perry Ellis, Calvin Klein, Levi's, Nike, dressbarn, Oshkosh B'Gosh, Carter's, Reebok, Jockey, Springmaid, Danskin, Van Heusen, Tommy Hilfiger, Royal Doulton, Waterford, Black & Decker, and Geoffrey Beene. There is also a carousel and a food court. Open Monday through Saturday from 10am to 9pm, Sunday from 10am to 8pm. 7400 Las Vegas Blvd. S. (at Warm Springs Rd.). ☎ **702/896-5599.** www.premium outlets.com.

Las Vegas Premium Outlets We had such high hopes for this, the most conveniently located, and largest, outlet mall in Vegas. We can say that it looks nice, in that pretty outdoor-mall kind of way. But the key here is "outdoor." It's fine on a regular day, but on a hot Vegas day—and there are plenty of those—this is an open oven of misery. They should put a roof over the thing or at least install a whole bunch of misters. You'll roast away while shopping among disappointingly dull stores, some of which are "outlets" only because they aren't in regular malls. Maybe we are just feeling bitter about that pair of Bass shoes that were half a size too small. Or that we can't quite fit into the Dolce & Gabbana sample sizes. Still, bring a lot of water if you go during the summer. Stores include Armani, Bernini, Brooks Brothers, Calvin Klein, Coach, Crabtree & Evelyn, Kenneth Cole, Lacoste, Nike, Perry Ellis, Ralph Lauren, Quiksilver, Samsonite, Timberland, Tommy Hilfiger, Wilson's Leather, and Zales. **Warning:** Parking here is often a nightmare. Consider taking a cab. Open Monday through Saturday from 10am to 9pm, Sunday from 10am to 8pm. 875 S. Grand Central Pkwy. (at I-15). © **702/474-7500.** www. premiumoutlets.com.

3 Hotel Shopping Arcades

Just about every Las Vegas hotel offers some shopping opportunities. The following have the most extensive arcades. The physical spaces of these shopping arcades are always open, but individual stores keep unpredictable hours.

Note: The Forum Shops at Caesars, The Grand Canal Shoppes at The Venetian, and Desert Passage at Planet Hollywood—as much sightseeing attractions as shopping arcades—are in the must-see category.

BALLY'S   Bally's **Avenue Shoppes** number around 20 emporia offering, you know, stuff. In addition, there are several gift shops, art galleries, and a pool-wear shop. A recent addition of a walkway to neighbor Paris Las Vegas features more stores and restaurants.

BELLAGIO ✩✩   **Via Bellagio** is where the high rollers go to spend their winnings or, at least, send their bored partners to amuse themselves during marathon gambling sessions. It's a veritable roll call of glossy magazine ads: Armani, Prada, Chanel, Tiffany, Hermès, Fred Leighton, Gucci, Dior, and Yves Saint Laurent. That's about it. You need anything else? Well, yes—money. We can't even afford the oxygen in these places. (Actually, we've discovered affordable, good-taste items in every store here, from a Tiffany's $30 silver key chain

---

Impressions

Tip Number 3: Win a bunch of money. I can't recommend this too highly. If it hasn't occurred to you, win $1,200 and see for yourself. It's very energizing and really adds to your Vegas fun.

—Merrill Markoe, *Viva Las Wine Goddesses!*

to a $100 Prada business card holder.) A nice touch is a parking lot by the far entrance to Via Bellagio, so you need not navigate the great distance from Bellagio's main parking structure, but can simply pop in and pick yourself up a little something.

CAESARS PALACE *★★★*   Until they got competition from The Venetian and Planet Hollywood, **The Forum Shops** were the pinnacle of silly shopping in Vegas, a 375,000-square-foot Rodeo-Drive-meets-the-Roman-Empire affair complete with a three-story courtyard entryway with its own circular escalator (has to be seen to be believed). Its architecture and sculpture span a period from 300 B.C. to A.D. 1700, so you get all your Italian ancient cityscape clichés. Then there is the Festival Fountain, where a scary-looking, tipsy Bacchus and some toga-clad Roman god and goddess pals come to animatronic life for 7 minutes once an hour, not that you can understand a word they say apart from vague urgings toward "revel." Which is just a fancy Roman-god way of saying "spend," and you can do that nicely.

In case that's not enough, there's the Roman Hall extension, which has for a centerpiece a 50,000-gallon circular aquarium and another fountain that also comes to life with a show of fire (don't stand too close—it gets really hot), dancing waters, and animatronic figures as the mythical continent of Atlantis rises and falls every hour. The production values are much higher than those of the Bacchus extravaganza, but it takes itself more seriously, so the giggle factor remains. It's in the multistoried extension, one that tries to move past "kitsch" and into "classy rich person's shopping experience"— though any sort of movement, literal or metaphoric, is tricky, what with all the giant marbled pillars, statues, and fountains, plus an atrium that actually admits sunlight. So with all the gawking opportunities it may be easy to forget that there are actually stores here where you can shop and buy things. Tenants are mostly of the exclusive variety although there are a few more Average Joe kind of stores (yes, of course there's a Gap). Some samples: Louis Vuitton, Bernini, Christian Dior, Christian Lacroix (sweetie darling), A/X Armani Exchange, Agent Provocateur, bebe, Gucci, Ann Taylor, Gianni Versace, Harry Winston, Brooks Brothers, Juicy Couture, Taryn Rose, a branch of the famed barbershop to the Royal Family Truefitt & Hill, a Playboy store, Kiehl's cosmetics, MAC, Vosges Haut-Chocolat, and many other clothing, shoe, and jewelry stores, a few of which get us more excited than the usual Vegas shopping experience, because they are stores with more limited availability. Most shops are open

Sunday to Thursday 10am to 11pm, Friday and Saturday 10am to midnight.

CIRCUS CIRCUS The shopping promenade here is adjacent to Adventuredome, so if your kids are old enough to be left in the theme park, you can browse through about a dozen shops, offering a selection of gifts and sundries, plus a newer shopping arcade themed as a European village, with cobblestone walkways and fake woods and so forth, decorated with replicas of vintage circus posters.

ESPLANADE AT WYNN LAS VEGAS Along the same rarified lines of the Bellagio shopping area, in that it's a Euro-style-esque (love those Vegas qualifiers!) shopping street lined with pricey places with famous names—Chanel, Cartier, Dior, Judith Leiber, Jean Paul Gaultier, Manolo Blahnik, Oscar de la Renta, La Flirt (a sort of mini-Sephora), Chocolat (excellent pastries and gourmet chocolates), and Jo Malone. We prefer it some to the one at Bellagio because it seems like it has just enough shops (like La Flirt) that nearly reach an average person's budget.

EXCALIBUR The shops of **The Realm** for the most part reflect the hotel's medieval theme. Dragon's Lair, for example, features items ranging from pewter swords and shields to full suits of armor, and Merlin's Mystic Shop carries crystals, luck charms, and gargoyles. Other shops carry more conventional wares—gifts, candy, jewelry, women's clothing, and Excalibur logo items. At Fantasy Faire, you can have your photo taken in Renaissance attire. And most importantly, there is a branch of that royal staple—Krispy Kreme!

HARRAH'S ✿ Harrah's **Carnaval Court** shopping center is the only outdoor shopping mall on the Strip, and it's a surprisingly pleasant place to browse through. Among the store highlights is a Ghirardelli Chocolate store, a branch of the famous San Francisco–based chocolate company. This store is remarkably like a smaller version of the one in SF (alas, without the vats of liquid chocolate being mixed up), and in addition to candy, you can get a variety of delicious sundaes and other ice-cream treats.

MONTE CARLO A cobblestone arcade of retail shops, the **Street of Dreams** includes several upscale clothing, timepiece, eyewear, and gift boutiques, plus a Lance Burton magic shop.

PLANET HOLLYWOOD ✿✿✿ Once the former **Desert Passage** of the Aladdin, a visually appealing rendition of the "come with me to the Casbah" architectural styles of northern Africa and Turkey, and once a fine example of the Vegas "shopping as amusement park" experience, it's now been transformed (in stages that may not be done by the time you read this) into an even gaudier, even glitzier, even less thematically coherent shopping "experience" called the "Miracle Mile." What? Think Fifth Avenue, except indoors. With big screens and other noisy electronics running continuous promos, and an entrance designed after that bastion of quiet good taste, Times Square. We're bitter, because we liked the previous incarnation so much. We are consoled because many of the stores will remain the same, plus a few new ones, like a branch of H&M.

RIO The 60,000-square-foot, two-story **Masquerade Village** is a nicely executed shopping arcade at Rio. It's done as a European village and features a wide variety of shops.

THE VENETIAN 🐧🐧 After you've shopped Ancient Rome at Caesars, come to **The Grand Canal Shoppes** and see if shopping in Renaissance-era (more or less) Venice is any different. Certainly the production values stay high; this is a re-created Italian village, complete with a painted, cloud-studded blue sky overhead, and a canal right down the center on which gondoliers float and sing. Pay them ($15), and you can take a lazy float down and back, serenaded by your boatman (actors hired especially for this purpose and with accents perfect enough to fool Roberto Benigni). As you pass by, under and over bridges, flower girls will serenade you and courtesans will flirt with you, and you may have an encounter with a famous Venetian or two, as Marco Polo discusses his travels and Casanova exerts his famous charm. The stroll (or float) ends at a miniature (though not by all that much) version of St. Mark's Square, the central landmark of Venice. Here, you'll find opera singers, strolling musicians, glass blowers, and other bustling marketplace activity. It's all most ambitious and beats the heck out of animatronic statues.

The Shoppes are accessible directly from outside via a grand staircase whose ceiling features more of those impressive hand-painted art reproductions. It's quite smashing.

Oh, the shops themselves? The usual high- and medium-end brand names: Jimmy Choo, Mikimoto, Movado, Davidoff, Kenneth Cole, Ann Taylor, BCBG, bebe, and more, plus Venetian glass and paper shops. Madame Tussauds (p. 119) is also located here, and so is the Canyon Ranch SpaClub.

And if that's not enough, sister shops at the Palazzo adjoining include a massive Barney's New York (the designer department store dear to the heart of many a fashionista), plus Christian Louboutin, Bottega Veneta, Chloe and more.

The shops are open Sunday through Thursday from 10am to 11pm, Friday and Saturday from 10am to midnight.

4 Vintage Clothing

The Attic ℛ   The former star of a Visa commercial, this store offers plenty of clothing choices on many racks. During a recent visit, a man came in asking for a poodle skirt for his 8-year-old. They had one. Open Monday through Thursday from 10am until 5pm, Friday from 10am until 6pm, Saturday from 11am until 6pm, and closed Sunday. 1018 S. Main St. ℂ **702/388-4088.** www.theatticlasvegas.com.

Buffalo Exchange ℛ   This is actually a branch of a chain of stores spread out across the western United States. Don't let the chain part worry you—this merchandise doesn't feel processed. Staffed by plenty of incredibly hip alt-culture kids (ask them what's happening in town during your visit), it is stuffed with dresses, shirts, pants, and so forth. As with any vintage shop, the contents are hit or miss. You can easily go in one day and come out with 12 fabulous new outfits, and go in another and come up dry. But it's still probably the most reliable of the local vintage shops. The store is open Monday through Saturday from 10am to 8pm and Sunday from 11am until 7pm. 4110 S. Maryland Pkwy. (at Flamingo Rd.). ℂ **702/791-3960.** www.buffalo exchange.com.

5 Souvenirs

Now, you'd think Vegas would be *the* place for kitschy souvenirs— the town itself is such a bastion of good taste, after all. But alas, even by generous standards, most of the crap sold is, well, crap. But there are a few places for some of your snow globe and fuzzy dice needs.

The **Arts Factory Complex** ℛℛℛ, 103 E. Charleston Blvd. (ℂ **702/382-3886**), has a gift shop full of pink flamingos (well, maybe not so many of those now that the pink flamingo factory has closed) and Vegas-specific items. There should be something here for every camp fancy.

If you prefer your souvenirs to be less deliberately iconic, head over to the **Bonanza Gift and Souvenir Shop** ℛℛ, 2460 Las Vegas Blvd. S. (ℂ **702/384-0005**). We looked, and we felt the tackiest item available was the pair of earrings made out of poker chips. Though we really liked the bracelets made out of dice.

For reverent camp, encrusted with sequins, do take a peek at the **Liberace Museum gift store** ✶✶, 1775 E. Tropicana Ave. (① **702/ 798-5595**). Encourage them to get even more out there (don't you think they should add Liberace mouse pads and screensavers?).

If you like your souvenirs with more style (spoilsports), **Cirque du Soleil's *O*** has a gift shop in the Bellagio, 3600 Las Vegas Blvd. S. (① **702/693-7444**), with Cirque-specific articles, but also fanciful pottery, masks, and other curiosities.

For mixed emotions, little can beat items emblazoned with vintage images of bomb tests and other glories to the good old days of atomic blasts, at the **Atomic Testing Museum gift store** ✶✶, 755 E. Flamingo Rd. (① **702/794-5161**).

6 Candy

M&M World ✶✶ *(Kids)* Everybody needs one vice, and for us, it's chocolate, by gosh. Its lure is so powerful, it overwhelms our usual snooty stance against anything even remotely resembling a tourist trap and leads us right to M&M World. What can one do when faced with a wall of M&Ms in colors never before seen by man (silver! hot pink! turquoise!)? Overpriced? But of course! Who cares? There are doodads galore, replete with the M&M logo, and a surprisingly enjoyable short film and comedy routine, ostensibly about the "history" of the candy but really just a cute little adventure with a decent budget behind it. Open Sunday through Thursday from 9am until 11pm, Friday and Saturday from 9am to midnight. In the Showcase Mall, 3785 Las Vegas Blvd. S. (just north of the MGM Grand). ① **702/ 736-7611**.

7 Antiques

Curiously, the one area where Vegas breaks out of the chain-store minimall mode is with antiques shops. There are quite a few—two dozen—of consistent quality and price, nearly all located within a few blocks of each other. We have one friend, someone who takes interior design very seriously, who comes straight to Vegas for most of her best finds (you should see her antique chandelier collection!). And we treasure our Charles and Diana wedding tea-cup-and-saucer set, purchased for next to nothing along this very street.

To get there, start in the middle of the **1600 block of East Charleston Boulevard** and keep driving east. The little stores, nearly all in old houses dating from the '30s, line each side of the street. Or you can stop in at **Silver Horse Antiques,** 1651 E.

Charleston Blvd. (© **702/385-2700**), and pick up a map to almost all the locations, with phone numbers and hours of operation.

Antiques at the Market   A newer antiques minimall (for lack of a better phrase) with a number of individuals operating stalls under one roof. Open Monday through Saturday from 10am to 6pm, Sunday from noon to 5pm. 6665 S. Eastern Ave. (btw. Sunset and Warm Springs roads). © 702/307-3960.

Antique Square 😘   A cruddy-looking collection of stores in several remodeled houses arranged in a square. But every good antiques shopper knows that these kinds of crammed junk stores are the place to find real treasures and to do real antiques hunting (because once they've been really picked through and prettily displayed by pros, you can kiss bargains and real finds goodbye). Individual store hours vary, but most are closed on Sunday and Monday. 2014–2034 E. Charleston Blvd. (at Eastern Ave.). © 702/471-6500.

Red Rooster Antique Mall   A minimall of sorts, only with "antiques" instead of a 7-Eleven and a nail salon. The place is older and battered, but features individual stalls selling all categories of stuff, from junk to treasures. Individual store hours vary, but most are open Monday through Saturday 10am to 6pm, Sunday from 11am to 5pm. 1109 Western Ave. (at Charleston and I-15). © 702/382-5253.

8 Wigs

Serge's Showgirl Wigs 😘   Oh, you probably thought all those showgirls just naturally had bountiful thick manes. Sorry to burst your bubble. If you have a desire to look like a showgirl yourself (and why not?), come to Serge's, which for more than 23 years has been supplying Vegas's wiggy needs, with more than 2,000 wigs to choose from. Wigs range in price from $130 to over $1,500, depending on quality and realness, and you can pick from Dolly Parton's wig line or get something custom-made. They also make hairpieces and toupees, and carry hair-care products. Open Monday through Saturday from 10am until 5:30pm.

And, if the prices at Serge's are too rich to bring your fantasy alive, right across the way is **Serge's Showgirl Wigs outlet,** with prices running from a more reasonable $60 to $70. 953 E. Sahara Ave., no. A-2. © 800/947-9447 or 702/732-1015. www.showgirlwigs.com.

7

Las Vegas After Dark

If there is anything Vegas has as much of as gambling, it's nightlife. You wouldn't be the first to make your visit entirely nocturnal. Every hotel has several bars and several free lounges with live music, plus a club or two. Elsewhere in the city are more bars, more clubs, plus strip joints, coffeehouses, and more. On top of that, Vegas is booming once again as a legitimate stop for concert acts and also has its own showy spectaculars and special theater productions.

Naturally, much of this will cost you, and naturally, we have ways of getting around that. While the production shows are comped freely to the high rollers who court Lady Luck at the slots and tables, you'll need to look instead at those free magazines (*What's On* and *Show Biz*) in your hotel room for discount coupons. Note that there are a few afternoon shows that are considerably cheaper than the nighttime events. Hotel bars can be more expensive than independent operators, but you can drink for free if you stand at a slot machine or sit in the keno lounge, pretending to play, until a cocktail waitress comes around, as drinks are free for gamblers. (Waitresses ought to make sure you are gambling before offering, but they almost never do.) Club admission tends to be free for Nevada residents, so try talking up people standing in lines with you, and see if they are from the state, and if so, if they are willing to pretend you are with them.

Several things to keep in mind: While Vegas is fairly casual, many of the dance clubs have dress codes, which basically means no jeans or sneakers or anything that makes you look like a gangster. Bar and club life doesn't kick in until quite late, when all the local restaurant staff and showgirls get off work. (Seriously, places can be dead at 10:30pm and unbelievably crowded at midnight—and stay that way until the wee, wee hours, thanks to the backward work schedules of a large portion of Young Vegas.) Also remember that a recently enacted smoking ban in Vegas prohibits smoking in bars that serve food. For more information, see p. 196.

To find out who'll be performing during your stay and for up-to-date listings of shows (prices change, shows close), you can call the various hotels, using their toll-free numbers. Or call the **Las Vegas Convention and Visitors Authority** (© 877/VISIT-LV [847-4858] or 702/892-0711) and ask them to send you free copies of *Showguide* or *What's On in Las Vegas* (one or both of which will probably be in your hotel room). You can also check out what's playing at **www.visit lasvegas.com**. It's best to plan well ahead if you have your heart set on seeing one of the most popular shows or catching a major headliner.

The hotel entertainment options described in this chapter include information on ticket prices, what's included in that price (drinks, dinner, taxes, and/or gratuities), showroom policies, and reservations. Whenever possible, reserve in advance, especially for shows on weekends and holidays. If the showroom has **maitre d' seating** (as opposed to preassigned seats), you may want to tip him to upgrade your seat. A tip of $15 to $20 per couple will usually do the trick at a major show, less at a small showroom. An alternative to tipping the maitre d' is to wait until the captain shows you to your seat. Perhaps it will be adequate, in which case you've saved some money. If not, you can offer the captain a tip for a better seat. If you do plan to tip, have the money ready; maitres d' and captains tend to get annoyed if you fumble around for it. You can also tip with casino chips (from the hotel casino where the show is taking place only) in lieu of cash. Whatever you tip, the proper etiquette is to do it rather subtly—a kind of palm-to-palm action. There's really no reason for this since everyone knows what's going on, but being blatant is in poor taste. Arrive early at maitre d' shows to get the best choice of seats.

If you buy tickets for an assigned-seat show in person, you can look over a seating chart. Avoid sitting right up by the stage if possible, especially for big production shows. Dance numbers are better viewed from the middle of the theater. With headliners, you might like to sit up close.

Note: All these caveats and instructions aside, most showrooms offer good visibility from just about every seat.

If you prefer rock or alternative music, your choices used to be limited, but that's changed. More of these bands are coming to town, attracted to the House of Blues and the Hard Rock Hotel's the Joint, which means you can actually see the likes of Marilyn Manson and Beck in Vegas. Check out the listings in this chapter for bars and coffeehouses, several of which offer live alternative or blues music. If you want to know what's playing during your stay, consult *Las Vegas Weekly,* with great club and bar descriptions in its listings. You can pick it up at restaurants, bars, music stores, and hip retail stores. If you're looking for good alt-culture tips, try asking the staff at the **Buffalo Exchange** vintage clothing store ((C) **702/791-3960;** p. 146); they have their fingers right on the pulse of the underground.

In addition to the listings below, consider the **Fremont Street Experience,** described on p. 113.

1 The Major Production Shows

The shows in Vegas are as glitzy and over-the-top as ever, but with a few exceptions, they aren't worth the ever-climbing ticket prices. We aren't talking Broadway caliber here, but there are some exceptions. Most of the Cirque du Soleil acts and the Blue Man Group can hold their own with the best. Three icons are in rotation doing very special shows at Caesar's: Bette Midler, Cher, and Elton John. Barry Manilow thrills his fanilows with his regular Las Vegas Hilton stint. Speaking of Broadway, in 2009, the much-lauded *Lion King* will be starting a residency at Mandalay Bay.

But for the most part, your money is better spent elsewhere, perhaps on a name act in town for a brief stand. Otherwise, the hotel shows are just heavily sequined versions of the classic vaudeville revue: a little song (lip-synced), a little dance (not going to knock your socks off), a little seltzer down the pants, if the pants are even there to begin with. Plus some magic acts.

Note: Although every effort has been made to keep up with the volatile Las Vegas show scene, keep in mind that the following reviews may not be indicative of the actual show you'll see, but the basic concept and idea will be the same. What's more, the show itself may have closed, so it's a good idea to call the venue and check.

Tips Our Favorites

Our vote for **best show?** It's a tossup between *KÀ* at MGM Grand, *O* at Bellagio, and *Mystère* at Treasure Island, all by Cirque du Soleil. Any must be seen to be believed—and even then you may not believe it, but you won't be forgetting the experience anytime soon. The **smartest show in town** is Penn & Teller at the Rio. The only reason we don't call it the **best magic show** is so that we can acknowledge the delightful Lance Burton at Monte Carlo. **Best classic Vegas topless revue** is *Jubilee!* at Bally's. **Best we-aren't-sure-what-the-heck-to-call-it** is Blue Man Group at The Venetian. **Best for the whole family** will be *The Lion King* at Mandalay Bay.

American Superstars *(Kids)*   One of a number of celebrity impersonator shows (well, it's cheaper than getting the real headliners), *American Superstars* is one of the few where said impersonators actually sing live. Five performers do their thing; the celebs impersonated vary, depending on the evening.

A typical Friday night would feature Britney, Christina, and Ricky Martin, not to mention staples like Madonna, Michael Jackson, and Diana Ross. The performers won't be putting the originals out of work anytime soon, but they aren't bad. Actually, they were closer in voice than in looks to the celebs in question (half the black performers were played by white actors), which is an unusual switch for Vegas impersonators. In the Stratosphere Casino Hotel & Tower, 2000 Las Vegas Blvd. S. ✆ 800/99-TOWER [99-86937] or 702/380-7711. www.stratospherehotel. com. Tickets $42 adults, $31 children 5–12 (including tax and handling fee); dinner and show packages available. Wed and Fri–Sat 6:30 and 8:30pm; Sun–Tues 7pm.

Bette Midler *★★★*   The Divine Miss M has brought her delicious self to a 2-year-plus residency in Caesars, taking over Céline Dion's remarkable run. Midler's bawdy jokes and belting vocals belie her 60-something age, as she delivers a classic *show*. You know, singing, dancing, joke telling, charisma, not to mention mermaid costumes and Sophie Tucker homages. Ticket prices are high for the good seats, to be sure, but the dame delivers; her voice and her stage presence are as strong as ever. This is Vegas entertainment as it was—a great performer doing what they do best, no gimmicks—unless you count those wheelchair dancing mermaids—and the only magic the kind that a great performer knows how to deliver, night after night. There will be 100 shows throughout the year, usually in 4-week blocks, Tuesday, Wednesday, and Friday through Sunday at 8pm. In Caesars Palace, 3570 Las Vegas Blvd. S. ✆ 877/7BETTEM [723-8836], or through www. ticketmaster.com. Tickets $95–$250 (plus booking fee).

Blue Man Group *★★★*   Are they blue? Indeed they are—three hairless, nonspeaking men dipped in azure paint, doing decidedly odd stunts with marshmallows, art supplies, audience members, tons of paper, and an amazing array of percussion instruments fashioned fancifully from PVC pipe. If that doesn't sound very Vegas, well, it's not. It's the latest franchise of a New York–originated performance-art troupe that seems to have slipped into town through a side door opened by Cirque du Soleil's groundbreaking successes. Don't get the wrong idea; this is no Cirque clone. There are no acrobatics or flowing choreography, no attempt to create an alternate universe, just a series of unconnected bits. But even if the whole is no greater than the sum of the parts, the parts are pretty great themselves. It's funny in the weirdest and most unexpected ways, and the crowd is usually roaring by the end. Fans of typical Vegas shows may leave scratching their heads, but we are glad there is another color in the Vegas entertainment spectrum. In The Venetian, 3355 Las Vegas Blvd. S. © 877/833-6423. www.venetian.com. Tickets $85–$140 plus tax and service fees. Nightly at 7:30pm with an additional 10:30pm show on Saturdays.

Cher 𝓚𝓚𝓚   Cherilyn Sarkisian has had a nice little career—the kind that gets you a headliner slot at Caesar's Palace in rotation with Elton John and Bette Midler. And the kind that gets you the ultimate status symbol of stardom, having the whole world know you on a first-name basis. That's Cher, who though at times has been dismissed as a mere "I Got You Babe" pawn of ex-hubby Sonny, a disco-era cartoon, high-profile serial romancer and anachronistic relic has time and again proven herself one of the most resilient figures in pop culture, almost on the force of her sheer will (and good sportsmanship) alone. Let's face it, she's not a great singer, can't really dance, isn't known as a songwriter or musician. Yet she's just plain likable—and

---

🄺 Family-Friendly Shows

Given the increasingly high cost of show tickets in Vegas, a family of four may have to think twice about taking the kids out for the night. And it doesn't help that Vegas is showing its preference for legal adults, with productions that are showing more and more bare skin. Even **Lance Burton** (p. 156), whose show is otherwise entirely suitable for kids, has showgirls with outfits that are rather skimpy in the back. Other than Burton, you're best off taking kids to impersonator show *American Superstars* (p. 152), which offers a children's price ticket, and the afternoon magic show **Mac King** (p. 160). Artistic kids will love either *KÀ* (p. 155), *Mystère* (p. 157), or *O* (p. 158), but wait until they're at least 8 years old because of the pacing and surreal imagery. And while grown-ups may roll their eyes, kids do adore the clash and clang of the knightly battles waged at the *Tournament of Kings* (p. 160); teens may like it, too, but be way too cool to admit it. And *The Lion King* (to open at Mandalay Bay) is an eye-popping spectacle that is sophisticated enough to please adults as well as kids.

knows how to make the most of her personality, sense of (often self-effacing) humor, and talents. Having her name on dozens of hits, one of the '70s top TV variety shows and a 1988 best actress Academy Award for her "Moonstruck" role are not things to sneeze at. Oh, and no one wears Bob Mackie gowns like she does! So can she excel with her own Vegas show? Just say the title of one of her signature comeback hits. No, not "Half Breed"! We mean "Believe." Tues, Wed, Sat, Sun at 7:30pm. In Caesars Palace. 3570 Las Vegas Blvd. S. © 866/510-2437. Tickets $95–$250 plus tax.

Criss Angel: *Believe with Cirque de Soleil* This recently opened collaboration between charismatic Angel and the always eye-catching Cirque got notices so atrocious there must be some doubt about the future of this production (its 10-year contract not withstanding). While "plot" may be too strong a word to associate with a Cirque production, this promised a narrative of sorts, probably paying dreamlike homage to Angel's love of Houdini (as does the title). That proved to be optimistic. As for Angel's hypnotic fantastical illusions and escapist scenarios, loud have been the complaints about their poor quality. At least Cirque's own surreal human-generated special effects remain thrilling. Fri–Tues 7pm and 10pm. In the Luxor, 3900 Las Vegas Blvd. S © 800/288-1000. Tickets $59–$150.

Crazy Girls *Crazy Girls,* presented in an intimate theater, is a typical example of a racy Strip revue. It features sexy showgirls with perfect bodies in erotic song-and-dance numbers enhanced by innovative lighting effects. Think of *Penthouse* poses coming to life. Perhaps one older man from Kentucky best summed it up: "It's okay if you like boobs and butt. But most of the girls can't even dance." In Riviera Hotel & Casino, 2901 Las Vegas Blvd. S. © 800/892-7469 or 702/794-9433. www.rivierahotel.com. Tickets $55–$75 (plus tax). Ages 18 and over only. Wed–Mon 9:30pm.

Danny Gans: *The Man of Many Voices* In a town where the consistent sellouts are costly, elaborate extravaganzas, it's a tribute to Danny Gans's charisma and appeal that his one-man variety act can draw the same crowds with nothing more than a backup band and a few props. Gans is "the man of many voices"—more than 400 of them—and his show features impressions of 80 different celebrities, usually a different mix each night, depending on audience demographics. He's a consistent crowd-pleaser, and the lack of bombast can be a refreshing change of pace. Wed and Fri–Sat at 8pm. In the Wynn, no ticket prices or times available at press time.

Jersey Boys Vegas ⭑⭑   Between 1962 and 1975, Frankie Valli and the Four Seasons racked up an astonishingly long string of catchy, well-crafted pop hits that are as well-known—and well-loved—as any in pop music. These time-tested songs are the central draw of the massively-popular, Tony-winning (for Best Musical) *Jersey Boys*. But this is far more than a rote musical revue, or just another re-creation of a popular oldies act. It's a real musical play, with a compelling street-to-suite storyline, a fair share of drama, and enough humor and uplift to satisfy both the theater veteran and the vacationing family (with a mild warning for some salty, Jersey-esque language). A dazzlingly visual production that crackles with energy and shines with precision stagecraft, *Jersey Boys* has already had an enthusiastic post-Broadway run. With its visual wow factor and an excitingly faithful rebirth of the Four Seasons' music, it just may be the perfect vehicle to break the theatrical Vegas jinx (which has seen other Tony winners such as *Hairspray, The Producers, Spamalot,* and *Avenue Q* slink off in defeat) and settle in for a long, flashy run. The Palazzo, 3325 Las Vegas Blvd. ✆ **866-641-SHOW [7469]. $65–$135. Mon, Thurs, Fri, Sat at 7pm, Tues and Sat at 7pm and 10pm.**

Jubilee! ⭑⭑   A classic Vegas spectacular, crammed with singing, dancing, magic, acrobats, elaborate costumes and sets, and, of course, bare breasts. It's a basic revue, with production numbers featuring homogenized versions of standards (Gershwin, Cole Porter, some Fred Astaire numbers) sometimes sung live, sometimes lip-synced, and always accompanied by lavishly costumed and frequently topless showgirls. Humorous set pieces about Samson and Delilah and the sinking of the *Titanic* (!) show off some pretty awesome sets. (They were doing the *Titanic* long before a certain movie, and recent attendees claimed the ship-sinking effect onstage here was a better production than the one in the movie.) The finale features aerodynamically impossible feathered and bejeweled costumes and headpieces designed by Bob Mackie. In Bally's Las Vegas, 3645 Las Vegas Blvd. S. ✆ **800/237-7469** or **702/739-4567. www.ballys.com. Ages 18 and over only. Tickets $68–$110. Sat–Thurs 7:30 and 10:30pm.**

KÀ ⭑⭑⭑ *Kids*   The fourth Cirque du Soleil show on the Strip is an Asian-themed affair (though its name is actually Egyptian and means "dual spirit," but we're not going to be picky about that) with an actual storyline (the plot about separated twins searching for each other is a little vague but easy enough to follow), making it perfect for those who like their entertainment a little less dadaist and a tad more literal. That's not to say that *KÀ* doesn't have the look and feel of a Cirque production. The divine artistry, technical wizardry, fabulous costumes, fast pacing, and acrobatics that are the hallmarks of Cirque du Soleil are still very much present and accounted for. But if its brethren lean more toward Fellini and Dalí, then *KÀ* is more Kabuki and kung fu. The opening two scenes, with their *Crouching Tiger, Hidden Dragon* choreography, are alone worth the steep price of admission. This show's probably the most accessible of the Cirque productions for the young set. In MGM Grand, 3799 Las Vegas Blvd. S. ℂ 877/880-0880 or 702/891-7777. www.ka.com. Ages 5 and over only. Tickets $69–$150. Fri–Tues 7:30 and 10:30pm.

Lance Burton: *Master Magician* ✸✸✸ *Kids*   Magic acts are a dime a dozen in Vegas of late. So when someone pops up who is original—not to mention charming and, yes, actually good at his job—it comes as a relief. Handsome and folksy, Burton is talented and engaging, for the most part shunning the big-ticket special effects that seem to have swamped most other shows in town. Instead, he offers an extremely appealing production that starts small, with "close-up" magic. These rather lovely tricks, he tells us, are what won him a number of prestigious magic competitions. They are truly extraordinary. (We swear that he tossed a bird up in the air, and the darned thing turned into confetti in front of our eyes. Really.) His dry, laconic, low-key delivery is plenty amusing and contrasts nicely to other performers in town, who seem as if they have been spending way too much time at Starbucks. He is joined by standout comic-juggler Michael Goudeau; the man juggles a chainsaw, a bowling ball, and a flaming torch *all at once*. In Monte Carlo Resort & Casino, 3770 Las Vegas Blvd. S. ℂ 877/386-8224 or 702/730-7160. www.montecarlo.com. Tickets $61–$73. Tues and Sat 7 and 10pm; Wed–Fri 7pm.

Le Rêve ✸   *Le Rêve,* named for the most significant of the paintings owned by Steve Wynn, is an extravaganza featuring all the usual elements: gorgeously sculpted athletic performers who twist, contort, and mostly pose in filmy tattered outfits before and after diving in and splashing out of a giant pool. Intermittently funny clowns do their thing. Magritte figures float by. Fountains rise out of the stage. The result is pure spectacle, with a slight narrative suggesting the proceedings are the dreams of a woman dealing with a turbulent romantic issue. It's like the biggest, most impressive Esther Williams production you can imagine. Speaking of which, you may wish to avoid sitting in the front rows, unless you don't mind spending 90 minutes huddling under the provided towels—not only does the in-the-round staging mean the performers routinely splash water, but

also that long, filmy costumes, when hauled out of said water and lifted high in the air, drip most impressively and most wetly on the first couple of rows. Since no seat is that far from the stage, and since the farther back, the more of the complex imagery you can take, there really isn't a bad seat, so stay back and stay dry. Monday, Thursday, and Sunday 7 and 9:30pm; Friday at 8:30pm; and Saturday at 8 and 10:30pm. In Wynn Las Vegas, 3131 Las Vegas Blvd. S. ✆ **888/320-7110**. www.wynnlasvegas.com. Ages 13 and over. Tickets $99–179.

LOVE ⚑   This is right on the edge between a Cirque success and the rare Cirque failure, and the measure of it really depends on what kind of Beatles fan you are. (We are operating under the assumption that there isn't anyone interested who isn't some level of fan—anyone who isn't won't be much drawn to this show.) If you are the sort who gets happy anytime you are within earshot of the Fab Four, you will enjoy this unfocused, lively bit of spectacle. If you are the sort of fan who finds any kind of commercialization of sacred music (regardless of official imprint by way of Sir George Martin's involvement and the stamp of approval by Paul, Ringo, Yoko, and George's widow, Olivia) repugnant, and/or is dismayed by literal representations of tunes (you can guess what happens during "Being for the Benefit of Mr. Kite"), then you might have mixed feelings. Still, the pedigree is undeniably impressive and the kids might goggle. At The Mirage, 3400 Las Vegas Blvd. S. ✆ **800/963-9637** or 702/792-7777. www.beatles. com. Tickets $94–$150. Nightly 7:30 and 10:30pm.

MGM Grand's *Crazy Horse Paris* ⚑   Further proof that Vegas is trying to distance itself from the "Vegas is for families" debacle, "classy adult entertainment" is the new watchword, with *Crazy Horse Paris* leading the pack. Allegedly the same show that has been running for years in a famous racy French nightclub, *Crazy Horse Paris* is just a bunch of girls taking their clothes off. Except that the girls are smashingly pretty, with the kind of bodies just not found on real live human beings, and they take their clothes off in curious and, yes, artistic ways: gyrating on *pointe* shoes while holding on to ropes or hoops, and falling over sofas while lip-syncing to French torch songs. In short, it's what striptease ought to be, and by gosh, if strip clubs were this well-staged, we'd go to them all the time. But at $60 a ticket, it's a great deal to pay for arty nudie fun. In MGM Grand, 3799 Las Vegas Blvd. S. ✆ **877/880-0880** or 702/891-7777. www.mgmgrand.com. Ages 18 and over only. Tickets $59. Wed–Mon 8 and 10:30pm.

Mystère ⚑⚑⚑ *Kids*   The in-house ads for Cirque du Soleil's *Mystère* (say miss-*tair*) proclaim "Words don't do it justice," and for once, that's not just hype. The show is so visual that trying to describe it is a losing proposition. And simply calling it a circus is like calling the Hope Diamond a gem or the Taj Mahal a building: It's accurate but doesn't begin to do it justice. The show features one simply unbelievable act after another (seemingly boneless contortionists and acrobats, breathtakingly beautiful aerial maneuvers), interspersed with dadaist/commedia dell'arte clowns, and everyone clad in costumes like nothing you've ever seen before.

The show is dreamlike, suspenseful, funny, erotic, mesmerizing, and just lovely. At times, you might find yourself moved to tears. For some children, however, it might be a bit too sophisticated and arty. Even if you've seen Cirque before, it's worth coming to check out, thanks to the large production values. It's a world-class show, no matter where it's playing; that this is playing in Vegas is astonishing. In TI at The Mirage, 3300 Las Vegas Blvd. S. ✆ **800/392-1999** or 702/894-7722. www.cirquedusoleil.com. Tickets $60–$95 (plus tax and service fee). Wed–Sat 7:30 and 10:30pm; Sun 4:30 and 7:30pm.

O (★★★ *Finds* *Kids*   How to describe the seemingly indescribable wonder and artistry of Cirque du Soleil's most dazzling display? An Esther Williams–Busby Berkeley spectacular on peyote? A Salvador Dalí painting come to life? A stage show by Fellini? The French troupe has topped itself with this production—and not simply because its breathtaking acrobatics are situated in, on, around, and above a 1.5-million-gallon pool (*eau*—pronounced O—is French for water). Even without those impossible feats, this might be worth the price just to see the presentation, a constantly shifting dreamscape tableau that's a marvel of imagination and staging. If you've never seen a Cirque show, prepare to have your brain turned inside out. We know—those ticket prices—*ouch*. We want to say that we can guarantee it's worth it, but that's a decision only you can make. We can say this: Watch this show, and you'll know where a good chunk of your money is going (in other words, they spend a bundle nightly to mount this thing). Note that no tank tops, shorts, or sneakers are allowed. In Bellagio, 3600 Las Vegas Blvd. S. ✆ **888/488-7111** or 702/693-7722. www.bellagio.com. Tickets $94–$150. Wed–Sun 7:30 and 10:30pm.

Penn & Teller (★★★ *Moments*   The most intelligent show in Vegas, as these two—magicians? illusionists? truth-tellers? BS artists? geniuses?—put on 90 minutes of, yes, magic and juggling, but also acerbic comedy, mean stunts, and great quiet beauty. Looking like two characters out of Dr. Seuss, big loud Penn and smaller quiet Teller (to reduce them to their basic characteristics) perform magic, reveal the secrets behind a few major magic tricks, discuss why magic is nothing but a bunch of lies, and then turn around and show why magic is as lovely an art form as any other. In Rio All-Suite Hotel & Casino, 3700 W. Flamingo Rd. ✆ **888/746-7784.** www.riolasvegas.com. Ages 5 and over only. Tickets $75–$85 (plus tax). Sat–Thurs 9pm.

Phantom of the Opera ✪   A 90-minute, no-intermission, boiled-down-to-the-basics—guy in mask, girl he loves, the guy she loves, caverns and canals and romance and tragedy and mystery and murder and light opera—of Andrew Lloyd Webber's biggest hit. Fans (and they are dedicated and opinionated) may yowl at this stripped-down version, but the production value (staged on the former site of the failed Guggenheim museum transformed into a $40 million theater, plus another $30 million to make the production even more high-tech than the original Broadway staging—expect pyrotechnics in addition to the famous chandelier crash) might please other potential attendees, not to mention add a legitimate bit of Broadway to a town that so far rarely supports it. At The Venetian, 3355 Las Vegas Blvd. S. ✆ **888/641-7469** or **702/414-7469.** www.venetian.com. Tickets $80–$150 (plus tax). Mon–Sat 7pm; Mon and Sat 9:30pm; Thurs 10:30pm.

Rita Rudner ✪✪   She stands in front of an audience for about an hour and tells the truth. It's that simple. It's also funny as heck, and oddly endearing, as Rudner's successful shtick is to present herself as Every Woman, not to mention the audience's Best Friend Forever. She wryly and dryly tosses out one-liners about gender relationships in an attempt to explain that age-old problem—What Do Women Want? And Why Don't Men Understand It's Shoes? At Harrah's, 3475 Las Vegas Blvd. S. ✆ **702/369-5222.** Tickets $54–$105.

The Second City ✪✪ *Value*   Second City is the Chicago-based comedy group that spawned not only *SCTV* but also some of the best modern-day comics (Gilda Radner, John Belushi, Martin Short, Mike Myers). This is an improv and sketch comedy show, with cast members performing stunts similar to those you might have seen on *Whose Line Is It Anyway?*—you know, taking suggestions from the audience and creating bizarre little skits and such out of them, all of it done at lightning speed with wit and a wink. Some of it can turn R-rated, so be careful bringing the kids, but do not hesitate to see it yourself. And join in—any improv group is only as good as the material fed it (so remember, there's only so much a group can do with jokes about sex and vomiting, especially if every single audience thinks that would be funny material with which to work). One of

---

(*Value* **Seeing the King . . . No, Not That One**

One of the best bargains in Las Vegas is an afternoon show at Harrah's. **Mac King** offers deliberately less-than-slick and charming, likable comedy as well as entertaining magic (Harrah's, 3475 Las Vegas Blvd. S.; ℂ **800/427-7247** or 702/369-5222; Tues–Sat 1 and 3pm; $25). *Tip:* You can make this an even bigger bargain if you sign up for Harrah's slot club. The club usually offers two free show tickets (you still have to pay the one-drink minimum) to new enrollees, and you won't have to gamble a cent.

---

the best values and highest-quality shows in Vegas. In Flamingo Las Vegas, 3555 Las Vegas Blvd. S. ℂ **800/221-7299** or 702/733-3333. www.second city.com. Tickets $45 (plus tax and fees). Thurs, Sat, Sun 8 and 10:30pm; Tues, Wed, Fri 8pm.

Tournament of Kings ⭐⭐ (*Kids*)   This one's for lovers of medieval yore or families looking for wholesome entertainment. For a fixed price, you get a dinner that's better than you might expect (Cornish game hen, very fine baked potato, and more), which you eat with your hands (in keeping with the theme), while Merlin (or someone like him) spends too much time trying to work up the crowd with a sing-along. This gives way to a competition between the kings of various medieval countries, competing for titles in knightly contests (jousting, horse races, and such) that are every bit as unrehearsed and spontaneous as a professional wrestling match. Eventually, good triumphs over evil and all that.

Each section of the arena is given a king to be the subject of and to root for, and the audience is encouraged to hoot, holler, and pound on the tables, which kids love, but teens will be too jaded for (though we know some from whom a spontaneous "way cool" slipped out a few times unchecked). Many adults might find it tiresome. Acrobatics are terrific, and certain buff performers make for a different sort of enjoyment. In Excalibur, 3850 Las Vegas Blvd. S. ℂ **800/933-1334** or 702/597-7600. Tickets $55 (includes dinner). Daily 6 and 8:30pm.

Zumanity   It's shocking how much goodwill Cirque du Soleil has squandered with this ill-conceived show. Purportedly dedicated to celebrating human sexuality, it's the least subtle show on the Strip (no easy feat, that), an erotic cabaret of the sort that stopped being shocking in *fin de siècle* Paris, not that that stops the crowd from eating up a bevy of acts which are all meant to be lewd or alluring or both. But if you pay attention, they are mostly just basic Cirque acts (and, worse, just basic striptease acts, which you can see anywhere in town for a great deal less money), though instead of giving the illusion of near-nakedness, they give the illusion of total nakedness (an illusion that works better the farther you sit from the stage). As they contort and writhe and feign pleasure or apathy, we feel sympathy for all the parents who spent money on gymnastics and ballet lessons over the years, only to have their poor kids end up in this. See, Cirque is naturally sexy and erotic, so all this is gilding the lily until it chokes from lack of oxygen and dies. Save your money for *La Femme* across the street or just go to Sapphire and tip the best dancer there. In New York–New York, 3790 Las Vegas Blvd. S. ℂ **866/606-7111** or 702/740-6815. www.zumanity.com. Ages 18 and over only. Tickets $85–$95 (theater seats), $69 (cabaret stools and balcony with partially obstructed views), $79 (upper orchestra), $99 (theater seats), $129 per person (duo sofas, sold in pairs), plus tax and service fee. Fri–Tues 7:30 and 10:30pm.

2 Headliner Showrooms

Vegas entertainment made its name with its showrooms, though its glory days are somewhat behind it, gone with the Rat Pack themselves. For a long time, Vegas headliners were something of a joke; only those on the downhill side of fame were thought to play there. But with all the new performance spaces—and high fees—offered by the new hotels, Vegas suddenly has credence again, especially in, of all things, the rock scene. Both the Hard Rock Hotel's The Joint and the House of Blues are attracting very current and very popular acts that find it hip, rather than humiliating, to play Sin City. However, the classic Vegas showroom itself does seem headed for the way of the dinosaurs; many of the hotels have shuttered theirs. As for the remainder, one is pretty much like the other, with the exception of the Hard Rock and HOB (hence their detailed descriptions), and in any case, audiences go based on the performer rather than the space itself. Check with your hotel or those free magazines in your room to see who is in town when you are.

Hard Rock Hotel's The Joint ℱ Formerly just about the only game in town in terms of good rock bookings, The Joint, with its 1,400-seat capacity, faces some stiff competition from the House of Blues. For example, when Alanis Morrisette came to town, she played the Hard Rock, but her opening act, Garbage, played the House of Blues. On the other hand, it was here the Rolling Stones chose to do a show during their arena tour—this was the smallest venue the band had played in years, and, as you can imagine, it was one hot ticket. When the Hard Rock Hotel opened in 1995, the Eagles were the first act to appear. Since then the facility has presented Bob Dylan, Ziggy Marley, Marilyn Manson, Green Day, the Black Crowes, David Bowie, Donna Summer, Stephen Stills, Jimmy Cliff, Tears for Fears, Lyle Lovett, and James Brown. The venue is not a preferred one, however; it's worth going only if a favorite performer is playing or if it's an opportunity to see a big artist play a smaller-than-usual room.

At press time, The Joint was closed for an entire reconception; the club is changing locations, which will allow for a much larger space when it reopens in late 2008. Expect a bigger rival to the House of Blues, which outstripped its rival some time ago.

Showroom policies: Seating is either preassigned or general, depending on the performer. **Price:** $20 to $500, depending on the performer (tax and drinks extra). **Show Times:** 8:30pm (nights of performance vary). **Reservations:** You can reserve up to 30 days in advance. In Hard Rock Hotel & Casino, 4455 Paradise Rd. ✆ 800/693-7625 or 702/693-5000. www.hardrockhotel.com.

House of Blues ✮✮   The House of Blues goes head-to-head with The Joint at the Hard Rock Hotel, which has translated into much better rock bookings overall, thanks to the competition. On its own merits, the House of Blues is a good, intimate room with a cozy floor surrounded by a bar area, and an upstairs balcony area that has actual theater seating. (The balcony might actually be a better place to see a show since the sightlines are unobscured, unlike down below, where posts and such can obstruct the view.) It's probably the most comfortable and user-friendly place to see a rock show in Vegas.

The House of Blues has rock and blues shows just about every night, with nationally recognized acts flocking to the place, including Bob Dylan, Seal, X, Garbage, Taylor Dayne, Etta James, Al Green, James Brown, the Go-Go's, and the Neville Brothers. During the summer Mandalay Bay hosts outdoor concerts on its poolside beach. Acts have included the Go-Gos and B-52s.

Showroom policies: Seating is either preassigned or general, depending on the performer (some shows are all general admission, with everyone standing on the floor). **Price:** $20 to $250, depending on the performer. **Show Times:** Vary, but usually 8pm. **Reservations:** You can buy tickets as soon as shows are announced; lead time varies with each artist. In Mandalay Bay, 3950 Las Vegas Blvd. S. ✆ 877/632-7400 or 702/632-7600. www.hob.com.

3 Comedy Clubs

Comedy Club   The Riviera's comedy club, on the second floor of the Mardi Gras Plaza, showcases several comedians nightly. They are usually nobody you've ever heard of and the place tends to draw a breed of comic that goes for the gross-out, insult-every-minority brand of "humor" instead of actual humor. In Riviera Hotel & Casino, 2901 Las Vegas Blvd. S. ✆ **800/634-6753** or 702/734-9301. Tickets $25. Daily 8:30 and 10:30pm.

Comedy Stop   Similar to the other comedy clubs in town, Comedy Stop features several "nationally known" comedy headliners nightly. In Tropicana Resort & Casino, 3801 Las Vegas Blvd. S. ✆ **800/468-9494** or 702/739-2411. Tickets $20 (includes tax, tip, and 1 drink). Daily 8 and 10:30pm.

The Improv ✸   These are talented performers—the top comics on the circuit, whom you're likely to see on Leno and Letterman. In Harrah's Las Vegas, 3475 Las Vegas Blvd. S. ✆ **800/392-9002** or 702/369-5111. Tickets $29 and $45 (plus tax). Weds–Fri and Sun 8:30 and 10:30pm, closed Mon, Tues, Thurs, Sat.

4 Gay Bars

Hip and happening Vegas locals know that some of the best scenes and dance action can actually be found in the city's gay bars. And no, they don't ask for sexuality ID at the door. All are welcome at any of the following establishments—as long as you don't have a problem with the people inside, they aren't going to have a problem with you. For women, this can be a fun way to dance and not get hassled by overeager lotharios. (Lesbians, by the way, are just as welcome at any of the gay bars.)

Rip-Off City.

You won't lack for hot nightclubs in Vegas, each one trying to outdo the other to the point that frankly, they are kind of all alike. One exceedingly dismaying way they resemble each other is the so-called "bottle service"; you may regret your fashionable heels when you realize you can't sit down at any of these venues unless you've reserved a table, where you are required to purchase a mininum of two bottles of booze, at around $350 per bottle. And that's after entrance fees, and not counting table fees, which can run into the thousands. It's a total racket. Unless you have plenty of discretionary income, do not reserve a table, and wear flat shoes.

If you want to know what's going on in gay Las Vegas during your visit, pick up a copy of the *QVegas,* a free gay-oriented newspaper that's available at any of the places described below. Or call ℰ **702/ 650-0636** or check out the online edition at **www.qvegas.com**. You can also find gay nightlife listings on the Web at **www.gaylasvegas. com** or **www.gayvegas.com**.

The Buffalo ℱ　Close to Gipsy, this leather/Levi's bar is popular with motorcycle clubs. It features beer busts (all the beer you can drink for a small cover) and other drink specials throughout the week. Pool tables, darts, and music videos play in an otherwise not-striking environment. It's very cheap, however, with long necks going for around $3, and it gets very busy, very late (3 or 4am). Open 24 hours. 4640 Paradise Rd. (at Naples Dr.). ℰ **702/733-8355**.

Gipsy ℱ　For years, Gipsy reigned supreme as the best gay dance place in the city, and for good reason: great location (Paradise Rd., near the Hard Rock), excellent layout (sunken dance floor and two bars), and very little competition. A few years ago, some fierce competition stole some of its spotlight, along with a good portion of the clientele, and so the Gipsy fought back with a $750,000 renovation that seemed to recapture past glories. But apparently they aren't willing to rest on their laurels. Drink specials along with special events, shows, male dancers, and theme nights have always made this place a good party bar. Open daily 10pm to 6am. 4605 Paradise Rd. (at Naples Dr.). ℰ **702/731-1919**. www.gipsylasvegas.com. Cover varies but is usually $5 and up on weekends, less or even free on weekdays.

Goodtimes Night Club ℱ　This quiet neighborhood bar is located (for those of you with a taste for subtle irony) in the same complex as the Liberace Museum, a few miles due east of the MGM Grand. There's a small dance floor, but nobody really uses it, the crowd preferring instead to take advantage of the cozy bar area. A small conversation pit is a perfect spot for an intimate chat. Of course, there's the omnipresent pool and video poker if you're not interested in witty repartee. We remember this place as being a lot more crowded than it was during our most recent visit (but perhaps we were there on an off night). It makes a nice respite after the Liberace Museum (after which you may very well need a stiff drink). Open 24 hours. In the Liberace Plaza, 1775 E. Tropicana Ave. (at Spencer St.). ℰ **702/736-9494**. www.goodtimeslv.com.

KRAVE ℱℱ　Most notably the first gay club on the Strip, not that anyone's admitting it's a gay club anymore. ("Alternative" is the winking buzzword.) The result is a more mixed crowd than you

Moments Lounge Lizard Supreme

All those faux-hipster artists doing woeful lounge-act characters in Hollywood and New York only wish they could be **Mr. Cook E. Jarr,** whose sincerity and obvious drive to entertain puts mere performance artists to shame. With George Hamilton's tan; Cher's first shag haircut (it's certainly not his factory-original coif); and a bottomless, borderless catalog of rock, pop, soul, swing, and standard favorites, he's more Vegas than Wayne Newton.

Cook has a cult following of blue-collar casino denizens and the youthful cocktail set, who listen enraptured as he plays human jukebox, complete with karaoke-style backing recordings, terrible jokes, an array of disco-era lights, and (his favorite) a smoke machine. He's actually a solid, throaty singer with a gift for vocal mimicry as he moves from Ben E. King to Bee Gees to Tony Bennett turf. And his tribute to the night Sinatra died—a version of "My Way" in which he voiced, alternatively, Sammy, Dino, and Elvis welcoming Ol' Blue Eyes to heaven—was priceless.

You can catch him at **Harrah's Carnaval Court Lounge** at 3475 Las Vegas Blvd. S. (© **702/369-5222**). Don't miss him! (And if he has left there by the time you read this, try to track him down.)

might get at other, openly gay clubs. The interior is a well-crafted Gothic explosion, with a dance floor and some go-go platforms that can feature dancers of either gender. Overall, a tossup; clearly, more money is going into the place, and the Strip access is important since most other local gay bars take some doing to get to. On the other hand, it has limited hours and a possibly even more competitive crowd. Note that if you don't pay the club valet, you have to park in the regular hotel parking, and that calls for a long jog through the evening-deserted Desert Passage shopping mall, which might be uncomfortable in club togs—limited access may well explain why there have already been two failed nightclubs in this space. Open Tuesday to Sunday from 8pm until late (after hours until dawn Fri and Sat). At Planet Hollywood Hotel & Casino, 3667 Las Vegas Blvd. S. (entrance on Harmon). © **702/836-0830**; www.kravelasvegas.com. Cover varies.

5 Other Bars

In addition to the venues below, consider hanging out, as the locals quickly began doing, at **Aureole, Red Square,** and the **House of Blues,** all in **Mandalay Bay** (p. 32). There's a separate bar at Aureole, facing the wine tower, where your wish for wine sends comely lasses flying up four stories, courtesy of Peter Pan–style harnesses, to fetch your desired bottle. At Red Square, keep your drink chilled on the ice bar, created from water that's poured and frozen daily. Or hang out and feel the blues at the small bottle-cap-bedecked bar in the corner of the House of Blues restaurant, which gets quite lively with off-duty locals after midnight. **Zuri** in the MGM Grand is the best of the casino-hotel bars that don't charge admission (although the drinks are expensive), probably because of its construction—a semicurtained enclave just off the elevators (as opposed to a space just plunked down right off, or right in the middle of, a casino). Amid swooping wood and red velvet couches, you can actually hear your partner's whispered sweet nothings.

You might also check out the incredible nighttime view at the bar atop the **Stratosphere**—nothing beats it.

There's also the **Viva Las Vegas Lounge** at the Hard Rock Hotel, where every rock-connected person in Vegas will eventually pass through.

And the **Petrossian Bar** in the Bellagio offers class along with its cocktails (to say nothing of caviar and other delicacies)—but come for the cocktails, as those in the know claim it's not only the best bar in Vegas for such matters, but maybe the best bar in the West.

Caramel 𝆄𝆄 It's small but worlds away from the Bellagio-business-as-usual just outside its doors. How happy the 20-somethings are that there is this hip-hop-spinning, caramel-and-chocolate-coated-drink-glasses, glowing-bar, nonthreatening (and non-Euro-stodgy), scene-intensive hangout in the middle of Bellagio. How much does this prove Bellagio is trying to lure the ghostbar crowd away from the Palms? Not that this will do it, but if you are here and young, it's where you should be. Open daily 5pm to 4am. In Bellagio, 3600 Las Vegas Blvd. S. ℂ **702/693-7111.**

Champagnes Cafe 𝆄𝆄 Wonder where old Vegas went? It ossified right here. Red-and-gold-flecked wallpaper and other such trappings of "glamour" never die—in fact, with this ultra-low-key lighting, they will never even fade. A seedy old bar with seedy old scary men leering away. Some might run screaming from the place, while others will think they've died and gone to heaven. Just remember—this is the kind of place director Quentin Tarantino, or this year's alt-cult hit movie, will make famous. It can't be long. And then it will be overrun with hipsters. Beat the rush, go there now, and brag that you knew about it back before it was so cool it became passé. Again. Open daily 24 hours. Karaoke Friday and Saturday 10pm to 2am. 3557 S. Maryland Pkwy. (between Twain Ave. and Desert Inn Rd.). ⓒ 702/737-1699.

Coyote Ugly ⓡ   You've seen the movie; now go have some of that prepackaged fun for yourself. Oh, come on—you don't think those bartender girls really dance on the bar and hose down the crowd just because they are so full of spontaneous rowdy high spirits, now do you? Not when the original locale built a reputation (and inspired a bad movie) for just such behavior, creating a success strong enough to start a whole chain of such frat-boy fun places? Open daily from 6pm until 4am. In New York–New York, 3790 Las Vegas Blvd. S. (at Tropicana Ave.). ⓒ 702/740-6969. Cover varies, usually $10 and up on weekends.

The Dispensary Lounge ⓡ   Stuck in a '70s time warp (the waterwheel and the ferns are the tip-off, though the songs on the Muzak confirm it), this is a fine place for a nice, long, quiet drink. One that lasts decades, perhaps. It's very quiet, low-key, and often on the empty side. Things pick up on weekends, but it still isn't the sort of place that attracts raucous drunks. (Of course, if it were on the Strip instead of being tucked away, it probably would.) "We leave you alone if you don't want to be bothered," says the proprietor. (We still worry about what happens if you sit here long enough.) If you are a hepcat, but one on the mild side, you'll love it. Open daily 24 hours. 2451 E. Tropicana Ave. (at Eastern Ave.). ⓒ 702/458-6343.

Double Down Saloon ⓡⓡ *Finds*   "House rule: You puke, you clean." Okay, that about sums up the Double Down. Well, no, it doesn't really do the place justice. This is a big local hangout, with management quoting an old *Scope* magazine description of its clientele: "Hipsters, blue collars, the well-heeled lunatic fringe." Rumored to have been spotted there: director Tim Burton and Dr. Timothy Leary. Need to know more? Okay, trippy hallucinogenic graffiti covers the walls, the ceiling, the tables, and possibly you if you sit there long enough. Decor includes Abby Rents–type chairs and thrift-store battered armchairs and sofa, a couple of pool tables, and a jukebox that holds everything from the Germs and Frank Zappa to Link Wray, Dick Dale, and the Reverend Horton Heat. On Wednesday night, they have a live blues band, while other nights might find local alternative, punk, or ska groups performing. There's no cover unless they have some out-of-town band that actually has a label deal. Open daily 24 hours. 4640 Paradise Rd. (at Naples Dr.). © 702/791-5775. www.doubledownsaloon.com.

Drop Bar ⚑   Smack in the middle of the Green Valley Ranch casino, with '60s-inspired go-go girls dancing away. Open daily 24 hours. In Green Valley Ranch Resort, 2300 Paseo Verde Pkwy., Henderson. © 702/221-6560. Cover varies, usually $10 and up.

Eiffel Tower Bar ⚑   From this chic and elegant room, in the restaurant on the 11th floor of the Eiffel Tower, you can look down on everyone (in Vegas)—just like a real Parisian! (Just kidding, Francophiles.) But really, this is a date-impressing bar, and, since there's no cover or minimum, it's a cost-effective alternative to the overly inflated food prices at the restaurant. Drop by for a drink, but try to look sophisticated. And then you can cop an attitude and dismiss everything as gauche—or droit, depending on which way you are seated. Open daily from 11am to 11:30pm. In Paris Las Vegas, 3655 Las Vegas Blvd. S. © 702/948-6937.

Forty Deuce ⚑⚑   Imported from Los Angeles, where it's a highly successful nightlife spot (and regular hangout for every hot young celebrity you can think of, and so very likely to be so in Vegas as well), this is part of the trend of new "burlesque" clubs—a bar with regular performances. Every 90 minutes or so, scantily clad girls come out and skillfully shake their groove thangs, stripping down to pasties, teeny boy shorts, and G-strings. There's both a bar (with obscenely expensive drinks) and a proper cabaret space—performers utilize both stage and bar top—where DJs spin in between performance spots. On weekends, you can't fit a piece of paper inside. Open Thursday through Monday from 10:30pm until dawn. Shows start at 12:30am and 3am. In Mandalay Bay, 3930 Las Vegas Blvd. S. © 702/632-9442. www.fortydeuce.com. Cover varies.

ghostbar ⚑⚑   Probably the most interesting aspect of this desperate-to-get-into-the-gossip-pages-as-the-trendy-bar-of-the-moment place (decorated in that '60s mod/futuristic silver gleam look) is that though much is made of the fact that it's on the 55th floor, it's really on the 42nd. Something about the number 4 being bad luck in Asian cultures. Whatever, the view still is fabulous, which is the main reason to come here, that and to peer at those tousled-hair beauties copping an attitude on the couches and see if any of them have the kind of names that will make tomorrow's gossip pages. It may be the hot bar of the moment by the time you get there (dress up), or everyone may have moved on. Open daily from 8pm until the early hours of the morning. In Palms Resort & Casino, 4321 W. Flamingo Rd. ⓒ **702/942-7778.** Cover varies, usually $10 and up.

Gordon Biersch Brewing Company ⚲   This is part of a chain, and while it does feel like it, it's better than the average such entry. The interior is both contemporary and rustic, warmer than its semi-industrial look might usually deliver. It's roomy, so you don't feel stacked up on top of other customers. The house lager (they specialize in German brews) is tasty and the noise level acceptable. A good place to go hoist a few. Open Sunday through Thursday from 11:30am until 2am, Friday and Saturday until they feel like closing. 3987 Paradise Rd. (just north of Flamingo Rd.). ⓒ **702/312-5247.** www.gordon biersch.com.

Griffin ⚲⚲   Part of a promising trend to revitalize the Fremont East District (just a couple of blocks from the Fremont Street Experience), the fun starts with the old stone facade and eponymous sign and continues inside with the stone pillars, arched cave ceiling and two fire pits. Just what you want in a stylish bar that revels in its history but at the same time doesn't try too hard. Given its proximity to other topnotch downtown hangouts such as Beauty Bar and Downtown Cocktail Lounge, this is a must-stop on the anti-Strip and hotel bar tour. There are DJ's on the weekends. Open Mon–Sat 5pm until close, Sun 9pm–close. 511 E. Fremont St. ⓒ **702/382-0577.**

Hogs & Heifers Saloon ⚲   While there is a chain of Coyote Ugly nightclubs (including one here in Vegas), the movie of the same name was actually based on the hijinks that happened at the New York version of this rowdy roadhouse saloon. New to Sin City as of 2005, the hogs here are of the motorcycle variety and the place definitely draws a crowd that can look intimidating, but is usually a friendly (and boisterous) bunch. Saucy, heckling bar maidens and outdoor barbecues on select weekends make this one of the few good options for nightlife in the Downtown area. Open usually daily 10am to 6am (call to check on hours, as they vary by month). 201 N. 3rd St. (between Ogden and Stewart, one block from the Fremont Street Experience.). ⓒ **702/676-1457.**

Peppermill's Fireside Lounge ⚲ *Finds*   Walk through the classic Peppermill's coffee shop (not a bad place to eat, by the way) on the Strip, and you land in its dark, plush, cozy lounge. A fabulously dated view of hip, it has low, circular banquette seats; fake floral foliage; low neon; and electric candles. But best of all is the water and fire pit as the centerpiece—a piece of kitsch thought long vanished from the earth, and attracting nostalgia buffs like moths to a flame. It all adds up to a cozy, womblike place, perfect for unwinding a bit after some time spent on the hectic Strip. The enormous, exotic froufrou tropical drinks (including the signature bathtub-size margaritas) will ensure that you sink into that level of comfortable stupor. Open 24 hours. 2985 Las Vegas Blvd. S. ⓒ **702/735-7635.**

Sand Dollar Blues Nightclub & Lounge 🏆   This is the kind of funky, no-decor (think posters and beer signs), atmosphere-intensive, slightly grimy, friendly bar you'll either wish your town has or hope it never does. Just up the road from Treasure Island, this is a great antidote to artificial Vegas. Attracting a solid mix of locals and tourists (employees claim the former includes everything from bikers to chamber of commerce members), the Sand Dollar features live blues (both electric and acoustic, with a little Cajun and zydeco thrown in) by local musicians every night. The dance floor is tiny and often full. The minimal cover always goes to the band. Depending on your desires, it's either refreshingly not Vegas or just the kind of place you came to Vegas to escape. Go before someone has the idea to build a theme hotel based on it. Open 24 hours. 3355 Spring Mountain Rd. (at Polaris Ave.). ⓒ **702/871-6651;** www.sanddollarblues.com. Cover varies but is usually no more than $7.

Triple 7 Brew Pub 🏆 *Finds*   Yet another of the many things Main Street Station has done right. Stepping into its microbrew pub feels like stepping out of Vegas. Well, maybe, except for the dueling piano entertainment. It has a partial modern warehouse look (exposed pipes, microbrew fixtures visible through exposed glass at back, and a very high ceiling), but a hammered tin ceiling continues the hotel's Victorian decor; the overall effect seems straight out of San Francisco's North Beach. It's a bit on the yuppified side but escapes being pretentious. And frankly, it's a much-needed modern touch for the Downtown area. This place has its own brewmaster, a number of microbrews ready to try, and an oyster and sushi bar, plus fancy burgers and pizzas. It can get noisy during the aforementioned piano duel act, but otherwise casino noise stays out. Since all of Downtown is too heavy on the old Las Vegas side (which is fine, but not *all* the time), this is good for a suitable breather. Open daily from 11am until 7am. In Main Street Station, 200 Main St. ⓒ **702/387-1896.**

Whisky Bar ⊛⊛   This is probably your best bet for a trendy place that might actually have either beautiful locals or out-of-town celebs looking for a cool time but wanting a lower profile, thanks to its very off-the-Strip location and also its creator, hip-bar-master Rande Gerber (Cindy Crawford's hubby). Think beds instead of couches, and you've got a sense of the gestalt. Open daily from 4pm until 4am. In Green Valley Ranch Resort, 2300 Paseo Verde Pkwy., Henderson. ⓒ 702/617-7560. Cover varies, usually $10 and up.

A KARAOKE BAR

Ellis Island Casino—Karaoke ⊛   Admit it. You sing in the shower. And when the acoustics are just right, you fancy you could give a Vegas lounge singer a run for his money. Here's your chance to test this theory without the comfort of tile acoustics. In this small, smoky den filled with leather and candles, any number of people from all walks of life get up and act out their lounge-singer fantasies. You can join them. With more than 6,000 titles, including multiple Engelbert Humperdinck, Mac Davis, and Tom Jones selections, there are plenty of cheesy numbers just perfect for this kind of environment. And if you stay here long enough, you'll hear them all. Karaoke is offered daily 9pm to 3am. 4178 Koval Lane (off Flamingo Rd., behind Bally's). ⓒ 702/733-8901.

6 Dance Clubs

In addition to the options listed below, country music fans might want to wander on over to **Toby Keith's I Love This Bar & Grill,** Harrah's, 3475 Las Vegas Blvd. S. (ⓒ 702/369-5084). Not for the grill part—the food is definitely on the overpriced and unexceptional side—but for the bar portion of the program with live entertainment Wednesday through Sunday from 9pm to 2am.

The Bank ⊛⊛   Because Vegas can never sit still, the otherwise alluring Light nightclub had to be demolished while it was still new-ish in order to make room for yet another hot spot. The entrance, lined with 500 bottles of Crystal, with crystal hanging from the ceiling, and the bar lined with gold crocodile skin puts a guest on notice; this is high end clubbing. Look for hefty cover charges (though ladies are often free), and as a result, it attracts the deep pocket crowd. Top of the line everything nearly justifies prices; the lights respond to the music, ten snow machines pump snow effects over the hot crowd, the staff are in couture suits. They may or may not let you in if you aren't dressed to the nines. Thursday through Sunday 10:30pm to 4am. In Bellagio, 3600 Las Vegas Blvd. S. ⓒ 702/693-8300.

Body English 🏆🏆   To our way of thinking, this is exactly what a Las Vegas club should be—because all the other hot nightclubs in town look exactly like a hot nightclub in any old town, and so we always want Vegas places to be *Vegas*—over the top and just a little bit wrong. So this clash of Anne Rice and Cher Gothic–themed wacky decadence, with fabrics on top of wood on top of mirrors, not to mention the sort of layout that allows for intimate corners and voyeuristic balcony viewing of the dance floor, is just the sort of overly rich dessert of a place we crave. So do many others; it's one of the hottest spots in town, and the wait in line is so long you might well polish off a Rice novel while standing in it. Well, you gotta pass the time somehow. Expect a hefty cover charge, too. Open Friday through Sunday 10pm to 4:30am. In the Hard Rock Hotel, 4455 Paradise Rd. ℂ 702/693-5000. www.bodyenglish.com. Cover varies, but can be as high as $30.

Cherry 🏆   All of Vegas is style over substance, and given how similar the city's nightclubs can look after awhile, this fantastically designed space—thank Rande Gerber again—is enough of said style to make it instantly fabulous. It echoes the red of the Red Rock Canyon and the titular fruit. The enveloping tunnel entrance just starts the experience. A circular bar and raised circular dance floor dominate the inside, while outside the decadent action takes in the pool area, including fire pit and rotating beds. Don't miss the bathrooms—we don't want to give anything away but there are several surprises waiting. In Red Rock Resort, 11011 W. Charleston Rd. ℂ 702/423-3112. Cover varies.

Cleopatra's Barge Nightclub 🏆   This is a small, unique nightclub set in part on a floating barge—you can feel it rocking. The bandstand, a small dance floor, and a few (usually reserved) tables are here, while others are set around the boat on "land." It's a gimmick, but one that makes this far more fun than other, more pedestrian, hotel bars. Plenty of dark makes for romance, but blaring volume levels mean you will have to scream those sweet nothings. Check out the bare-breasted figurehead on the ship's prow who juts out over the hallway going past the entrance. She could put someone's eye out. Open nightly from 10:30pm until 4am. In Caesars Palace, 3570 Las Vegas Blvd. S. ℂ 702/731-7110. 2-drink minimum.

Drai's After Hours 🏆   Young Hollywood film execs and record-company types are likely to be found here, schmoozing and dancing it up to house, techno, and tribal music. Open Wednesday through Sunday from midnight until dawn. In the Barbary Coast, 3595 Las Vegas Blvd. S. ℂ 702/737-0555. Cover varies, usually $20.

Jet 🐇 Take everything they've done right at a smaller club and throw more money, more space, and more everything at it, with mixed results. The club is stunning, with three dance floors and four bars on multiple levels to keep you entertained and give you something to look at, but the combination of higher-than-average cover charges and the "club of the moment" vibe can be a bit exhausting for anyone looking for a less competitive experience. If that's you, visit the sister club instead. Open Friday, Saturday, and Monday from 10:30pm until late. In The Mirage, 3400 Las Vegas Blvd. S. ℂ **702/632-7600**. Cover varies, usually $30 and up.

Monte Carlo Pub & Brewery 🐇 *Finds* After 9pm nightly, this immense warehouselike pub and working microbrewery (see details in chapter 4) turns from a casual restaurant into something of a dance club. Rock videos blare forth from a large screen and 40 TV monitors around the room, while onstage, dueling pianos provide music and audience-participation entertainment. The Pub is cigar-friendly and maintains a humidor. There's a full bar, and, of course, the house microbrews are featured; you can also order pizza. Open Wednesday, Thursday, and Sunday until 1am, Friday and Saturday 'til 2am. In Monte Carlo Resort & Casino, 3770 Las Vegas Blvd. S. ℂ **702/730-7777**.

Playboy Club 🐇 It's understandable that after a long stint in Vegas, doing the sorts of things that make you not look at your watch, you might not know what time it is. Or even what day. But this makes us seriously consider what year it is. Yes, the first and ultimate Gentlemen's Club, when those words meant something, kinda, is back, and as cottontailed as ever. The future is now everywhere except here, where retro is king and the serving wenches do that little dip when they drop off your drinks. Gloria Steinem is wondering where it all went wrong, but everyone else is having too good a time to care. Secretly, we don't blame them. Open daily at 8pm. In the Palms, 4321 W. Flamingo Rd. ℂ **702/942-7777**. Cover varies, usually $40, including entrance to Moon nightclub upstairs.

Privé and the Living Room 🐇🐇🐇 For once, a user-friendly club that's hot but not intimidating. While as dazzling as any of the other high end joints on the Strip, this one is surprisingly egalitarian. There is no dress code (though dress up anyway, because it's more fun), which means all manner of patrons are mingling together. And mingle they do; with the exception of one row of bottle tables, all seating, and all areas of the club are open to all patrons—no VIP ropes or other barriers, just move about the spacious, amphitheatre-inspired set-up as you will. No matter where you stand, there is a good view. For that matter, if the spirit moves you, jump on the tables and couches and dance; they encourage that. Smashing visuals include a stage (they claim spontaneous performances bust out occasionally), two-story fireplace, projection screens showing Godzilla movies and the like, plus actual dance coordinators for the table-top dancing waitresses. Because of the eclectic mix of clientele, the energy is great. Plus, one cover gets you two clubs: the Living Room is a much smaller space, evoking its name with a fireplace, leather couches, chandeliers, and a booming, deafening sound system. Open Monday, Friday, Saturday 10pm to 4am. In Planet Hollywood, 3667 Las Vegas Blvd. S. ℭ **702/492-3960.** Cover $20 for women, $30 for men.

PURE 𝆄𝆄𝆄   The biggest club on the Strip (it occupies the former home of the late, lamented, and much more family-friendly Caesars Magical Empire), PURE is everything a big loud nightclub ought to be. The theme is reflected in the decor—or lack of it, since just about everything is as white as Ivory Soap (get the name?)—which is either minimalist brilliant or reflects the fact that even Vegas designers get tired. In any event, the noise and lack of cushy corners mean this is a definite get-your-booty-in-motion kind of place, though there is ample space (there are airline hangars that are smaller) for just standing around watching other booties in motion. There is also a rooftop club, itself bigger than most regular Vegas clubs, with views of the Strip, for those who need a little fresh air. Open Friday through Sunday and Tuesday 10pm to 4am. In Caesars Palace, 3570 Las Vegas Blvd. S. ℭ **702/731-7110.** Cover varies.

Rain 𝆄𝆄𝆄   One of the hottest nightclubs in Vegas—at least, until everyone moves to the next one. Which means you (and us—don't think we aren't standing there with you, shoulder to shoulder in solidarity) probably will spend most of your time trying to convince someone, anyone, to let you in. But we also have to be honest: If you can brave the wait, the crowds, and the attitude, you will be inside a club that has done everything right, from the multilevel layout that allows them to pack the crowds in and allows those crowds to peer up and down at their brethren, to DJs who play the right house and techno cuts (at a pulse-thumping tempo, so don't expect your good pickup lines to be heard), to the scaffolding that holds pyrotechnic and other mood-revvers, to the ubiquitous-of-late go-go girls dressed like strippers. If this is your choice, then note that they start lining up way before the opening time. Open Thursday from 11pm and Friday and Saturday from 10pm until dawn. In the Palms, 4321 W. Flamingo Rd. ℭ **702/940-7246.** Cover $25 and up.

rumjungle ★★ Now, normally our delicate sensibilities wince at such overkill, and we tend to write off efforts such as this as just trying a bit too hard. But surprisingly, rumjungle really delivers the great fun it promises. The fire-wall entrance gives way to a wall of water; a two-story bar is full of the largest collection of rum varieties anywhere, each bottle illuminated with a laser beam of light; go-go girls dance and prance between bottles of wine, to dueling congas; and the food all comes skewered on swords. It's all a bit much, but it works, really it does. Get there early (before 10pm) to avoid lines/guest lists/the cover charge, and consider having dinner (served 'til 11pm); it's costly, but it's a multicourse, all-you-can-eat feast of flame-pit-cooked Brazilian food. For the amount of food and the waiving of the cover charge, dinner is a good deal. Then dance it off all night long (the club is open 'til 4am Fri–Sat nights and 2am the rest of the week). In Mandalay Bay, 3950 Las Vegas Blvd. S. ✆ 702/632-7408. Cover varies, usually $10–$20, "ladies always free."

Studio 54 The legendary Studio 54 has been resurrected here in Las Vegas, but with all the bad elements and none of the good ones. Forget Truman, Halston, and Liza doing illegal (or at least immoral) things in the bathroom stalls; that part of Studio 54 remains but a fond memory. The snooty, exclusive door attitude, however, has been retained. Hooray. Red-rope policies are all well and good if you're trying to build a mystique in a regular club, but for a tourist attraction, where guests are likely to be one-time-only (or, at best, once-a-year), it's obnoxious. The large dance floor has a balcony overlooking it, the decor is industrial (exposed piping and the like), the music is hip-hop and electronic, and there is nothing to do other than dance. If the real Studio 54 had been this boring, no one would remember it today. Open Tuesday through Saturday from 10pm until dawn. In MGM Grand, 3799 Las Vegas Blvd. S. ✆ 702/891-1111. www.studio54lv.com. Cover varies, usually $20 and up.

Tabu ★ This hot nightclub is, despite the name, less stripper-saucy than the other new "ultra lounges" (which here means "noisy, high-priced bar"), and consequently is more grown up—and just as loud. With an interior of late-'90s-high-tech/industrial-meets-cheesy-'80s-bachelor's den, it's nothing aesthetically special, though there are some nice spots for canoodling. But do find a wall or the circular couch if you want to hear yourself think. Open Tuesday through Saturday from 10pm until "early morning." In MGM Grand, 3799 Las Vegas Blvd. S. ✆ 702/891-7183. Cover varies, but about $10 for men, free for women.

Tao ⊛ As of this writing, this is the hottest of the Vegas hot spots. Yes, that has been mentioned in other reviews here and yes, it changes on an almost-daily basis, but welcome to the Las Vegas club scene. Done as a Buddhist temple run amok, this multilevel club is drawing the party faithful and the celebrity entourages in droves, so expect long lines and very high cover charges. Some may find the wall-to-wall crowds, flashing lights, pounding music, and general chaos overwhelming but they are obviously doing something right. Open Thursday through Saturday from 10pm until dawn. At The Venetian, 3355 Las Vegas Blvd. S. ℂ **702/388-8588.** Cover varies.

Tryst ⊛ Wynn's first stab at a nightclub, La Bete, tanked. Months after it opened in April 2005 they shut it down, brought in new management, revamped the place, and tried again. The result is much more subtle than the beast-themed original, but this is the Vegas nightclub scene, so it's definitely a sliding scale. After all, the dance floor opens up onto a 90-foot waterfall, so it's all relative. Expect a slightly more refined crowd than you'll usually find at such places, which may be a good or bad thing depending upon your viewpoint. Open Thursday through Sunday 10pm to 4am. At Wynn Las Vegas, 3131 Las Vegas Blvd. S. ℂ **702/770-3375.** Cover varies.

VooDoo Lounge ⊛ Occupying, along with the VooDoo Cafe, two floors in the new addition to the Rio, the Lounge almost successfully combines Haitian voodoo and New Orleans Creole in its decor and theme. There are two main rooms: one with a large dance floor and stage for live music, and a disco room, which is filled with large video screens and serious light action. Big club chairs in groups form conversation pits, where you might actually be able to have a conversation. The big seller? The bartenders put on a show, a la Tom Cruise in *Cocktail.* They shake, jiggle, and light stuff on fire. Supposedly, the live music includes Cajun acts, but when it comes down to it, rock seems to rule the day. The mid- to late-20s crowd is more heavily local than you might expect; the dress code calls for "business casual," with no shorts, jeans, or shirts without collars for men. Open nightly 5pm to 3am or later. In Rio, 3700 Las Vegas Blvd. S. ℂ **702/252-7777.** Cover $10 and up.

7 Strip Clubs

No, we don't mean entertainment establishments on Las Vegas Boulevard South. We mean the other kind of "strip." Yes, people come to town for the gambling and the wedding chapels, but the lure of Vegas doesn't stop there. Though prostitution is not legal within the city, the sex industry is an active and obvious force in town. Every other cab carries a placard for a strip club, and a walk down the Strip at night will have dozens of people thrusting flyers at you for clubs, escort services, phone sex lines, and more. And some of you are going to want to check it out.

And why not? An essential part of the Vegas allure is decadence, and naked flesh would certainly qualify, as does the thrill of trying something new and daring. Of course, by and large, the nicer bars aren't particularly daring, and if you go to more than one in an evening, the thrill wears off and the breasts don't look quite so bare.

In addition to the listings below, keep an eye out for a new addition to the scene, **Tommy Rocker's Mojave Beach Topless Bar.** In a "If you can't beat 'em, join 'em" move, longtime bar owner and local musician Tommy Rocker decided to revamp his frat-boy fave, at 4275 Dean Martin Dr. (© **702/261-2688;** www.tommyrocker. com; daily 24 hrs.; happy hours 6am–6pm; $20 cover), and turn it into a strip club, gleefully saying his new place's motto will be "Fun for the whole family, except for your wife and kids." Tommy plays on Saturday nights, in addition to the other attractions.

Cheetah's 🍸   This is the strip club used as the set in the movie *Showgirls,* but thanks to the magic of Hollywood and later renovations by the club, only the main stage will look vaguely familiar to those few looking for Nomi Malone. There's also a smaller stage, plus three tiny "tip stages" so that you can really get close to (and give much money to) the woman of your choice. Eight TVs line the walls; the club does a brisk business during major sporting events. The management believes that if you treat people right, they will keep coming back, so the atmosphere is friendlier than at other clubs. Lap dances are $20. Open 24 hours. 2112 Western Ave. © 702/384-0074. Topless. Cover $20 after 8pm until 5am. Unescorted women allowed.

Club Paradise 🍸   Until the new behemoths moved into town, this was the nicest of the strip clubs. Which isn't to say it isn't still nice—it's just got competition. The interior and atmosphere are rather like those of a hot nightclub where most of the women happen to be topless. The glitzy stage looks like something from a miniature showroom: The lights flash and the dance music pounds, there are two big video screens (one featuring soft porn, the other showing sports!), the chairs are plush and comfortable, the place is relatively bright by strip-club standards, and they offer champagne and cigars. Not surprisingly, they get a very white-collar crowd here. The result is not terribly sleazy, which may please some and turn others off. Lap dances are $20. Open Monday to Friday 5pm to 8am, and Saturday and Sunday 6pm to 8am. 4416 Paradise Rd. ⓒ **702/ 734-7990**. Topless. Cover $20, 2-drink minimum (drinks $4.50 and up). Unescorted women allowed.

Déjà Vu Showgirls 𝓡𝓡 Owned by the same people as Little Darlings (see below), this place both deeply perturbs us and amuses the heck out of us. The latter because it's one of the rare strip clubs where the women actually perform numbers. Instead of just coming out and taking off an article or two of clothing and then parading around in a desultory manner before collecting a few tips and running off to solicit lap dances, each stripper comes out and does an actual routine—well, okay, maybe not so much, but she does remove her clothes to personally chosen music, shedding an outfit tailored to her music selection. And so it happened that we have now seen a punk-rock chick strip to "Anarchy in the U.K." Lap dances are $20 to $30. Open Monday through Saturday from 11am to 6am, and Sunday from 6pm to 4am. 3247 Industrial Rd. ⓒ **702/894-4167**. Totally nude. Unescorted women allowed. Cover charge $15. 18 and over. No alcohol.

Glitter Gulch 𝓡 Right there in the middle of the Fremont Street Experience, Glitter Gulch is either an eyesore or the last bastion of Old Las Vegas, depending on your point of view. Given its convenient location, this is the perfect place for the merely curious—you can easily pop in, check things out, goggle and ogle, and then hit the road, personal dignity intact. Table dances are $20. Open daily 1pm to 4am. 20 Fremont St. ⓒ **702/385-4774**. Topless. 2-drink minimum (drinks $7 and up) before 8pm. After 8pm cover is $20 and includes 1 drink. Unescorted women allowed.

Little Darlings 𝓡 They call themselves the "Pornocopia of Sex," and given the number of services they offer, you can see why. In addition to a fully stocked adult store, they have private nude dances in booths. This is one of the few clubs where the women are not allowed any physical contact with the customers. There are also rooms where you can watch a nude woman take a shower (in theory doing erotic things with soap), and "Fantasy Rooms" where a glass pane separates you from a woman performing still more erotic stunts. Despite all the nude offerings, the resultant atmosphere is not especially dirty, just rowdy. Totally nude private dance in booth $20,

Fantasy Room $100 to $300. Open Monday through Saturday 11am to 6am; Sunday 6pm to 4am. 1514 Western Ave. ✆ **702/366-0145.** Totally nude. Cover $20 (includes soda and juice). No unescorted women.

Olympic Gardens Topless Cabaret ✰ Once the largest of the strip clubs, this almost feels like a family operation, thanks to the middle-aged women handling the door. It also has a boutique that sells lingerie and naughty outfits. The crowd is a mix of 20s to 30s blue-collar guys and techno geeks. As the place fills up and the chairs are crammed in next to each other, it's hard to see how enjoyable or intimate a lap dance can be when the guy next to you is getting one as well. Oh, and by the way, they also have male strippers most nights of the week, so you ladies don't feel left out. Lap dances are $20, more in VIP room. Open daily 24 hours. 1531 Las Vegas Blvd. S. ✆ **702/385-8987.** Topless. Cover $30 after 6pm. Unescorted women allowed.

Palomino Club ✰ Once the nicest strip club in town, this place now edges into the seedy end of things. It's also a bit out of the way. On the other hand, it does offer total nudity in a classic red-walled setting. And its location outside the Vegas city limits means that it's one of the only clubs that offers both total nudity *and* alcohol. Topless lap dances are $20; totally nude dances are $40. Open daily 5pm to 5am. 1848 Las Vegas Blvd. N. ✆ **702/642-2984.** Totally nude. Cover $20. Unescorted women allowed.

Sapphire Gentleman's Club ✰✰✰ Ladies and gentlemen, particularly the latter, Las Vegas, home of the largest everything else, now brings you—drum roll—the largest strip club *in the world!* That's right, 71,000 square feet of nakedidity. Of course, you have to see it—and, of course, that's what they are counting on. But let's say this: While really, it's nothing you haven't seen before, strip-club-wise, if you haven't seen a strip club, this is the place to start because it's modern and clean—although, frankly, it's not all that different, looks-wise, from Rain, the superhot nightclub at the Rio. Lap dances are $20. Open 24 hours. 3025 S. Industrial Rd. ✆ **702/796-0000.** Topless. Cover $30. 6pm–6am. Unescorted women allowed.

Spearmint Rhino ✰ Did you know that even strip bars come in chains? They do, and this is a familiar brand to those in the know or who read billboards close to airports. The runway (where some of the dancers get a little personal with each other) is actually in a separate back area, so it is possible to have a drink at the front (where there are many TVs and other manly accouterments) and never see a naked girl (save for the smaller stage and pole nearby). On a busy night, it's crammed with grown-up frat boys enjoying a clubby space. There can be a veritable factory assembly line of lap dances during these busy periods, which, frankly, seems the opposite of a turn-on to us. Lap dances are $20. Open 24 hours. 3444 Highland Dr. Ⓒ 702/ 796-3600. Topless. Cover $30. Unescorted women allowed.

8

Side Trips from Las Vegas

You might not know it, but there is a big wide world outside of Vegas, and some of it is extraordinary—especially if your aesthetic sensibilities favor the stark and surprising mysteries of desert landscapes. There is every bit as much to marvel at out there as there is within the confines of Vegas, and the two settings make for a curious contrast of the entirely artificial and the wholly natural.

But apart from simple admiration, there's a lot to do, from touring the true architectural marvel that is Hoover Dam, to hiking Red Rock Canyon, to swimming and boating on Lake Mead. You'll get a dose of much-needed fresh air—possibly even some exercise—and your kids can get their ya-yas out.

The excursions covered in this chapter, with the exception of the Grand Canyon trips mentioned below, will take you from 20 to 60 miles out of town. Every one of them offers a memorable travel experience.

GRAND CANYON TOURS

Dozens of sightseeing tours depart from the city daily. The major operator, **Scenic Airlines** (© **800/634-6801** or 702/638-3300; www.scenic.com), runs deluxe, full-day guided air-ground tours for $279 per person ($249 for children 2–11); the price includes a bus excursion through the national park, a flight over the canyon, and lunch. All scenic tours include flightseeing. The company also offers both full-day and overnight tours with hiking. Scenic also offers tours to other points of interest and national parks, including Bryce Canyon and Monument Valley. Ask for details when you call.

Gray Line Tours (© **800/634-6579;** www.grayline.com) also operates tours to the Grand Canyon. Call or visit their website for details.

1 Hoover Dam & Lake Mead

30 miles SE of Las Vegas

This is one of the most popular excursions from Las Vegas, visited by 2,000 to 3,000 people daily. Why should you join them? Because

Hoover Dam is an engineering and architectural marvel, and it changed the Southwest forever. Without it, you wouldn't even be going to Vegas. Kids may be bored, unless they like machinery or just plain big things, but expose them to it anyway, for their own good. (Buy them an ice cream and a Hoover Dam snow globe as a bribe.) Obviously, if you are staying at Lake Mead, it's a must.

The tour itself is a bit cursory and commercialized, but you do get up close and personal with the dam. Wear comfortable shoes; the tour involves quite a bit of walking. Try to take the tour in the morning to beat the desert heat and the really big crowds. You can have lunch out in Boulder City and then perhaps drive back through the **Valley of Fire State Park** (described later in this chapter), which is about 60 magnificently scenic miles from Lake Mead (purchase gas before you start!). Or you can spend the afternoon in Lake Mead pursuits—hiking, boating, even scuba diving in season—or perhaps taking a rafting trip down the Colorado River.

GETTING THERE

Drive east on Flamingo or Tropicana to U.S. 515 south, which automatically turns into I-93 south and takes you right to the dam. This will involve a rather dramatic drive, as you go through Boulder City, come over a rise, and Lake Mead suddenly appears spread out before you. It's a beautiful sight. At about this point, the road narrows down to two lanes, and traffic can slow considerably. On busy tourist days, this means the drive can take an hour or more.

Go past the turnoff to Lake Mead. As you near the dam, you'll see a five-story parking structure tucked into the canyon wall on your left. Park here ($5 charge) and take the elevators or stairs to the walkway leading to the new visitor center.

If you would rather go on an **organized tour,** check out **Gray Line** (℡ **800/634-6579;** www.grayline.com), which offers a Hoover Dam package that includes admission and a tour of the dam plus a buffet lunch and a side trip to the Ethel M Chocolate Factory. When you're in Las Vegas, look for discount coupons in the numerous free publications available at hotels. The 7½-hour **Deluxe Hoover Dam Tour** departs daily at 7:30am; the price is $49, with admission to the dam's Discovery Tour an additional $11.

HOOVER DAM ✹✹✹

There would be no Vegas as we know it without the Hoover Dam. Certainly not the neon and glitz. In fact, the growth of the entire Southwest can be tied directly to the electricity created by the dam.

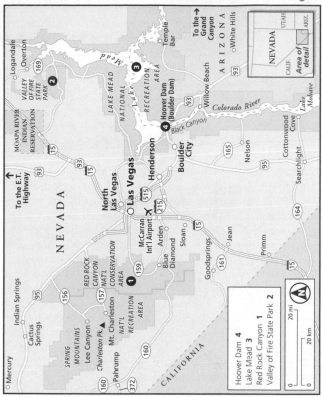

Until the Hoover Dam was built, much of the southwestern United States was plagued by two natural problems: parched, sandy terrain that lacked irrigation for most of the year, and extensive flooding in spring and early summer, when the mighty Colorado River, fed by melting snow from its source in the Rocky Mountains, overflowed its banks and destroyed crops, lives, and property. On the positive side, raging unchecked over eons, the river's turbulent, rushing waters carved the Grand Canyon.

In 1928, prodded by the seven states through which the river runs during the course of its 1,400-mile journey to the Gulf of California, Congress authorized construction of a dam at Boulder Canyon (later moved to Black Canyon). The Senate's declaration of intention was that "A mighty river, now a source of destruction, is to be curbed and put to work in the interests of society." Construction began in

1931. Because of its vast scope and the unprecedented problems posed in its realization, the project generated significant advances in many areas of machinery production, engineering, and construction. An army of more than 5,200 laborers was assembled, and work proceeded 24 hours a day. Completed in 1936, 2 years ahead of schedule and $15 million under budget (it is, no doubt, a Wonder of the Modern Fiscal World), the dam stopped the annual floods and conserved water for irrigation and industrial and domestic use. Equally important, it became one of the world's major electrical generating plants, providing low-cost, pollution-free hydroelectric power to a score of surrounding communities. Hoover Dam's $165-million cost has been repaid with interest by the sale of inexpensive power to a number of California cities and the states of Arizona and Nevada. The dam is a government project that paid for itself—a feat almost as awe-inspiring as its engineering.

The dam itself is a massive curved wall, 660 feet thick at the bottom and tapering to 45 feet where the road crosses it at the top. It towers 726 feet above bedrock (about the height of a 60-story skyscraper) and acts as a plug between the canyon walls to hold back up to 9.2 trillion gallons of water in Lake Mead, the reservoir created by its construction. Four concrete intake towers on the lake side drop the water down about 600 feet to drive turbines and create power, after which the water spills out into the river and continues south.

All the architecture is on a grand scale, and the design has beautiful Art Deco elements, unusual in an engineering project. Note, for instance, the monumental 30-foot bronze sculpture, *Winged Figures of the Republic,* flanking a 142-foot flagpole at the Nevada entrance. According to its creator, Oskar Hansen, the sculpture symbolizes "the immutable calm of intellectual resolution, and the enormous power of trained physical strength, equally enthroned in placid triumph of scientific achievement."

Seven miles northwest of the dam on U.S. 93, you'll pass through **Boulder City,** which was built to house managerial and construction workers. Sweltering summer heat (many days it is 125°F/52°C) ruled out a campsite by the dam, and the higher elevation of Boulder City offered lower temperatures. The city emerged within a single year, turning a desert wasteland into a community of 6,000. By 1934, it was Nevada's third-largest town.

TOURING THE DAM

The very nice **Hoover Dam Visitor Center,** a vast three-level circular concrete structure with a rooftop overlook, opened in 1995.

You'll enter the Reception Lobby, where you can buy tickets; peruse informational exhibits, photographs, and memorabilia; and view three 12-minute video presentations (about the importance of water to life, the events leading up to the construction of Hoover Dam, and the construction itself, as well as the many benefits it confers). Exhibits on the Plaza Level include interactive displays on the environment, habitation, and development of the Southwest; the people who built the dam; and related topics.

Yet another floor up, galleries on the Overlook Level demonstrate, via sculpted bronze panels, the benefits of Hoover Dam and Lake Mead to the states of Arizona, Nevada, and California. The Overlook Level additionally provides an unobstructed view of Lake Mead, the dam, the power plant, the Colorado River, and Black Canyon. (There are multiple photo opportunities throughout this trip.)

You can visit an exhibit center across the street where a 10-minute presentation in a small theater focuses on a topographical map of the 1,400-mile Colorado River. It also has a cafeteria. Notice, by the way, how the restrooms in the center have only electric dryers, no paper towels. A tribute?

The center closes at 6pm, and 5:15pm is the last admission time, though hours vary seasonally. There are two tours available, the Power Plant Tour and the Hoover Dam Tour. Admission to the former is $11 for adults; $9 for seniors, military personnel and their dependents, all children 4 to 16; and free for military in uniform and children 3 and under. The more extensive Hoover Dam Tour is $30 per person, no children 7 and under allowed; parking is $7 no matter which tour you take, and the lot takes cash only. There is no need to call ahead to reserve a place, but for more information, call ℭ **866/ 730-9097** or 702/494-2517.

Tours, by the way, are "not recommended for claustrophobics or those persons with defibrillators."

At this writing, thanks to post–September 11, 2001, terrorist attacks security measures, tours of the dam keep changing format and are somewhat restricted. On the Power Plant tour visitors go to the center, see a movie, walk on top of the dam. While both tours includes a 530-foot descent via elevator into the dam to view the massive generators, the Power Plant tour is a self-guided tour aided by the occasional information kiosk or guide/docent planted at intervals along the way; the pricier tour offers the same attractions and viewing opportunities, but it is guided, lasts an hour and a half, and is limited to 20 people. If you plan on taking that tour, be aware that it covers over a mile and a half of walking on concrete and gravel, with no handicapped access. The Hoover Dam tour is offered every half hour, with the last tour at 3:30, while the final Power Plant admission is at 5:15.

Neither of these is quite as thrilling as the former "hard hat" tours but there are still plenty of curious little tidbits of info to be learned. Obviously, access to the current setup could at any moment be further decreased, or security further tightened, though the decrease in access is sadly more likely.

Some fun facts you might hear along the way: It took 6½ years to fill the lake. Though 96 workers were killed during the construction, contrary to popular myth, none were accidentally buried as the concrete was poured (it was poured only at a level of 8 in. at a time). Look for a monument to them outside—"they died to make the desert bloom"—along with one for their doggy mascot who was also killed, although after the dam was completed. Compare their wages of 50¢ an hour to those of their Depression-era peers, who made 5¢ to 30¢.

For more information on the dam, and sometimes discount coupons, visit **www.usbr.gov/lc/hooverdam**.

LAKE MEAD NATIONAL RECREATION AREA 𝕬𝕬

Under the auspices of the National Park Service, the 1.5-million-acre Lake Mead National Recreation Area was created in 1936 around Lake Mead (the reservoir lake that resulted from the construction of Hoover Dam) and later Lake Mohave to the south (formed with the construction of Davis Dam). Before the lakes emerged, this desert region was brutally hot, dry, and rugged—unfit for human habitation. Today it's one of the nation's most popular playgrounds, attracting about 9 million visitors annually. The two lakes comprise 291 square miles. At an elevation of 1,221 feet, Lake Mead itself extends some 110 miles upstream toward the Grand Canyon. Its 550-mile shoreline, backed by spectacular cliff and canyon scenery, forms a perfect setting for a wide variety of watersports and desert hiking.

The **Alan Bible Visitor Center,** 4 miles northeast of Boulder City on U.S. 93 at NV 166 (ⓒ **702/293-8990**), can provide information on all area activities and services. You can pick up trail maps and brochures here, view informative films, and find out about scenic drives, accommodations, ranger-guided hikes, naturalist programs and lectures, bird-watching, canoeing, camping, lakeside RV parks, and picnic facilities. The center also sells books and videotapes about the area. It's open daily 8:30am to 4:30pm except Thanksgiving, Christmas, and New Year's Day.

For information on accommodations, boat rentals, and fishing, call **Seven Crown Resorts** (© **800/752-9669** or 702/293-3484; www. sevencrown.com). You can also find Lake Mead info on the Web at **www.nps.gov/lame**.

The **entry fee** for the area is $5 per vehicle, which covers all passengers, or $3 per person if you're walking, motorcycling, or biking in.

OTHER OUTDOOR ACTIVITIES

This is a lovely area for scenic drives amid the dramatic desert scenery. One popular route follows the Lakeshore and Northshore Scenic drives along the edge of Lake Mead. From these roads there are panoramic views of the blue lake, set against a backdrop of the browns, blacks, reds, and grays of the desert mountains. Northshore Scenic Drive also leads through areas of brilliant red boulders and rock formations, and you'll find a picnic area along the way.

BOATING & FISHING   A store at **Lake Mead Resort and Marina,** under the auspices of Seven Crown Resorts (© **800/752-9669** or 702/293-3484; www.sevencrown.com), rents fishing boats, ski boats, personal watercraft, and patio boats. It also carries groceries, clothing, marine supplies, sporting goods, water-skiing gear, fishing equipment, and bait and tackle. Nonresidents can get a fishing license here ($69 a year, or $18 for 1 day plus $7 for each additional day; discounts for children 14 and under are available; additional fees apply for special fishing classifications including trout, which require a $10 stamp for taking or possessing that fish). The staff are knowledgeable and can apprise you of good fishing spots. Largemouth bass, striped bass, channel catfish, crappie, and bluegill are found in Lake Mead; rainbow trout, largemouth bass, and striped bass in Lake Mohave. You can also arrange here to rent a fully equipped houseboat at **Echo Bay,** 40 miles north.

Other convenient Lake Mead marinas offering similar rentals and equipment are **Las Vegas Boat Harbor** (© **702/565-9111;** www.las vegasbaymarina.com), which is even closer to Las Vegas, and **Callville Bay Resort & Marina** (© **800/255-5561** or 702/565-8958; www.callvillebay.com), which is the least crowded of the five on the Nevada Shore.

Note: Several years of drought have drastically reduced the size of Lake Mead and moved its shoreline. As a result, several of the lake's marinas are threatened with relocation or even closure, and some activities on and around some areas of the lake have been restricted. Be sure to call ahead to verify the latest lake conditions.

CAMPING   Lake Mead's shoreline is dotted with campsites, all of them equipped with running water, picnic tables, and grills. Available on a first-come, first-served basis, they are administered by the **National Park Service** (② **702/293-8990;** www.nps.gov). There's a charge of $10 per night at each campsite.

CANOEING   The **Alan Bible Visitor Center** (see above) can provide a list of outfitters that rent canoes for trips on the Colorado River. There's one catch, however: A canoeing permit ($10 per person) is required in advance for certain areas near the dam and is available from the **Bureau of Reclamation.** Call ② **702/293-8204** or visit **www.usbr.gov/lc** for information.

HIKING   The best season for hiking is November to March (it's too hot the rest of the year). Some ranger-guided hikes are offered via the **Alan Bible Visitor Center** (see above), which also stocks detailed trail maps. Three trails, ranging in length from .75 miles to 6 miles, originate at the visitor center. The 6-mile trail goes past remains of the railroad built for the dam project. Be sure to take all necessary desert-hiking precautions (see "Desert Hiking Advice," in chapter 5).

LAKE CRUISES   A delightful way to enjoy Lake Mead is on a cruise aboard the **Lake Mead Cruises** boat *Desert Princess* ⊙ (② **702/293-6180;** www.lakemeadcruises.com), a Mississippi-style paddle-wheeler. Cruises depart year-round from a terminal near **Lake Mead Lodge** at 322 Lake Shore Rd. in Boulder City. It's a relaxing, scenic trip (enjoyed from an open promenade deck or one of two fully enclosed, climate-controlled decks) through Black Canyon and past colorful rock formations known as the "Arizona Paint Pots" en route to Hoover Dam, which is lit at night. Options include narrated midday cruises ($22 adults, $10 children), cocktail/dinner cruises ($46 adults, $25 children), sunset dinner/dance cruises with live music ($58 adults, children not allowed), and Sunday brunch cruises ($37 adults, $18 children). Dinner is served in a pleasant, windowed, air-conditioned dining room. There's a full bar onboard. Call for departure times.

BOULDER CITY

You might want to consider poking around Boulder City on your way back to Vegas. Literally the company town for those building Hoover Dam, it was created by the wives who came with their husbands and turned a temporary site into a real community, since aided by the recreational attractions and attendant businesses of Lake Mead. It doesn't look like much as you first approach it, but once you are in the heart, you'll discover that it's quite charming. There are some antiques and curio shops, and a number of family-style restaurants and burger and Mexican joints, including **Totos,** a reasonably priced Mexican restaurant at 806 Buchanan Blvd. (© **702/ 293-1744**); it's in the Von's shopping center.

2 Valley of Fire State Park ★★

60 miles NE of Las Vegas

Most people visualize the desert as a vast expanse of undulating sands punctuated by the occasional cactus or palm-fringed oasis. But the desert of America's Southwest bears little relation to this Lawrence of Arabia image. Stretching for hundreds of miles around Las Vegas in every direction is a seemingly lifeless tundra of vivid reddish earth, shaped by time, climate, and subterranean upheavals into majestic canyons, cliffs, and ridges.

The 36,000-acre Valley of Fire State Park typifies the mountainous red Mojave Desert. It derives its name from the brilliant sandstone formations that were created 150 million years ago by a great shifting of sand, and continues to be shaped by the geologic processes of wind and water erosion. These are rock formations like you'll never see anywhere else. There is nothing green, just fiery flaming-red rocks, swirling unrelieved as far as the eye can see. No wonder various sci-fi movies have used this as a stand-in for another planet. The whole place is very mysterious, loaded with petroglyphs, and totally inhospitable. It's not hard to believe that for the American Indians it was a sacred place, where the men came to test their manhood. It is a natural wonder that must be seen to be appreciated.

Although it's hard to imagine in the sweltering Nevada heat, for billions of years these rocks were under hundreds of feet of ocean. This ocean floor began to rise some 200 million years ago, and the waters became shallower. Eventually the sea made a complete retreat, leaving a muddy terrain traversed by ever-diminishing streams. A great sandy desert covered much of the southwestern part of the American continent until about 140 million years ago. Over eons, winds, massive fault action, and water erosion sculpted fantastic formations of sand and limestone. Oxidation of iron in the sands and mud—and the effect of ground water leaching the oxidized iron— turned the rocks the many hues of red, pink, russet, lavender, and white that can be seen today. Logs of ancient forests washed down from faraway highlands and became petrified fossils, which can be seen along two interpretive trails.

Human beings occupied the region, a wetter and cooler one, as far back as 4,000 years ago. They didn't live in the Valley of Fire, but during the Gypsum period (2000 B.C.–300 B.C.) men hunted bighorn sheep (a source of food, clothing, blankets, and hut coverings) here with notched sticks called *atlatls* that are depicted in the park's petroglyphs. Women and children caught rabbits, tortoises, and other small game. In the next phase, from 300 B.C. to A.D. 700, the climate became warmer and dryer. Bows and arrows replaced *atlatls,* and the hunters and gatherers discovered farming. The ancestral Puebloan people began cultivating corn, squash, and beans, and communities began replacing small nomadic family groups. These ancient people wove watertight baskets, mats, hunting nets, and clothing. Around A.D. 300, they learned how to make sun-dried ceramic pottery. Other tribes, notably the Paiutes, migrated to the area. By A.D. 1150, they had become the dominant group. Unlike the ancestral Puebloans, they were still nomadic and used the Valley of Fire region seasonally. These were the inhabitants whom white settlers found when they entered the area in the early to mid-1800s. The newcomers diverted river and spring waters to irrigate their farmlands, destroying the nature-based Paiute way of life. About 300 descendants of those Paiute tribespeople still live on the Moapa Indian Reservation that was established along the Muddy River in 1872.

GETTING THERE

From Las Vegas, take I-15 north to exit 75 (Valley of Fire turnoff). However, the more scenic route is to take I-15 north, then travel Lake Mead Boulevard east to Northshore Road (NV 167), and proceed north to the Valley of Fire exit. The first route takes about an hour, the second 1½ hours.

There is a $5 per-vehicle admission charge to the park, regardless of how many people you cram inside.

Plan on spending a minimum of an hour in the park, though you can spend a great deal more time. It can get very hot in there (there is nothing to relieve the sun beating down on all that red and reflecting off it) and there is no water, so be certain to bring a liter, maybe two, per person in the summer. Without a guide, you must stay on paved roads, but don't worry if they end; you can always turn around and come back to the main road again. You can see a great deal from the car, and there are also hiking trails.

Numerous **sightseeing tours** go to the Valley of Fire. Inquire at your hotel tour desk. Char Cruze of **Creative Adventures** (p. 133) also offers a fantastic tour.

The Valley of Fire can also be visited in conjunction with Lake Mead. From **Lake Mead Lodge,** take NV 166 (Lakeshore Rd.) north, make a right turn on NV 167 (Northshore Rd.), turn left on NV 169 (Moapa Valley Blvd.) west—a spectacularly scenic drive—and follow the signs. The Valley is about 65 miles from Hoover Dam.

WHAT TO SEE & DO

There are no food concessions or gas stations in the park; however, you can obtain meals or gas on NV 167 or in nearby **Overton** (15 miles northwest on NV 169). Overton is a fertile valley town replete with trees, agricultural crops, horses, and herds of cattle—quite a change in scenery. On your way in or out of the teeming metropolis, do stop off at **Inside Scoop** ✸, 395 S. Moapa Valley Blvd. (© **702/ 397-2055**), open Monday through Saturday from 10am until 8pm and Sunday from 11am to 7pm. It's a sweet, old-fashioned ice-cream parlor run by extremely friendly people, with a proper menu that, in addition to classic sandwiches and the like, features some surprising choices—a vegetarian sandwich and a fish salad with crab and shrimp, for example. Everything is quite tasty and fresh. They also do box lunches, perfect for picnicking inside the park. We strongly recommend coming by here on your way in for a box lunch, and then coming by afterward for a much-needed ice cream.

At the southern edge of town is the **Lost City Museum** ✸, 721 S. Moapa Valley Blvd. (© **702/397-2193**), a sweet little museum, very nicely done, commemorating an ancient ancestral Puebloan village that was discovered in the region in 1924. Reconstructed wattle-and-daub pueblos surround the museum. Admission is $3 for adults, $2 for seniors 65 and over, and free for children 17 and under. The museum is open daily 8:30am to 4:30pm. Closed Thanksgiving, Christmas, and New Year's Day.

Information headquarters for the Valley of Fire is the **Visitor Center** on NV 169, 6 miles west of Northshore Road (© **702/397-2088;** http://parks.nv.gov/vf.htm). It's open daily 8:30am to 4:30pm and is worth a quick stop for information and a bit of history before entering the park.

There are **hiking trails, shaded picnic sites,** and **two campgrounds** in the park. Most sites are equipped with tables, grills, water, and restrooms. A $12 per-vehicle per-night camping fee is charged for use of the campground.

Petroglyphs at Atlatl Rock and Petroglyph Canyon are both easily accessible. In summer, when temperatures are usually over 100°F (38°C), you may have to settle for driving through the park in an air-conditioned car.

3 Red Rock Canyon ⊀⊀⊀
19 miles W of Las Vegas

If you need a break from the Vegas hubbub, Red Rock Canyon is balm for your overstimulated soul. Less than 20 miles away—but a world apart—this is a magnificent unspoiled vista that should cleanse and refresh you. You can drive the panoramic 13-mile **Scenic Drive** (open daily 7am–dusk) or explore it in more depth on foot, making it perfect for athletes and armchair types. There are many interesting sights and trail heads along the drive. The **National Conservation Area** (© 702/515-5350; www.nv.blm.gov/redrockcanyon) offers hiking trails and internationally acclaimed rock-climbing opportunities (especially notable is the 7,068-ft. Mt. Wilson, the highest sandstone peak among the bluffs). There are picnic areas along the drive and in nearby **Spring Mountain Ranch State Park** (© 702/875-4141; http://parks.nv.gov/smr.htm), 5 miles south, which also offers plays in an outdoor theater during the summer.

GETTING THERE
Just drive west on Charleston Boulevard, which becomes NV 159. Virtually as soon as you leave the city, the red rocks begin to loom around you. The visitor center will appear on your right.

You can also go on an **organized tour. Gray Line** (© 800/634-6579; www.grayline.com), among other companies, runs bus tours to Red Rock Canyon. Inquire at your hotel tour desk.

Finally, you can go **by bike.** Not very far out of town (at Rainbow Blvd.), Charleston Boulevard is flanked by a bike path that continues for about 11 miles to the visitor center/scenic drive. The path is hilly but not difficult if you're in reasonable shape. However, only exceptionally fit and experienced bikers should attempt to explore Red Rock Canyon by bike.

Just off NV 159, you'll see the **Red Rock Canyon Visitor Center** (© 702/515-5350), which marks the entrance to the park. There, you can pick up information on trails and view history exhibits about the canyon. The center is open daily 8:30am to 4:30pm.

WHAT TO SEE & DO
Begin at the **visitor center;** not only is there a $5 per-vehicle fee to pay, but you can pick up a variety of helpful literature: history, guides, trail maps, and exhibits of local flora and fauna. You'll see a fascinating video here about Nevada's thousands of wild horses and burros, protected by an act of Congress since 1971. Furthermore, you can obtain permits for hiking and backpacking. Call ahead to

> **⟨ Tips ⟩ Wild Weather**
>
> Although it can get very hot in Red Rock during the summer, it can also get very cold there during the winter. A recent trip in March to Red Rock found it closed—due to snow!

find out about ranger-guided tours as well as informative guided hikes offered by groups like the Sierra Club and the Audubon Society. And, if you're traveling with children, ask about the free *Junior Ranger Discovery Book* filled with fun family activities.

The easiest thing to do is to **drive the 13-mile scenic loop** ⟨⟨. It really is a loop, and it goes only one way, so once you start, you are committed to driving the whole thing. You can stop the car to admire any number of fabulous views and sights along the way, or have a picnic, or take a walk or hike. As you drive, observe how dramatically the milky-white limestone alternates with iron-rich red rocks. Farther along, the mountains become solid limestone, with canyons running between them, which lead to an evergreen forest—a surprising addition to the desert.

If you're up to it, however, we can't stress enough that the way to really see the canyon is by **hiking.** Every trail is incredible—glance over your options and decide what you might be looking for. You can begin from the visitor center or drive into the loop, park, and start from points therein. Hiking trails range from a .7-mile-loop stroll to a waterfall (its flow varying seasonally) at Lost Creek to much longer and more strenuous treks. Actually, all the hikes involve a certain amount of effort, as you have to scramble over rocks on even the shorter hikes. Unfit or undexterous people should be aware. Be sure to wear good shoes, as the rocks can be slippery. You must have a map; you won't get lost forever (there usually are other hikers around to help you out, eventually), but you can get lost. It is often tough to find a landmark, and once you're deep into the rocks, everything looks the same, even with the map. Consequently, give yourself extra time for each hike (at least an additional hour), regardless of its billed length, to allow for the lack of paths and getting disoriented, and simply to slow down and admire the scenery.

Biking is another option; riding a bicycle would be a tremendous way to travel the loop. There are also terrific off-road mountain biking trails, with levels from amateur to expert.

See chapter 5 for further details on **climbing.**

Appendix: Fast Facts

AMERICAN EXPRESS   There is an Amex Travel office located at
The Fashion Show Mall, 3200 Las Vegas Blvd. S., Las Vegas, NV
89109 (© **702/739-8474**).

BABYSITTERS   Contact **Around the Clock Child Care** (© **800/
798-6768** or 702/365-1040). In business since 1987, this reputable
company clears its sitters with the health department, the sheriff,
and the FBI, and it carefully screens references. Charges are $70 for
4 hours for one or two children, and $15 for each additional hour,
with surcharges for additional children and on holidays. Sitters are
on call 7 days a week, 24 hours a day, and they will come to your
hotel. Call at least 3 hours in advance. Office hours are 10am to
10pm.

BANKS   Banks are generally open 9 or 10am to 5 and sometimes
6pm, and most have Saturday hours. ATMs are plentiful all around
town. When the banks are closed, note that most casino cashiers will
cash personal checks and can exchange foreign currency.

CAR RENTALS   See "Getting Around," in chapter 2.

CONVENTIONS   Las Vegas is one of America's top convention destinations. Much of the action takes place at the **Las Vegas Convention Center,** 3150 Paradise Rd., Las Vegas, NV 89109 (© **702/892-
7575**), which is the largest single-level convention center in the
world. Its 3.2 million square feet house 144 meeting rooms. And this
immense facility is augmented by the **Cashman Field Center,** 850
Las Vegas Blvd. N., Las Vegas, NV 89101 (© **702/386-7100**).
Under the same auspices, Cashman provides another 98,100 square
feet of convention space. Additionally, there are massive convention
facilities at many of the big hotels, including the MGM Grand, The
Mirage, Mandalay Bay, The Venetian, and more.

DENTISTS & DOCTORS   Hotels usually have lists of dentists and
doctors. In addition, they are listed in the Centel Yellow Pages. See
also "Hospitals," below.

For dentist referrals, you can call the **Southern Nevada Dental
Society** (© **702/733-8700**) weekdays 9am to noon and 1 to 5pm;
when the office is closed, a recording will tell you whom to call for
emergency service.

For physician referrals, call **Desert Springs Hospital** (© 702/ **388-4888;** www.desertspringshospital.net). Hours are Monday to Friday 8am to 8pm, and Saturday from 9am to 3pm.

EMERGENCIES   Dial © **911** to contact the police or fire departments or to call an ambulance.

HIGHWAY CONDITIONS   For recorded information, call © **702/ 486-3116.**

HOSPITALS   Emergency services are available 24 hours a day at **University Medical Center,** 1800 W. Charleston Blvd., at Shadow Lane (© **702/383-2000;** www.umc-cares.org); the emergency room entrance is on the corner of Hastings and Rose streets. **Sunrise Hospital & Medical Center,** 3186 Maryland Pkwy., between Desert Inn Road and Sahara Avenue (© **702/731-8080;** www.sunrise hospital.com), also has a 24-hour emergency room.

For more minor problems, try the **Harmon Medical Center,** the closest to the Strip, with doctors and X-ray machines; it's located at 105 E. Harmon at Koval, near the MGM Grand (© **702/796-1116;** www.harmonmedicalcenter.com). It's open 24 hours, and there is a pharmacy on-site.

HOT LINES   Emergency hot lines include the **Rape Crisis Center** (© 702/366-1640), **Suicide Prevention** (© 702/731-2990), and **Poison Emergencies** (© 800/446-6179).

LIQUOR & GAMBLING LAWS   You must be 21 to drink or gamble; proof of age is required and often requested at bars, nightclubs, casinos, and restaurants, so it's always a good idea to bring ID when you go out. There are no closing hours in Las Vegas for the sale or consumption of alcohol, even on Sunday. Don't even think about driving while you're under the influence or have an open container of alcohol in your car. Beer, wine, and liquor are all sold in all kinds of stores pretty much around the clock; you won't have a hard time finding a drink in this town. It's even legal to have an open container outside on the Strip and Fremont Street, but not Downtown.

NEWSPAPERS & PERIODICALS   There are two Las Vegas dailies: the *Las Vegas Review-Journal* and the *Las Vegas Sun.* The *Review-Journal*'s Friday edition has a helpful "Weekend" section with a comprehensive guide to shows and buffets. A free alternative paper—the *Las Vegas Weekly*—has club listings and many unbiased restaurant and bar reviews. And at every hotel desk, you'll find free local magazines that are chock-full of helpful information—although probably of the sort that comes from paid advertising. They also often have excellent bargain coupons for dining and second (and third) tier shows—it's worth going through them for these alone.

PARKING   Valet parking is one of the great pleasures of Las Vegas and well worth the dollar or two tip (given when the car is returned) to save walking a city block from the far reaches of a hotel parking lot, particularly when the temperature is over 100°F (38°C). Another summer plus: The valet will turn on your air-conditioning so that you don't have to get in an "oven on wheels."

PHARMACIES   There's a 24-hour **Walgreens** (which also has a 1-hr. photo) at 3763 Las Vegas Blvd. S. (© **702/739-9638**), almost directly across from the Monte Carlo. **Sav-On** is a large 24-hour drugstore and pharmacy close to the Strip at 1360 E. Flamingo Rd., at Maryland Parkway (© **702/731-5373** for the pharmacy, 702/737-0595 for general merchandise). **White Cross Drugs,** 1700 Las Vegas Blvd. S. (©**702/382-1733**), open daily 7am to 1am, will make pharmacy deliveries to your hotel during the day.

POLICE   For non-emergencies, call © **702/795-3111.** For emergencies, call © **911.**

POST OFFICE   The most convenient post office is immediately behind the Stardust Hotel at 3100 Industrial Rd., between Sahara Avenue and Spring Mountain Road (© **800/297-5543**). It's open Monday to Friday 8:30am to 5pm. You can also mail letters and packages at your hotel, and there's a full-service U.S. Post Office in The Forum Shops in Caesars Palace.

SAFETY   In Las Vegas, vast amounts of money are always on display, and criminals find many easy marks. Don't be one of them. At gaming tables and slot machines, men should keep wallets well-concealed and out of the reach of pickpockets, and women should keep handbags in plain sight (on laps). If you win a big jackpot, ask the pit boss or slot attendant to cut you a check rather than give you cash—the cash may look nice, but flashing it can attract the wrong kind of attention. Outside casinos, popular spots for pickpockets and thieves are restaurants and outdoor shows, such as the volcano at The Mirage or the Treasure Island pirate battle. Stay alert. Unless your hotel room has an in-room safe, check your valuables in a safe-deposit box at the front desk.

SMOKING LAWS   In December 2006, Las Vegas voters passed the Nevada Clean Indoor Air Act, prohibiting smoking in all restaurants, all bars that serve food, grocery stores, schools, malls, and retail establishments, among other places. Essentially, the act bans smoking wherever minors might be present or where food is served. Note that smoking is still permitted in casinos of a certain amount of floor space (nearly all casinos in Vegas) and bars, but is banned in bars that serve food.

TAXES   Clark County hotel room tax is 9%, and in Henderson, it's 10%; the sales tax is 7%.

TIME ZONE   Las Vegas is on Pacific Standard Time, 3 hours earlier than the East Coast, 2 hours earlier than the Midwest.

VETERINARIAN   If Fido or Fluffy gets sick while traveling, go to the **West Flamingo Animal Hospital,** 5445 Flamingo Rd., near Decatur Boulevard (© **702/876-2111;** www.westflamingo.vetsuite. com). They're open 24 hours; they take Discover, MasterCard, and Visa; and they have an ATM.

VISAS   For information about U.S. visas go to **http://travel.state. gov** and click on "Visas."

WEDDINGS   Las Vegas is one of the easiest places in the world to tie the knot. There's no blood test or waiting period, the ceremony and license are inexpensive, chapels are open around the clock (though you can no longer get a wedding license 24 hours on the weekends, which is probably just as well), and your honeymoon destination is right at hand. More than 101,000 marriages are performed here each year. Get a license downtown at the **Clark County Marriage License Bureau,** 201 Clark Ave. (© **702/455-4415**), which is open daily from 8am to midnight. The cost of a marriage license is $55; the cost of the ceremony varies depending on where you go to have it done. See "Getting Married," in chapter 5, for details on the local wedding chapels.

Index

See also Accommodations and Restaurants indexes, below.

GENERAL INDEX

A
ARP, 28
Accommodations, 29–61. *See also*
  Accommodations Index
    best, 4–6
    casino-free hotels, 52–55
    casino hotels, 38–51
    East of the Strip, 35–36
        casino hotels, 50–51
    Mid-Strip, 43–49, 55, 57–58
    North Strip, 55–58
    pools, 37
    South Strip, 31–35
        casino hotels, 39–43
    top hotels, 31–38
    West of the Strip, 36–38
Active pursuits, 135–138
The Adventuredome, 129–130
Alamo, 18
Alan Bible Visitor Center, 186–188
American Airlines Vacations, 26
American Express, 194
    emergency number, 24
American Express Vacations, 26
American Golf, 133
American Superstars, 152
Amtrak, 16
Angel, Criss, 154
Angel Park Golf Club, 134
Antiques, 147–148
Antiques at the Market, 148
Antique Square, 148
Arcades, 131
The Arts Factory Complex, 110, 146
The Atomic Testing Museum, 110, 112
Atomic Testing Museum gift store, 147
The Attic, 146
Australia, customs regulations, 11
Avenue Shoppes, 142
Avis, 18

B
abysitters, 194
Bali Hai Golf Club, 134
Bally's
    shopping, 142
    tennis, 138
The Bank, 171
Banks, 194
Bars, 166–171
    gay, 163–165
Bathhouse at THEhotel Mandalay
  Bay, 56
Bellagio, shopping, 142–143
Bellagio Conservatory, 114
Bellagio Fountains, 114
Bellagio Gallery of Fine Art, 112
Bell Trans, 16
Biking, 192, 193
Black Mountain Golf & Country Club,
  134–135
Blue Man Group, 152–153
Boat cruises, Lake Mead, 188
Boating, 187
Bodies, 112–113
Body English, 172
Bonanza Gift and Souvenir Shop, 146
Bonnie Springs Ranch, 138
Boulder City, 188–189
The Boulevard, 139–140
Bowling, 136
Budget, 18
The Buffalo, 164
Buffalo Exchange, 146
Buffets and sunday brunches, 102–107
Burton, Lance, 156

C
aesars Palace
    for kids, 129
    shopping, 143–144
Calendar of events, 12–15
Callville Bay Resort & Marina, 187
Camping, 188

Canada, customs regulations, 10
Canoeing, 188
Canyon Ranch Spa at The Venetian, 56
Caramel, 166
Carnaval Court, 144
Car rentals, 18–20
Car travel
   in Las Vegas, 17
   to Las Vegas, 15
Cashman Field Center, 194
Casino-free hotels, 52–55
Casino hotels, 38–51
Chamber of Commerce, 12
Champagnes Cafe, 166–167
Chapel of the Bells, 125
Cheetah's, 132, 177
Cher, 153–154
Cherry, 172
CineVegas Film Festival, 13
Circus Circus
   for kids, 129
   shopping, 144
Cirque du Soleil's O, 147
Citizens Area Transit (CAT), 17
Clark Country Marriage License
   Bureau, 123
Cleopatra's Barge Nightclub, 172
Climate, 11–12
Clothing, vintage, 146
Club Paradise, 177–178
Comedy Club, 163
Comedy clubs, 163
The Comedy Festival, 13–14
Comedy Stop, 163
Coney Island Emporium, 131
Continental Airlines Vacations, 26
Conventions, 194
Cook E. Jarr, 165
Cowboy Trail Rides, 136, 138
Coyote Ugly, 167
Craig Ranch Golf Club, 135
Crazy Girls, 154
Creative Adventures, 133
Criss Angel: Believe with Cirque de
   Soleil, 154
Cupid's Wedding Chapel, 125
Customs regulations, 10–11

Dance clubs, 171–176
Danny Gans: The Man of Many Voices,
   154
Déjà Vu Showgirls, 178

Delta Vacations, 25, 26
Desert Cab Company, 20
Desert Passage, 144–145
Desert Rose Golf Course, 135
The Deuce, 20
Dining, 62–107. See also Restaurants
   Index
   best, 6–7
   buffets and Sunday brunches,
      102–107
   Downtown, 100–101, 107
   East of the Strip, 88–96
   Mid-Strip, 73–84, 103–107
   North Strip, 85–88
   South Strip, 62–73, 102–103
   with views, 78
   West Las Vegas, 96–100
   for wine lovers, 90–91
Disabilities, travelers with, 27
The Dispensary Lounge, 167
Doctors and dentists, 194–195
Dollar car rentals, 18
Dolphin Habitat, 120–121
Dolphin Spa at Green Valley, 56
Double Down Saloon, 167–168
Downtown ("Glitter Gulch"), 22, 24
   restaurants, 100–101, 107
Drai's After Hours, 172
Drop Bar, 168

East of the Strip, 22
   accommodations, 35–36
   casino hotels, 50–51
   restaurants, 88–96
Echo Bay, 187
Eiffel Tower Bar, 168
Eiffel Tower Tour, 113
Ellis Island Casino-Karaoke, 171
Emergencies, 195
Enterprise, 18
Entry requirements, 9–10
Esplanade at Wynn Las Vegas, 144
Excalibur
   for kids, 129
   shopping, 144
Expedia, 26

Families with children, 28
   arcades, 131
   attractions for, 128–131
Fantasy Faire, 131

Fashion Outlets Las Vegas, 141
Fashion Show, 140
Festivals and special events, 12–15
Film Festival, CineVegas, 13
Fishing, 187
The Flamingo Las Vegas, tennis, 138
Food courts, 73
Football
    Las Vegas Bowl Week, 15
    Western Athletic Conference (WAC)
    Football Championship, 14
Forty Deuce, 168
The Forum Shops at Caesars Palace,
    132, 143–144
Forum Shops Fountain Shows, 114
Free attractions, 114–115
Fremont Street Experience, 113
Frys.com Open, 13

Galleria at Sunset, 140
Gambling, 118
GameWorks, 113, 116, 132
Gans, Danny, 154
Gateway District, 22
Gay bars, 163–165
Gays and lesbians, information and
    resources, 27–28
Ghostbar, 168–169
Gipsy, 164
Glitter Gulch, 178
Gold Coast Hotel, bowling, 136
Golf, 133–135
    Frys.com Open, 13
Goodtimes Night Club, 164
Gordon Biersch Brewing Company,
    169
Graceland Wedding Chapel, 125
The Grand Canal Shoppes, 145–146
Grand Canyon, tours, 132–133, 181
Gray Line Tours, 131, 181
Green Valley, Dolphin Spa at, 56
Greyhound, senior discounts, 28
Griffin, 169

Hard Rock Hotel & Casino, 132
Hard Rock Hotel's The Joint, 161–162
Harrah's, shopping, 134
Harrah's Carnaval Court Lounge, 165
Help of Southern Nevada, 16

Hertz, 18
Hiking, 137, 188, 191, 193
Hogs & Heifers Saloon, 169
Hoover Dam, 181–186
Hoover Dam Visitor Center, 184–185
Horseback riding, 136, 138
Hospitals, 195
Hot lines, 195
House of Blues, 162

Improv, The, 163
Inside Scoop (Overton), 191
Insurance, car-rental, 19–20
Ireland, customs regulations, 11
Itineraries, suggested, 109–110

Jersey Boys Vegas, 155
Jet, 173
Jubilee!, 155

KA, 155–156
Keith's I Love This Bar & Grill, 171
King, Mac, 160
KRAVE, 164–165

Lake Mead Cruises, 188
Lake Mead National Recreation Area,
    186–187
Lake Mead Resort and Marina, 187
Lance Burton: Master Magician, 156
Las Vegas Boat Harbor, 187
Las Vegas Bowl Week, 15
Las Vegas Chamber of Commerce, 8
Las Vegas Convention and Visitors
    Authority, 8, 12, 150
Las Vegas Convention Center, 194
Las Vegas Cyber Speedway/SPEED:
    The Ride, 116
Las Vegas Mini Gran Prix, 117
Las Vegas Monorail, 21
Las Vegas Motor Speedway,
    12–13, 117
Las Vegas National Golf Club, 135
Las Vegas Natural History Museum,
    130
Las Vegas Outlet Center, 141
Las Vegas Premium Outlets, 141–142

Las Vegas Strip Trolley, 21
Las Vegas Weddings and Rooms, 124
Las Vegas Weekly, 150
Le Rêve, 156–157
Liberace Museum, 117, 119
Liberace Museum gift store, 147
Liberty Travel, 26
Lied Discovery Children's Museum, 130–131
Lion Habitat, MGM Grand, 120
Liquor and gambling laws, 195
Little Chapel of the Flowers, 126–127
Little Darlings, 178–179
Little White Wedding Chapel, 127
Lost City Museum (Overton), 191
LOVE, 157
Lucky Strike at the Rio, 136

Madame Tussauds Las Vegas, 119
Malls, 139–140
Mandara Spa at Planet Hollywood, 56
M&M World, 147
Marjorie Barrick Museum, 119–120
Marriage, 123–127
Masquerade Show in the Sky, 114
Masquerade Village, 145
MasterCard, emergency number, 24
McCarran International Airport, 15
    arriving at, 16–17
Mead, Lake, 129
Meadows Mall, 140
MGM Grand Lion Habitat, 120
MGM Grand's Crazy Horse Paris, 157
Midler, Bette, 152
Mid-Strip, 22
    accommodations, 43–49, 55, 57–58
    restaurants, 73–84, 103–107
Mirage Volcano, 114–115
Money and costs, 24–26
Monorail, Las Vegas, 21
Monte Carlo Pub & Brewery, 173
Monte Carlo shopping, 144
Mount Charleston Resort, Oktoberfest, 13
Mystère, 157–158

NASCAR/Winston Cup, 12–13
National, 18
National Conservation Area, 192
National Finals Rodeo, 14–15

Natural History Museum, Las Vegas, 130
Nevada Commission on Tourism, 9, 27
Newspapers and magazines, 195
New Year's Eve, 14, 15
New York-New York, food court, 73
New Zealand, customs regulations, 11
NFR Cowboy Christmas Gift Show, 15
Nightlife, 149–180
    bars, 166–171
    dance clubs, 171–176
    family-friendly shows, 153
    favorite shows, 151
    gay bars, 163–165
    headliner showrooms, 161–162
    major production shows, 151–161
    strip clubs, 176–180
North Strip, 22
    accommodations, 55–58
    restaurants, 85–88

O, Cirque du Soleil's, 158
Oktoberfest, 13
Olympic Gardens Topless Cabaret, 179
Orbitz, 26
Organized tours, 131–133
The Orleans, bowling, 136
Outlet centers, 141–142
Overton, 191

Package deals, 24–26
Palomino Club, 179
Parking, 196
Passports, 10
Payless, 18
Penn & Teller, 158–159
Peppermill's Fireside Lounge, 132, 169–170
Petroglyphs, 191
Petrossian Bar, 166
Phantom of the Opera, 159
Pharmacies, 196
Photo ops, 126
Pit Pass Arcade, 131
Planet Hollywood
    Mandara Spa at, 56
    shopping, 144–145
Planning your trip, 8–28
    customs regulations, 10–11
    entry requirements, 9–10

Planning your trip *(cont.)*
  getting around, 16–21
  layout of Las Vegas, 21–24
  money and costs, 24–26
  specialized travel resources, 27–28
  traveling to Las Vegas, 15–16
  visitor information, 8–9
  when to go, 11–12
Playboy Club, 173
Poker, World Series of, 13
Police, 196
Pools, 37
Post office, 196
Precipitation, average, 12
Privé and the Living Room, 173–174
PURE, 174

Q *Vegas,* 27–28

R ain, 174
Rainfall, average, 12
The Realm, 144
Red Rock Canyon, 132, 138, 192–193
Red Rooster Antique Mall, 148
Restaurants, 62–107. *See also*
  Restaurants Index
    best, 6–7
    buffets and Sunday brunches,
      102–107
    Downtown, 100–101, 107
    East of the Strip, 88–96
    Mid-Strip, 73–84, 103–107
    North Strip, 85–88
    South Strip, 62–73, 102–103
    with views, 78
    West Las Vegas, 96–100
    for wine lovers, 90–91
Rio All-Suite Hotel & Casino
    golf course, 133
    shopping, 145
    World Series of Poker, 13
Rock climbing, 138
Rodeos, National Finals Rodeo, 14–15
Rudner, Rita, 159
Rumjungle, 175

S afety, 196
Sam's Town, bowling, 136
Sand Dollar Blues Nightclub & Lounge,
  170

Santa Fe Station, bowling, 136
Sapphire Gentleman's Club, 179
Scenic Airlines, 181
The Second City, 159–160
Seniors, 28
Serge's Showgirl Wigs, 148
Seven Crown Resorts, 187
Shark Reef at Mandalay Bay, 120
Shopping, 139–148
    antiques, 147–148
    candy, 147
    hotel arcades, 142–146
    malls, 139–140
    outlet centers, 141–142
    souvenirs, 146–147
    vintage clothing, 146
    wigs, 148
Siegfried & Roy's Secret Garden, 120
Sights and attractions, 108–133
    free, 114–115
    for kids, 128–131
    organized tours, 131–133
    suggested itineraries, 109–110
    top attractions, 110–123
Silver Horse Antiques, 147–148
Sirens of TI, 115
Smoking laws, 196–197
Southern Nevada Center for
  Independent Living, 27
South Strip, 21–22
    accommodations, 31–35
      casino hotels, 39–43
    restaurants, 62–73, 102–103
Southwest Airlines Vacations, 25, 26
Souvenirs, 146–147
Spas, 56
Spearmint Rhino, 179–180
Special events and festivals, 12–15
Spring Mountain Ranch State Park,
  192
Springs Preserve, 121–122
Star Trek: The Experience, 129
Stratosphere Thrill Rides, 122
Street of Dreams, 144
The Strip, 21–22
Strip clubs, 176–180
Studio 54, 175
Suncoast, 136
Sunset Station, bowling, 136

Tabu, 175
Tao, 176
Taxes, 197
Taxis, 20
Temperatures, average, 12
Tennis, 138
Texas Station, bowling, 136
THEhotel Mandalay Bay, Bathhouse
    at, 56
Thrifty, 18
Time zone, 197
Titanic: The Exhibition, 122–123
Tommy Rocker's Mojave Beach Topless
    Bar, 177
Tourist information, 8–9
Tournament of Kings, 160
Tours, organized, 131–133
Train travel, to Las Vegas, 16
Transportation, 16
Travelaxe, 30
Traveler's Aid Society, 16
Traveling to Las Vegas, 15–16
Travelocity, 26
Triple 7 Brew Pub, 170
Trolley, Las Vegas Strip, 21
Tryst, 176

United Kingdom, customs
    regulations, 11
United Vacations, 26
US Airways Vacations, 26

Vacation Together, 26
Valley of Fire State Park, 182, 189–191
The Venetian
    Canyon Ranch Spa at, 56
    shopping, 145–146
Veterinarian, 197
Via Bellagio, 142–143
Vintage clothing, 146
Visa, emergency number, 24
Visa Waiver Program, 9–10
Visitor information, 8–9
Viva Las Vegas Lounge, 166
VooDoo Lounge, 176

Weather, 11–12
Websites, 9
Weddings, 123–127, 197

Wee Kirk O' the Heather, 127
"Welcome to Las Vegas" sign, 126
Western Athletic Conference (WAC)
    Football Championship, 14
West of the Strip
    accommodations, 36–38
    restaurants, 96–100
Whisky Bar, 171
Whittlesea Blue Cab, 20
Wigs, 148
Women travelers, 28
World Series of Poker, 13
Wynn Conservatory, 115
Wynn Lake of Dreams, 115
Wynn Las Vegas, shopping, 144

Yellow/Checker Cab, 20

Zumanity, 160–161
Zuri, 166

ACCOMMODATIONS

Bally's Las Vegas, 57
Bellagio, 43–44
Caesars Palace, 44
Circus Circus, 58
Courtyard by Marriott, 52
Desert Rose Resort, 53
Excalibur, 39
The Flamingo Las Vegas, 55
Four Seasons Las Vegas, 31–32
Green Valley Ranch Resort, 35
Hard Rock Hotel & Casino Note, 50
Harrah's Las Vegas, 57
Hyatt Place, 53
La Quinta, 53–54
Las Vegas Hilton, 50–51
Las Vegas Marriott Suites, 54
Luxor, 39–40
Mandalay Bay, 32, 34
MGM Grand Hotel & Casino, 40–41
The Mirage, 44–45
Monte Carlo Resort & Casino, 41
New York-New York Hotel & Casino,
    41–42
Palazzo, 45–46
Palms Casino Resort, 46
Paris Las Vegas, 46–47
Planet Hollywood Resort & Casino, 42

Red Rock Resort, 36, 38
Residence Inn, 54–55
Rio All-Suite Hotel & Casino, 58
Ritz-Carlton, Lake Las Vegas, 36
South Point, 42–43
Stratosphere Casino Hotel & Tower, 55–57
THEhotel at Mandalay Bay, 34–35
TI-Treasure Island Las Vegas, 47–48
The Venetian, 48–49
The Westin Casuarina Las Vegas Hotel and Spa, 51
Wynn Las Vegas, 49

RESTAURANTS

Alex, 85
Alizé, 73–74
Aureole, 62, 64, 91
Austins Steakhouse, 96, 98
Bally's Sterling Sunday Brunch, 103–104
B&B Ristorante, 74
Bartolotta Ristorante di Mare, 85–86
Bellagio's Buffet, 104
Border Grill, 67
Bouchon, 79–80
Bougainvillea, 93–94
Burger Bar, 68
Cafe Heidelberg German Deli and Restaurant, 86
Canaletto, 80
Canter's, 84
Capriotti's, 87
Carluccio's Tivoli Gardens, 92–93
Cathay House, 98–99
Charlie Palmer Steak, 64
Circo, 80–81
Cypress Street Marketplace, 84
Delmonico Steakhouse, 74–75
Dick's Last Resort, 69
Doña María Tamales, 87–88
Dragon Noodle Co., 69
Earl of Sandwich, 72
Eiffel Tower, 78
Einstein Bros. Bagels, 94
El Sombrero Cafe, 101
Emeril's New Orleans Fish House, 65
ESPN Zone, 71
Fellini's, 86–87
Fin, 75

Fix, 75–76
Fleur de Lys, 65, 91
Golden Nugget's Buffet, 107
Grand Wok and Sushi Bar, 69–70
Hash House A Go Go, 99–100
House of Blues, 70–71
Hugo's Cellar, 100
Ice House Lounge, 101
Isla, 81–82
Jason's Deli, 94
Jody Maroni's Sausage Kingdom, 72
Joël Robuchon at the Mansion, 66
Krispy Kreme, 73
LA Pizza Kitchen, 73
L'Atelier de Joël Robuchon, 66–67
Lawry's The Prime Rib, 88, 90–91
Le Cirque, 76
Lotus of Siam, 94–95
Main Street Station's Garden Court, 107
Mandalay Bay's Bay Side Buffet, 102
M&M Soul Food, 101
Memphis Championship Barbecue, 93
Mesa Grill, 76–77
MGM Grand Buffet, 102–103
Mirage's Cravings, 105–106
Mon Ami Gabi, 82
Monte Carlo Pub & Brewery, 72–73
Monte Carlo's Buffet, 103
MORE, The Buffet at Luxor, 103
New York-New York, 73
Olives, 82–83
The Palm, 77
Palms Fantasy Market Buffet, 106–107
Pamplemousse, 92
Paris Las Vegas's Le Village Buffet, 104–105
Payard Patisserie & Bistro, 83
Paymon's Mediterranean Café & Lounge, 95–96
Petrossian Bar, 90
Picasso, 77–78
Pink Taco, 93
Pinot Brasserie, 81
The Range Steakhouse, 78–79
Red Square, 67
Rio's Carnival World Buffet, 106
Rosemary's Restaurant, 91, 98
Salt Lick, 99
Sensi, 83–84
Spago, 79

Stratosphere's Top of the World, 78
Table 10, 68
Tiffany's at the White Cross
    Pharmacy, 88
Toto's, 96
Totos (Boulder City), 189
Valentino, 90–91

The Venetian, 73
Viva Mercado's, 99
The Wine Cellar & Tasting Room, 90
Wolfgang Puck Bar & Grill, 70–71
Wynn Las Vegas Buffet, 105

FROMMER'S® COMPLETE TRAVEL GUIDES

Alaska
Amalfi Coast
American Southwest
Amsterdam
Argentina
Arizona
Atlanta
Australia
Austria
Bahamas
Barcelona
Beijing
Belgium, Holland & Luxembourg
Belize
Bermuda
Boston
Brazil
British Columbia & the Canadian
  Rockies
Brussels & Bruges
Budapest & the Best of Hungary
Buenos Aires
Calgary
California
Canada
Cancún, Cozumel & the Yucatán
Cape Cod, Nantucket & Martha's
  Vineyard
Caribbean
Caribbean Ports of Call
Carolinas & Georgia
Chicago
Chile & Easter Island
China
Colorado
Costa Rica
Croatia
Cuba
Denmark
Denver, Boulder & Colorado Springs
Eastern Europe
Ecuador & the Galapagos Islands
Edinburgh & Glasgow
England
Europe
Europe by Rail

Florence, Tuscany & Umbria
Florida
France
Germany
Greece
Greek Islands
Guatemala
Hawaii
Hong Kong
Honolulu, Waikiki & Oahu
India
Ireland
Israel
Italy
Jamaica
Japan
Kauai
Las Vegas
London
Los Angeles
Los Cabos & Baja
Madrid
Maine Coast
Maryland & Delaware
Maui
Mexico
Montana & Wyoming
Montréal & Québec City
Morocco
Moscow & St. Petersburg
Munich & the Bavarian Alps
Nashville & Memphis
New England
Newfoundland & Labrador
New Mexico
New Orleans
New York City
New York State
New Zealand
Northern Italy
Norway
Nova Scotia, New Brunswick &
  Prince Edward Island
Oregon
Paris
Peru

Philadelphia & the Amish Country
Portugal
Prague & the Best of the Czech
  Republic
Provence & the Riviera
Puerto Rico
Rome
San Antonio & Austin
San Diego
San Francisco
Santa Fe, Taos & Albuquerque
Scandinavia
Scotland
Seattle
Seville, Granada & the Best of
  Andalusia
Shanghai
Sicily
Singapore & Malaysia
South Africa
South America
South Florida
South Korea
South Pacific
Southeast Asia
Spain
Sweden
Switzerland
Tahiti & French Polynesia
Texas
Thailand
Tokyo
Toronto
Turkey
USA
Utah
Vancouver & Victoria
Vermont, New Hampshire & Maine
Vienna & the Danube Valley
Vietnam
Virgin Islands
Virginia
Walt Disney World® & Orlando
Washington, D.C.
Washington State

FROMMER'S® DAY BY DAY GUIDES

Amsterdam
Barcelona
Beijing
Boston
Cancun & the Yucatan
Chicago
Florence & Tuscany

Hong Kong
Honolulu & Oahu
London
Maui
Montréal
Napa & Sonoma
New York City

Paris
Provence & the Riviera
Rome
San Francisco
Venice
Washington D.C.

PAULINE FROMMER'S GUIDES: SEE MORE. SPEND LESS.

Alaska
Hawaii
Italy

Las Vegas
London
New York City

Paris
Walt Disney World®
Washington D.C.

FROMMER'S® PORTABLE GUIDES

Acapulco, Ixtapa & Zihuatanejo
Amsterdam
Aruba, Bonaire & Curacao
Australia's Great Barrier Reef
Bahamas
Big Island of Hawaii
Boston
California Wine Country
Cancún
Cayman Islands
Charleston
Chicago
Dominican Republic

Florence
Las Vegas
Las Vegas for Non-Gamblers
London
Maui
Nantucket & Martha's Vineyard
New Orleans
New York City
Paris
Portland
Puerto Rico
Puerto Vallarta, Manzanillo &
    Guadalajara

Rio de Janeiro
San Diego
San Francisco
Savannah
St. Martin, Sint Maarten, Anguila &
    St. Bart's
Turks & Caicos
Vancouver
Venice
Virgin Islands
Washington, D.C.
Whistler

FROMMER'S® CRUISE GUIDES

Alaska Cruises & Ports of Call

Cruises & Ports of Call

European Cruises & Ports of Call

FROMMER'S® NATIONAL PARK GUIDES

Algonquin Provincial Park
Banff & Jasper
Grand Canyon

National Parks of the American West
Rocky Mountain
Yellowstone & Grand Teton

Yosemite and Sequoia & Kings
    Canyon
Zion & Bryce Canyon

FROMMER'S® WITH KIDS GUIDES

Chicago
Hawaii
Las Vegas
London

National Parks
New York City
San Francisco

Toronto
Walt Disney World® & Orlando
Washington, D.C.

FROMMER'S® PHRASEFINDER DICTIONARY GUIDES

Chinese
French

German
Italian

Japanese
Spanish

SUZY GERSHMAN'S BORN TO SHOP GUIDES

France
Hong Kong, Shanghai & Beijing
Italy

London
New York
Paris

San Francisco
Where to Buy the Best of Everything.

FROMMER'S® BEST-LOVED DRIVING TOURS

Britain
California
France
Germany

Ireland
Italy
New England
Northern Italy

Scotland
Spain
Tuscany & Umbria

THE UNOFFICIAL GUIDES®

Adventure Travel in Alaska
Beyond Disney
California with Kids
Central Italy
Chicago
Cruises
Disneyland®
England
Hawaii

Ireland
Las Vegas
London
Maui
Mexico's Best Beach Resorts
Mini Mickey
New Orleans
New York City
Paris

San Francisco
South Florida including Miami &
    the Keys
Walt Disney World®
Walt Disney World® for
    Grown-ups
Walt Disney World® with Kids
Washington, D.C.

SPECIAL-INTEREST TITLES

Athens Past & Present
Best Places to Raise Your Family
Cities Ranked & Rated
500 Places to Take Your Kids Before They Grow Up
Frommer's Best Day Trips from London
Frommer's Best RV & Tent Campgrounds in the U.S.A.

Frommer's Exploring America by RV
Frommer's NYC Free & Dirt Cheap
Frommer's Road Atlas Europe
Frommer's Road Atlas Ireland
Retirement Places Rated